Multimedia Stardom in Hong K

I0004945

This book details original research into the practices and discourse of multimedia stardom alongside changing social and cultural landscapes in Hong Kong since 1980. It examines the cultural and sociological significance of stardom in the region, and the conditions which gave rise to such famous stars as Jackie Chan and Chow Yun-fat. This book elaborates the distinction between multimedia stardom and celebrity, asserting that in Hong Kong stardom has been central in the production and consumption of local media, while demonstrating the importance of multimedia stardom as part of the 'cultural Chinese' mediascape and transnational popular culture from both historical and contemporary contexts.

Leung Wing-Fai is a Lecturer in Contemporary Chinese Studies at University College Cork, Ireland.

Media, Culture and Social Change in Asia

The aim of this series is to publish original, high-quality work by both new and
established scholars in the West and the East, on all aspects of media, culture and
social change in Asia.

Multimedia Stardom in Hong Kong

Image, performance and identity

Leung Wing-Fai

Routledge
Taylor & Francis Group

LONDON AND NEW YORK

First published 2015 by Routledge

2 Park Square, Milton Park, Abingdon, Oxfordshire OX14 4RN
711 Third Avenue, New York, NY 10017

Routledge is an imprint of the Taylor & Francis Group, an informa business

First issued in paperback 2017

British Library Cataloguing in Publication Data
A catalogue record for this book is available from the British Library

Library of Congress Cataloging in Publication Data
Leung, Wing-Fai, 1970-
Multimedia stardom in Hong Kong : image, performance and identity /
Leung Wing-Fai.
pages cm. — (Media, culture and social change in Asia series; 42)
Includes bibliographical references and index.
1. Performance art—China—Hong Kong. 2. Entertainers—China—Hong
Kong. 3. Multimedia (Art)—China—Hong Kong. 4. Popular culture—
China—Hong Kong. 5. Culture diffusion—China—Hong Kong. 6. Social
change—China—Hong Kong. 1. Title
NX583.C6L48 2014
791.095125—dc23
2014025677

ISBN: 978-0-415-70912-5 (hbk)
ISBN: 978-0-8153-6704-8 (pbk)

Typeset in Times New Roman
by Swales & Willis Ltd, Exeter, Devon, UK

Contents

Illustrations

Figures

Tables

Acknowledgements

In the process of conducting the research that led to this book, I have received encouragement and support from more people than I can name here. I am grateful to my parents Leung Shui Cheung and Law Wan Tai and my brothers Percy and John for having fed me a diet of Hong Kong media and popular culture over the years. A special thank you is due to Benjamin J. Heal for standing by me and supporting my writing, and Audrey Pearl Yan Heal who has been amazing.

My thanks go to Dr Kevin Latham, Professor Mark Hobart, the Centre for Media and Film Studies and my colleagues at the School of Oriental and African Studies, University of London; Dr Leon Hunt, Dr Stefano Locati and Dr Norbert Morawetz for friendship and help; colleagues at the Department of Journalism and Communication, Chinese University of Hong Kong who hosted me in 2005; the National Media Museum; Dr Richard Howells and Dr Jeremy Taylor; Professor Daria Berg, Universität St. Gallen; colleagues at the School of Asian Studies, University College Cork, Ireland.

I would like to thank all the anonymous informants and interviewees, Carol, David, Jo C, Jo H, Jo M, Kit, Ophelia, Simon Broad, Fruit Chan, Chan Pak-sun, Rowena Chan, Sylvia Chang, Bede Cheng, Cheung Tung-joe, Jimmy Choi, Robert Chua, Ann Hui, Dr David Jiang, Carol Lai Miu-suet, Edward Lam, Karena Lam, Andrew Lau, Jeff Lau, Olivia Lau, Angelica Lee Sinje, Philip Lee, Bey Logan, Gary Mak, Carl Ng, R. Ng, Sally Nicholls, P. Sze, Dr Stephen Sze Man-hung, Diego Swing, Ted Thomas, Jason Tobin, Angie Tsang, Charles Wang, Flora Wu; the support of Broadway Cinemas, Hong Kong Film Critics Society, Red on Red; Lam Tze-chung, Viann Liang, Wai Ka-fai, Johnnie To, Lam Suet, Lau Ching-wan and the colleagues at Far East Film.

I received generous grant support from several sources to conduct and write up the research project that led to this book. I am grateful to Central Research Fund, University of London (2005), The British Federation of Women Graduates Foundation Grant (2006) and University College Cork publication research fund (2013). I also want to thank the confidence and patience of Professor Stephanie Donald, anonymous reviewers of the manuscripts; Peter Sowden, Helena Hurd and staff at Routledge for bringing this book through the review, editing and production process.

Grateful acknowledgement is made to those who gave their kind permission to reproduce material in this book: *Eastweek* (Figure 2.1), Film Unlimited Production (Figure 3.1) and Qixinran (Cheerland Entertainment Inc.), especially Ms Yuan Mei and Ms Ann Hui (Figure 6.1). The case study on the Edison Chen scandal was adapted from the article with permission,

'Discourse of *Nǚ Mingxing*: Womanhood and Female Sexuality in 1930s Shanghai and 2000s Hong Kong', Journal of Chinese Studies/Zhongguo Yanjiu, 7 (2013).

In memory of Kevin Law who left in 2005.

Note on romanization and translation

Personal and place names follow the spellings usually used in existing publications, which come from different systems of the Romanization of Cantonese, where standardization is inappropriate. English titles of films, programmes and songs follow those already in existence in English publications, on DVD and album covers. The Chinese names of the interviewees and titles of events cited are included in Appendix 1. A list of Chinese names, titles, terms and Chinese translations of English terms is given in Appendix 2, excepting commonly known names such as Kowloon.

The Romanization of Chinese names, terms and titles is in *hanyu pinyin*, based on Mandarin Chinese, and presented in italic, except those in quotations from existing sources that sometimes contain instances of other methods. All translations of magazine, newspaper articles and texts in Chinese are my own unless otherwise stated.

Abbreviations

APA	Academy for Performing Arts
ATV	(see RTV)
CEO	Chief Executive Officer
CEPA	Closer Economic Partnership Agreement
CPPCC	Chinese People's Political Consultative Conference
CTV	Commercial Television
CTV	China Television
EEG	Emperor Entertainment Group
EYT	*Enjoy Yourself Tonight*
HKD	Hong Kong Dollars
HKFA	Hong Kong Film Archive
HKIFF	Hong Kong International Film Festival
IFPI	International Federation of the Phonographic Industry
IVS	Individual Visit Scheme
KMT	Nationalist party; Kuomintang or Guomindang
PRC	People's Republic of China
RTHK	Radio Television Hong Kong
RTV	Rediffusion Television, then Asia Television (ATV)
SAR	Special Administrative Region
SARS	Severe Acute Respiratory Syndrome
SCMP	*South China Morning Post*
TVB	Television Broadcasts Company
TVBS	TVB Superstation
VCD	video compact disc

Introduction

Stars and the collective in Hong Kong

Bruce Lee (1940–73), Chow Yun-fat (b.1955), Jackie Chan (b.1954), Jet Li (Li Lianjie, b. 1963) and Maggie Cheung (b.1964) are among the most globally recognizable stars who have either come from or established their careers in Hong Kong's media industry. This book is about multimedia stardom in Hong Kong conceptualized in relation to a range of media practices, including advertising, film, new media (such as the Internet), pop music, the printed press and television. The cultural and sociological significance of stardom in the region are examined along with the conditions that gave rise to these famous stars.

In this book I distinguish multimedia stardom from celebrity. Celebrity refers to fame or notoriety; in Hong Kong celebrity is best translated as *mingren* ('famous people'), a term that can refer to wealthy business people and politicians as well as pop stars. Celebrity culture is one aspect of stardom, but in this book I define multimedia stardom as a concept connected exclusively to the entertainment industry rather than to other fields such as sport, the business world, politics or government. As celebrity culture is part of stardom, the concept of multimedia stardom serves as a bridge between scholarship on stardom and celebrity. Looking at celebrity as a facet of multimedia stardom allows my analysis to examine 'the public' in Hong Kong, because celebrity can be thought of as 'the embodiment of the collective power of an invested audience in a particular person' (Marshall 2006, p.316).

Clifford Geertz defines culture as an 'ensemble of stories we tell ourselves about ourselves' (1973, p.448), and Raymond Williams states, 'Culture is ordinary' (1989, p.3). Multimedia stars participate in the telling of stories about a specific society, whether in entertainment news reports, film narratives, television drama or pop song lyrics, all of which are pervasive in everyday life. Williams (2002), reflecting Marxist ideas, further states that the underlying production system of a culture must be interpreted, because culture is 'a whole way of life' (p.95) and an aspect of social organization that is clearly affected by economic change. The production context, meanwhile, is not static. For instance, Sonia Livingstone and Tim Markham (2008) contend that media forms and contents are increasingly globalized, commercialized and diversified. My study therefore investigates multimedia stardom within its production and consumption contexts and examines the transformation of stardom-related popular cultural forms over time.

Why research the production and consumption of stardom as an investigation into culture? My study of stars in Hong Kong stems from the argument that stars, as public figures who tell us something about the social contexts in which they operate and about how private individuals are governed by culturally acceptable models of behaviour, are vital subjects in understanding Hong Kong culture and society. Stars exist in an intersection between the public and private spheres. They bring the news and the personal together by being both public and intimate, by being news only because they are individuals (Ellis 1997). In his rationale for the analysis of stardom, Francesco Alberoni (2007) contends that stars should be regarded as a powerless elite made possible by large-scale societies experiencing economic development and greater social mobility. He focuses on the ruling power elite that includes politicians and the wealthy, and in this sense, as role models of social mobility but without political power, stars can distract public scrutiny away from the power elite. For example, stars in Hong Kong are often expected to get involved in public campaigns, fundraising concerts or other large-scale charity events. Collectively, stars might illustrate the individual values that are revered or under threat in a given society over time (Dyer 1979). If stars represent social values, how stardom changes over time tells us about transformations within the wider cultural contexts that give rise to these famous individuals.

Stars are often considered exemplary individuals, as illustrated by a media incident in Hong Kong in January and February 2008. A scandal erupted in the city concerning the illegal distribution over the Internet of private photographs of the young star Edison Chen (b.1980) and several female stars and models, including Gillian Chung (of the girl band Twins, b.1981) and Cecilia Cheung (b.1980), who were Chen's sexual partners. The photographs were stolen when Chen's computer was taken to a shop for repairs. The scandal prompted a media frenzy, with one online discussion generating more than 25 million page views and 140,000 comments (Watts 2008). On 21 February 2008 the singer-actor publicly apologized to the female victims and announced that he would retire from the Hong Kong entertainment world 'indefinitely'. Part of his statement during the press conference stressed the point that stars are thought of as exemplary individuals even though many fail in this capacity:[1]

> I know young people in Hong Kong look up to many figures in our society. And in this regard, I have failed. I failed as a role model . . . To all the young people in our community, let this be a lesson for you all. This is not an example to be set for you.

Several characteristics of contemporary multimedia stardom in Hong Kong can be deduced from this example. First, contemporary stars may find themselves in public roles that have little to do with their performances; instead, their image as circulated in the entertainment press has become an important facet of their stardom. This incident forced the entertainment world, the police and the public to evaluate the cultural and social practices associated with the circulation of image and fame in cyberspace. Second, the case demonstrates how new means of communication, such as the Internet and social media, can affect stardom, which used to be associated with the traditional media practices of film, television and pop music. Third, stars, as shown by Chen's announcement, seem to understand their position in society not only as performers or entertainers but also as 'role models'. Scandals arise when private transgressions become public (Adut 2009) and in the case of Edison Chen, he also failed as a representative of the collective.

Hong Kong, as a Chinese society that spent over 150 years under Western colonial rule, has been influenced by ideas about the individual that problematize the dichotomized and essentialistic conceptions of individualism and collectivity. It has been argued that culture in Hong Kong came to be characterized by utilitarianism and consumerism as opposed to the received perception of the importance of collectivity in Chinese society (Sun 1989). This book focuses on the period since the 1970s, a time of dramatic change for Hong Kong citizens. The 1970s was a decade of social and economic transformation brought about by government policies responding to the coming of age of a population enlarged by post-war mass migration and to the emergence of a middle class resulting from better educational and economic opportunities.[2] The relative economic prosperity and social stability of the early 1980s, however, was disrupted by apprehension associated with the expected handover of Hong Kong to Chinese rule in 1997.[3] British Prime Minister Margaret Thatcher visited Beijing in 1984 to sign the Joint Declaration specifying the terms of the transfer of sovereignty to China. Residents were indifferent to the politics of identity as a collective notion until the question of the handover to China arose (Chun 1996), and the handover continued to affect the social, political and personal lives of Hong Kong residents throughout the transition period.[4]

Much has been written about the term 'Hong Kong identity' as a collective notion, especially about the formation of such an identity and changes in its meanings in the run up to the handover.[5] These writers focus their debates on whether people in Hong Kong accepted the city's changing relationship with Mainland China as a result of the handover. Allen Chun (1996) suggests that as 1997 approached, a crisis of culture occurred that called into question Hong Kong's autonomy and its 'identity' and forced young people brought up in Hong Kong's apolitical culture to examine their 'Chinese' identity.

Ackbar Abbas (1996, p.1) describes 'the cultural self-invention of the Hong Kong subject' before the handover in what he calls 'a space of disappearance'.[6] This 'last-minute' search for the Hong Kong subject was a collective response to the return of Chinese rule, an event citizens feared might cause the disappearance of their local way of life. I argue that the process of identity-searching became even more pronounced after the handover due to the political and economic problems in the city. In mid-1997 the economy of Hong Kong was hit by the Asia-wide economic crisis. Although Hong Kong recovered better than its Asian neighbours, the poor economy, high unemployment and a property slump left lasting effects on the public psyche. Tensions between the most recent wave of new migrants, mainland visitors and existing Hong Kong citizens similarly raised questions about local identity after the city's first 15 years as a Special Administrative Region (SAR) of China. Hong Kong identity should therefore be considered as a conception that is transformative and historically specific.

In this book I contextualize the importance of China within the constructions of identity in Hong Kong as part of the complexity encompassing social, cultural and economic conditions, but I also carry out an 'interrogation of local experience' (Abbas 2001, p.626) found in indigenous cultural forms and practices. The 1980s saw dramatic growth in commercially successful and prolific cultural products, including cinema, pop music and television, which were consumed by the emerging middle class, and so these media, along with the centrality of stardom, are local cultural practices that are useful for an examination of identity in Hong Kong. I seek to address three main questions in this book: What were the relationships between the practices and discourse of stardom;[7] how did the changing social and cultural landscapes of the city affect the development of multimedia stardom; and how did stardom change from the early 1980s to the post-handover context?

Beyond film stardom

The main concerns addressed by literature on Hong Kong's popular culture in the 1980s and 1990s are the handover and the connections between Hong Kong and China. A large number of such commentaries written in English are dominated by a discussion of the collective search for a unified Hong Kong identity.[8] For example, Benjamin Leung observes that 'the rise of the Hong Kong identity is a dual process of dissociation from colonial cultural domination as well as from the social and political life of the mainland' (1996, p.68). This process was exemplified by an indigenization of popular culture in the city that took place in the 1970s (examined in Chapters 1 and 2). Television drama series and other entertainment programmes portrayed the modern, capitalist, glamorous city lifestyle of Hong Kong as something opposed to the traditionalism and socialism of China (Chu 2003). A range of popular cultural practices ought to be of central concern in the exploration of post-1970 Hong Kong society, and yet the content of locally produced films tends to dominate the existing literature.

There are numerous examples of writers, using textual analysis as their main tool, arguing that the films made during this transitional period are allegories of Hong Kong's political future (Brett Erens 2000; Chua 1998; Lee 1994; Li 1994; Stringer 1997; Teo 1997; Williams 1995; Williams 1997; Williams 1998; Yau 1994).[9] Allegory is also applied to geographical displacement, as in Ann Hui's Vietnam trilogy (the television programme, *The Boy from Vietnam*, and the films, *The Story of Woo Viet*, 1981, and *Boat People*, 1982), which is seen as a metaphor for Hong Kong's future (Li 1994; Williams 1998).[10] These writers tend to map predetermined ideas about the geopolitics of Hong Kong onto the cinematic worlds presented, rather than viewing the films' action and aesthetics as interactions with their context (Robinson 2006). This is particularly pertinent when writers focus on Hong Kong's relationship with China at the expense of Hong Kong's own rich cultural and social history. In this book I explore stardom and a variety of media practices in order to uncover the social and cultural life of Hong Kong, rather than examining the macro-level political relationships with China that pre-handover literature tends to focus on.

Similarly, the writings on post-1997 Hong Kong cinema are also dominated by handover-related themes. Chu Yingchi (2003) briefly surveys several films from the period in order to examine Hong Kong's relationship with China in terms of memory, sense of loss, and identity. The writings cited thus far, mainly examining the content of films from Hong Kong, tend to treat film narratives as if they were literary works and directly reflective of the collective sentiments of audience members who all view each film in exactly the same way. Textual analysis is only a partial way of examining cultural phenomena because the phenomena are generally analysed without considering the conditions under which they were produced and received (Thompson 1995). The meaning of the media message is not static but varies from one socio-historical context to another, an aspect of particular relevance to my retrospective analysis of multimedia stardom as a cultural phenomenon.

The sociologist Chan Hoi-man suggests that Hong Kong's popular culture from the 1970s performs several functions, including offering reflections of a collective ethos and conveying a sense of increased material wealth (cited in Leung 1996). While Hong Kong pop culture reflects the quests for individual success and collective survival against overwhelming historical odds, it also provides relaxation and relief from the frustrations of urban life. As such, popular culture is thought to counteract the reality of individuals' struggle for economic success, especially for the majority who do not achieve it (Leung 1996). This position assumes a homogeneity of both the producers and consumers of popular culture.

This kind of assumption about producers and consumers is often replicated in star studies, because stardom can be approached both as a phenomenon of production and as a phenomenon of consumption (Dyer 1979). Existing examinations of the images, fans and local audiences of Hong Kong stars assume that stars function as compensation for everyday stress without specific reference to the historical or cultural contexts. Day Wong's (2005) article on women's reception of Hong Kong cinema, relying on an extensive collection of interviews, focuses on the audiences' responses to specific stories within the films. To illustrate fan responses to storylines and characters as evidence of star-identification, Wong cites the job insecurity experienced by one of her informants and suggests that 'watching *Police Story* [Jackie Chan, 1985] provided her with a kind of comfort and compensation' (2005, p.256, my parenthesis). Wong's interpretation therefore assumes that stars are functional in relation to the audiences' needs and frustrations. This is an example of how critics and academics often treat local consumers as a homogeneous entity.

Where studies move away from a focus on stars' onscreen image towards the production and consumption of stardom, they provide more complex analyses of empirical evidence. Some writers apply an approach to the study of media consumers that situates their experiences historically and away from an assumption of their needs. For example, films do not hold the same meanings for the audience, director, actors, distributor and producer, and these meanings change over time (Wong & McDonogh 2001a, 2001b). The consumption of Cantonese opera in Hong Kong has undergone significant changes since the 1930s, with the advent and subsequent decline of opera films. While the commercial value of opera stars' performances almost ceased to exist in the 1990s, the stars' image as respected entertainers continued in the media world (Latham 2000). Ruan Jihong's (2003) examination of the changing relationship between journalists and entertainment stars in Hong Kong shows that as the printed press changed in the 1990s, so did the ways that news about the stars was reported, which had an impact on their image. My analysis treats stardom as a set of practices involving producers and audiences, two parties that may attach very different meanings to stardom. I then interrogate how changes in the cultural and social contexts affected production and consumption as two interdependent dimensions of stardom.

There has been more reliance on empirical research in the study of media such as television and popular music than of film in Hong Kong. Eric Ma (1995) compares the text, production and consumption of local television drama series from the 1970s with those from the 1990s and concludes that television played a role in the formation and maintenance of identity in Hong Kong as affected by the anticipated handover, while also influencing perceptions of the city's relationships with China more generally. Within the literature on Cantonese pop music, aspects of identity, such as ethnicity and gender, have been discussed (Erni 2007; Fung & Curtin 2002; Witzleben 1999). Although pop stars are an important part of some of these studies, the research often examines a particular form of identity using stars as examples rather than studying stardom per se. For example, much of the existing literature on journalism in Hong Kong focuses on political communication (Chan & Lee 1991; Lee 1998; Lee 2000), contrasting journalism practices employed in the city with those of the press media in China. The entertainment press rarely features in these studies except for a few short journalistic articles (Lee 2003). The chapters that follow refocus the study of a range of media in Hong Kong, including film, television, pop music and the printed press, and examine the medias' most celebrated personnel.

Existing English-language literature on stardom tends to concentrate on Hollywood,[11] one of the largest producers of commercial films. Nevertheless, the definitions of film stardom point to the existence of a star discourse across different media and to meanings beyond stars' participation in films:

> Stars are only of significance because they are in films and therefore are part of the way films signify . . . The sociological concern can only make headway when informed by a proper engagement with . . . their specific signification as realised in media texts (including films, but also newspaper stories, television programmes, advertisements, etc.).
>
> (Dyer 1979, p.1)

This offers a starting point for an attempt to understand the practices of multimedia stardom, albeit with a focus on film stars as individuals who are engaged in making, usually commercial, films in which they are presented as the major attraction. Despite the acknowledgement that stars' specific signification is realized in different media texts, film continues to be seen as the privileged form of signification within star studies, as a medium that provides the ultimate confirmation of stardom (Gledhill 1991). The stars' image outside of film is incomplete without their screen performance because film performance presents the completeness of the star, the real mystery that other star texts can only hint at (Ellis 1997). As a result of the privileged status of screen presence, star studies have been dominated by the analysis of texts with a central focus on the appearances of individual stars in films, while their cross-media images are placed on the periphery. Film studies often treat the content of film texts as if created by one author. Similarly, the related field of star studies tends to treat stars as 'texts' that can be analysed without considering the conditions under which they were produced and consumed (Thompson 1995, p.37). This approach lends itself well to debates that rely on the construction of a set of dominant meanings associated with the individual stars.

Existing literature on Chinese stars similarly privileges film stardom and case studies of individual examples. Zhang Yingjin and Mary Farquhar's edited collection, *Chinese Film Stars* (2010), for example, is based on individual case studies and contains chapters on many male Hong Kong stars: Bruce Lee, Jackie Chan, Chow Yun-fat, Leslie Cheung (1956–2003) and Jet Li. Sabrina Yu's (2012a) monograph examines Jet Li as a key case study of transnational film stardom. Her work signals an emerging direction of research on the transnational nature of stardom,[12] an aspect that will also be examined as part of my analysis of multimedia stardom. Similarly, while celebrity studies tend to consider famous persons from other media and popular cultural products, Graeme Turner (2010) is insightful in pointing out that existing studies are based mostly on the textual analysis of representations of individual celebrities rather than on the production and consumption contexts and the social implications of celebrity culture.[13]

In focusing on one of the central features of contemporary stardom, its multimedia nature, this book analyses an area that is acknowledged but often underresearched in star studies. For instance, Martin Barker and Thomas Austin (2003), writing about Hollywood, say that stardom is an intertextual and multimedia phenomenon with overlapping political, economic, technological and discursive dimensions, and these interrelating fields of activity can be termed '*star systems*' (Barker & Austin 2003, p.25, original emphasis) because they each play a part in the production and circulation of star images and narratives. Richard Allen and Douglas Gomery (cited in Geraghty 2000) state that the term 'stars' in the West, currently referring to a wide range of celebrities including rock stars, athletes and soap opera actors, is overused and almost meaningless. On the contrary, I contend that it is precisely the diffused, cross-media presence of contemporary stars in Hong Kong, a unique feature of the cultural and social life in the city, which makes stardom an important research subject. Stardom in media industries, such as those in Hong Kong, is under-researched due to the domination of studies on

Hollywood cinema. Star studies remain largely confined to the relationship with a specific medium (film) and the American studio production system rather than examining stardom as practices that are culturally and historically specific. Paul McDonald warns:

> The star image approach, reading the meaning of a single star in isolation, has tended to lose sight of the ways in which the meaning or professional power of one star are conditional upon a system of differences and distinctions between stars and other performers . . . analysis of stars in context shows how these differences change historically and culturally.
>
> (1998, p.200)

It is an oversimplification to state that particular stars are products of only their contemporaneous times and societies. In this study I therefore locate stardom within its cultural context through a retrospective evaluation of earlier generations of stars in comparison to contemporary stars.

In summary, several issues are apparent in relation to current approaches to studying popular culture and stardom in Hong Kong. Writers tend to focus on Hong Kong's relationship with China at the expense of the city's unique cultural and social history. While some of the themes in prevailing scholarship are relevant, such as identity and retrospective re-evaluations of the recent cultural and social history of Hong Kong, existing literature fails to consider changes throughout the pre- and post-1997 period by placing too much emphasis on the handover. In addition, star studies remain largely film-centric and mostly about Hollywood. Even though it is acknowledged that star studies should be time- and space-specific, empirical work and substantive studies from outside of the USA and Europe are rare. In relation to Hong Kong, stars are under-researched in comparison to the interest in the content of the films produced in the city, especially those from the pre-1997 period. Finally, existing writings do not acknowledge the close relationships between the different forms of media in Hong Kong, and authors tend to assume that the media products they examine have a unified audience.

In contrast, I present empirical evidence from a group of interlocking media practices as they relate to stardom and in conjunction with the changing social and cultural landscapes in pre- and post-handover Hong Kong in order to investigate what makes stardom in this city unique. Stardom in Hong Kong is a changing set of practices that involves different cultural products and their consumption, including advertising, films, magazine images, pop music, television and inter-media commentaries. Analysis of the practices of multimedia stardom needs to go beyond attempting to map Hong Kong culture and society onto predetermined issues, such as the handover and the relationship with China, while still acknowledging the impact of those issues on the development of the city and its media industry. My analysis thus extends beyond 1997 to include recent changes in the cultural and social landscapes of Hong Kong, especially Hong Kong media stars' growing significance in China and international popular culture.

Understanding multimedia stardom

While conducting the research that led to this book, a question that I was often asked and that I kept in mind was what stardom tells us about Hong Kong society. From the early days of star studies, ideological debates have been firmly embedded in the Hollywood paradigm, as Richard Dyer writes, 'The primary concern of any attention to Hollywood must be with the dominant ideology of western society. Any dominant ideology in any society presents itself as the ideology of that society as a whole' (1979, p.2). The assumption of stars' ability to reflect a society's ideology is not unproblematic because, as Alan Lovell (2003) asserts, a change occurred between the publication of Dyer's *Stars* (1979, revised 1998) and *Heavenly Bodies* (1986), in that the latter shifts the terminology to discourse. While the term discourse is often used interchangeably with ideology, the shift in usage reflects the academic interests of the two periods (Althusser 1971, Foucault 1983). Lovell (2003) also notes that Dyer does not explain why ideology has to be central in the study of stars. Ideology can be seen simply as 'a society's ideas' (Gledhill 1997, p.347) – but ideas about what, whose ideas, and is there a limit to these ideas? How are stars best in telling us about these ideas? Michel Foucault offers a direct critique of the notion of ideology:

> The notion of ideology appears to me to be difficult to make use of, for three reasons. The first is that, like it or not, it always stands in virtual opposition to something else which is supposed to count as truth . . . The second drawback is that the concept of ideology refers . . . to something of the order of a subject. Thirdly, ideology stands in a secondary position relative to something which functions as its infrastructure, as its material, economic determinant, etc. For these three reasons, I think that this is a notion that cannot be used without circumspection.
>
> (1980, p.118)

Within Foucault's conceptualization of discourse (1983), therefore, there is no constant limit of 'society', identifiable truth or a unified subject; rather, the subject is continuously made and remade and is historically situated. Lovell (2003) also voices objections to the assumption of the centrality of ideology in Dyer's work, in that it relies on an essentialist account of individuality embodied by the stars. Stardom in a society at a particular time is a discursive construction and is constantly in flux. The subjects, producers and consumers involved in the creation of stardom are discursively constructed in relationship to each other. Film stars often provide evidence that opposes the conception of a stable, unique identity (Lovell 2003), while the changing theoretical frames in star studies, as outlined above, destabilize notions of subjectivity and problematize and complicate an essential view of society. My study, using explanatory frameworks of image, performance and identity, is a prime example of how stars and their presence across media create a set of questions related to the changing constitution and recognition of cultural subjects (Butler 1993; Foucault 1987).

The debates about multimedia stardom described in this book demonstrate how the subject area has changed alongside developments in cultural studies, which have shifted away from the analysis of stars as ahistorical texts. As McDonald observes:

> Contextualising the meaning of stars is always open to the charge of present-ing a simple 'reflectionist' history of stardom: societies change historically and stars reflect those changes . . . This raises questions of what defines and delimits a 'context', and what forms of context are to be judged as of most relevance to the study of stardom.
>
> (1998, p.179)

By conducting interviews with media professionals and considering the changing social and cultural contexts in Hong Kong over the decades since the early 1980s, I treat stardom not as something static but as a context-specific discursive construc-tion. Those I interviewed over the course of researching this book participated in the discursive construction of this knowledge through articulatory practice: 'any practice establishing a relation among elements such that their identity is modi-fied as a result of the articulatory practice. The structured totality resulting from the articulatory practice [is] *discourse.*' (Laclau & Mouffe 1985, p.105, original emphasis). In sharing their thoughts on stardom, the mediasphere,[14] culture and society in Hong Kong with me, my interviewees constructed and organized social realities and, as a result, modified their own identity as Hong Kong subjects. In the chapters that follow, I shall delimit and define the most relevant contexts for understanding multimedia stardom in Hong Kong as the city faced successive challenges since the early 1980s.

Methods

The predominant approach to the research that led to this book was the use of qualitative methods that allow researchers to get close to the data and provide opportunities for them to derive their concepts from the gathered information, with a constant interplay of data collection and analysis (Burgess 1984; Wiseman 1979). I began in 2001, and this decade-long research project included a ten-month period of fieldwork in Hong Kong in 2005, supplemented by shorter visits in 2009, 2012 and 2014. The most important primary materials came from interviews with media professionals, journalists and actors. The research was complemented by my work as a freelance film journalist, most importantly at Asian and European film festivals, including the Hong Kong International Film Festival (HKIFF), Taipei International Film Festival, Hong Kong Independent Short Film and Video Awards and Far East Film, Udine, Italy. I attended industry events, public screenings and seminars and became an observer-participant. As a journalist and during the periods of fieldwork, I undertook in-depth interviews with professionals from the Hong Kong media industries who were connected with the production of stars' onscreen roles and on- and off-screen images, including film- and programme-makers, a television and commercial producer, stars and actors, agents and thespians.[15] I also interviewed scholars, local writers and journalists, who, in the context of this research, can be thought of as expert witnesses. Some of these interviews were one or two hours long. Most of the interviewees were professionals from a cohort born in the years after the Second World War and up to 1980. The older research subjects would have experienced the changes in Hong Kong since the 1970s as adults, while the younger interviewees, who would have been in their late teens at the time, also had some recollection of the transitional period and handover. The sample of interviewees was selected for its relevance and appropriateness for the research questions and by data- and theory-driven sampling, with a focus on industry veterans who were already working in the media sector in the 1980s and early 1990s. There was access to mainstream industry insiders: Miriam Yeung's (b.1974) management company granted me an interview, as did the actresses Sylvia Chang (b.1953) and Lee Sinje (b.1976), television and commercial producer Robert Chua, and producer-directors Jeff Lau and Andrew Lau.

Stardom in Hong Kong is circulated in different entertainment formats and through associated merchandizing, effectively forming a nexus of different media: feature films, television programmes, music recordings and videos, the printed press, advertising and the Internet. I therefore gathered data from all these media, including stars' interviews from other published sources, relevant materials from the printed press, Internet sites, the Hong Kong Film Archive (HKFA) and the trade press. This combination of methods (triangulation) is designed to generate verbal, textual and visual data that can support, refute and complement each other to better clarify the specific nature of multimedia stardom in Hong Kong.

Stardom-related practices and discourses are symbolic cultural forms, the meanings of which are subject to interpretation rather than being static and intrinsic; therefore, these forms, alongside the conditions under which they are produced and consumed, must be analysed in a systematic and detailed way (Thompson 1995). The transcripts and collected evidence were used to determine the key concepts and further categorize the evidence in a process that follows the grounded theory approach, an analytical procedure that induces from research findings, develops conceptual categories and identifies patterned relationships (Schrøder & Jensen 2002). As such, the theoretical constructions and conceptions are achieved through an interplay between collection and analysis of robust, context-specific data.

Overview of the book

The chapters that follow begin with a historical contextualization of multimedia stardom followed by an examination of the decades since the early 1980s, when the question of the handover of Hong Kong from British to Chinese rule was first raised, concluding with the post-handover mediasphere. I examine multimedia stardom through the key concepts of image, performance and identity. After an in-depth analysis of the data, I argue that stardom is influenced by and helps us to understand the cultural and social contexts in Hong Kong.

In Chapter 1, 'Transformations in Hong Kong society and popular culture', I examine the historical development of Hong Kong society and culture, the process of the indigenization of local popular media that took place in the 1970s, and changes since the mid-1990s, and argue for the close and unique relationships between media and the social and cultural landscapes of the city. Chapter 2, 'Multimedia stardom in Hong Kong', considers the specific characteristics of stardom in Hong Kong through a historical review. In this chapter I focus on an examination of a group of indigenous stars and the subsequent transformations in stardom from the 1990s, taking into account Hong Kong stars' developing presence in China and international popular culture.

Stars are symbolic forms carrying cultural meanings that also reveal ideas about individuals in capitalist societies (Gledhill 1991). The next three chapters therefore focus on an examination of several emerging themes that provide the basis of my argument for the significance of multimedia stardom in Hong Kong. McDonald (2000) suggests that Hollywood stars' work in films and as image makes them both commodity and capital, which the studios and the stars themselves, often through agents, can exploit. In other words, stars' performances and other activities, such as the production of image, should be considered their work in the commercial media industries. In existing paradigms of star studies, film performances are considered 'privileged instances' (Dyer 1979, pp.88) of stardom. My conceptualization of multimedia stardom addresses this assumption as it interrogates two of the main themes connected to this type of stardom, namely image and performance. The scandal involving Edison Chen showed that the multimedia nature of stardom was changing in contemporary Hong Kong through a shift in prominence from performances towards image production. This shift had a direct impact on the discourse of stardom against the social and cultural backgrounds. Chapter 3, 'Image', explores the stars' existence as images sold in commercials and entertainment news and investigates contemporary notions about the commodification of individuals and the anxiety that it raises. In this chapter I also examine the changing practices of advertising, multimedia corporations, newspaper and magazine publishing, and the creation of young stars in Hong Kong.

Chapter 4, 'Performance', explores the unique traditions in the practice and discourse of performance in Hong Kong, framed against ideas about work and success. Evidence is provided of stardom as a symbolic form in an analysis of the individual's role in capitalist society. In Chapter 5, 'Identity', I take into account the specific historical and cultural transformations of the city, focusing on the 2000s and early 2010s. I argue that stars can be analysed in relation to notions of identity and examine the significance of the expectation that Hong Kong stars be model individuals and representatives of the collective at times of crisis.

The concluding chapter draws lessons from my discussion of image, performance and identity, illustrating the relationships between the shifting practices and discourse of stardom and the social and cultural landscapes in Hong Kong. I demonstrate the importance of multimedia stardom as part of transnational popular culture and the 'cultural Chinese' (Tu 1991) mediascape, using evidence from both historical and contemporary contexts. Multimedia stars in Hong Kong, as the most visible people working in popular cultural forms in the city, have a significant presence in the Greater Chinese and global popular culture nexus.

1 Transformations in Hong Kong society and popular culture

In the Introduction I argued that the distinctive cultural and social development of Hong Kong is a relevant context for understanding multimedia stardom. In this chapter I therefore detail the indigenization of popular culture in Hong Kong from the 1970s onwards, the subsequent decline of the local media since the mid-1990s, and the developing roles of the city's media in relation to Chinese and international popular culture. I contextualize these developments against changes in the culture in order to demonstrate the close and unique relationship between media in Hong Kong and the social and cultural landscapes of the city.

The social and cultural development of Hong Kong

Hong Kong Island was ceded to Great Britain by China under the Treaty of Nanking in 1842 after the First Opium War between Britain and the Qing Government. In 1860 Britain acquired Kowloon following the Second Opium War (1856–60). The New Territories, leased to Britain for 99 years in 1898 under the Second Convention of Peking, completed the geographical makeup of the colony. It is suggested that there was racial segregation between the colonists and the Chinese and that little indigenous Hong Kong culture existed in the nineteenth century because neither group regarded the city as their permanent home (Leung 1996). This is not strictly correct because the farming communities of Hakka and Punti settlers, as well as other ethnic groups such as the Tanka (boat dwellers), had arrived long before the nineteenth century and had distinctive cultural and social customs.[1]

During the Second World War, Hong Kong was occupied by Japan from 1941 to 1945, and the Chinese population suffered military and cultural oppression. After the war, Hong Kong remained a British colony, but its cultural and social development was inseparable from what happened in Mainland China. The 1950s was a period of rapid social change in Hong Kong, particularly after establishment of the People's Republic of China (PRC) in 1949 stimulated mass migration into the British colony. The population of Hong Kong jumped from 1.6 million in 1940 to 3 million in 1960, reaching 5.2 million in 1980 (Morris 1988). Hong Kong also grew as a manufacturing and export centre from the 1950s, benefiting from laissez-faire conditions (Jarvie & Agassi 1969) that provided jobs and opportunities for the new migrants. Among the migrants were wealthy merchant families, many from Shanghai, who brought with them business know-how. Despite this economic growth, many post-war immigrants busied themselves with economic survival. The sociologist Lau Siu-kai called their survival strategy 'utilitarian familism', meaning that the refugee families were culturally and economically conservative, with strong political apathy toward the larger society (cited in Siu 1996, p.182). Family was an important source of support as government provisions were inadequate (Leung 1996), and the number of refugees would soon force the colonial government to begin social and welfare programmes to provide housing, education and transportation. The increase in population and the poor quality of many dwellings culminated in the great fire of the Shek Kip Mei slums in 1953, and rebuilding the area defined public housing policy in subsequent decades. Despite the general post-war hardship and poverty, a small middle class began to emerge, indicative of a society that would become increasingly divided between rich and poor.

From 1967 to 1976, Mainland China was embroiled in the Cultural Revolution. While many new migrants in Hong Kong might previously have sent goods to relatives in their home villages, contact and communication were made difficult during this time, resulting in a greater sense of distance between Hong Kong and the Mainland. After the introduction of China's Open Door Policy in 1978, increasing numbers of migrants from the Mainland arrived in Hong Kong, providing additional low-wage workers. Those who considered themselves Hong Kong *ren* ('people') often looked down on new migrants and mainlanders, whom they regarded as the 'other'. The 1970s was a decade of further social and economic transformation in Hong Kong, the effects of which prompted the government to increase its intervention in social welfare. Leung sums up the significance of the period: 'the Hong Kong experience as we know it today has its roots in the society's political and economic transformations beginning in the early 1970s' (1996, p.51). The same decade also saw the coming of age of the children of 1950s refugees; for the first time, a generation born and bred in Hong Kong formed the majority of the population (Yahuda 1995). They were generally better educated than their parents and became the new middle/professional class.

In reference to all these changes, Esther Cheung warns about what she calls colonialist historical writings (Birch 1991; Cameron 1991; Welsh 1997) that suggest a 'grand narrative of Hong Kong history characterized by the dominant representation of Hong Kong as a capitalist success and the miraculous transformation of it from a remote fishing village to a world-class metropole' (Cheung 2001, p.565). This kind of linear history is based on a discourse of progress idealizing colonialism as a developmental, modernizing project (Cheung 2001). In particular, Cheung (2001) points out that Hong Kong is often depicted in these writings with natal metaphors, the city being 'a miraculous offspring' and the result of 'a true marriage of Confucian values and British colonial ethics' (Birch 1991, pp.22–3). However, many 'local fishing and farming villages had never transformed themselves into the world metropolis' (Siu 1996, p.177), and original fishing communities suffered marginalization and economic exploitation in Hong Kong under colonial rule (Cheung 2001). Unfortunately for such communities, fishing and farming activities have been replaced by major development projects, the most obvious examples being the opening of Hong Kong International Airport in 1998 and Disneyland on Lantau Island in 2005. A grand narrative of Hong Kong as a capitalist success therefore obscures the divisions within its society resulting, most often, from stratification by economic status.

Jonathan Grant (2001) discusses how the colonial government intervened during the industrialization process in post-war Hong Kong to reinvent public culture, partly in response to a series of riots by civilians that caused great concern for the stability of the city. In 1956 a riot led by Nationalists resulted in 44 deaths (Grant 2001). A 1966 riot, triggered by plans for a fare increase on the Star Ferry, was a result of underlying discontent felt by the young generation raised in Hong Kong by immigrant parents, especially with the difference between social and economic realities and aspirations (Jarvie 1969). Influenced by the Cultural Revolution on the Mainland, the 1967 anti-colonial riots started as a strike and saw the most prolonged and violent clashes between Communist sympathizers and the police in the recent history of the city, with 51 deaths and 2,000 convictions. The emerging Cold War, the Civil War in China and the riots in Hong Kong prompted several ordinances from 1948 to 1970 that sought to control trade union activities and large-scale gatherings and give the government power to incarcerate or deport 'troublemakers' (Grant 2001, pp.160–1). As an example, 20 'progressive' (the euphemism for left-wing) actors and filmmakers were expelled by the colonial government in 1952 (p.161). In spite of the turmoil, the combination of cultural discourse, high availability of cheap labour, government legislation to avoid wage inflation and weak trade union organization encouraged and maintained economic growth (Jarvie & Agassi 1969).

Public housing and social welfare policies contributed to the break-up of the extended family and engendered the idea of the nuclear family (Grant 2001). In addition, sociologists in Hong Kong believe that a shift occurred from extended family networks to a more nuclear family orientation as a result of adaptation to the industrial and commercial contexts (an idea reflected in Lau Siu-kai's use of the term utilitarian familism) (Leung 1996). From the 1970s onwards this trend continued towards utilitarian or egotistical individualism, though collectivism continued to find favour in support for a social order that would allow for individual development (Leung 1996). Grant suggests that 'the imagining of reciprocal and imbricated industrial and societal "development" . . . in which all had a share, was a powerful image of social progress which was wholly depoliticized' (2001, p.167). To prevent future disturbances and sustain industrial and societal development, the government needed a cultural discourse that avoided the question of inequalities of power and wealth. Government policies in this regard were successful to the extent that, according to a sociological study from 1988, 69.3 per cent of respondents agreed that 'the rights possessed by a person in society are not in-born. It is because of his good performance that society gives him the rights as rewards' (Lau & Kuan 1988, p.51). The Hong Kong Chinese were supposed to be motivated to work hard by the perceived possibility for social mobility, and their efforts were put forth to fulfil the 'rags-to-riches' Hong Kong dream (Leung 1996, pp.55–60). The implication is that social mobility in a meritocratic society could be achieved through hard work, and therefore an important personal ethic emerged that was based on self-reliance, materialism and a pragmatic orientation.

This discourse of a collective ethos explains Hong Kong's economic progress while obscuring social and cultural differences. For example, Chun suggests that there was 'a media-oriented popular culture that was financed by large capitalist interests . . . which neatly reproduced the utilitarian values of a free-market society' (1996, p.58). Furthermore, the people of Hong Kong had a unique view of the world and their place in it, where everything, including culture, could be given a price (Chun 1996). Chun's notion of Hong Kong culture essentializes it through the stereotypical view of a market-oriented culture entirely resulting from capitalist ideology. This perspective assumes one unified, highly commercialized Hong Kong culture, a notion that has been criticized by Abbas (1997) as a cliché.

Rather than being homogeneous, cultural and social formations in Hong Kong were marked by class differences. Hong Kong society had only gradually started to prosper after the Second World War, so the collective ethos of materialist success through labour helped to explain the achievements of the emerging middle class. Annie Chan (2000) uses the term 'middle class' to refer to the professional and managerial classes and to those who have benefited by the recent expansion of further and higher education, although she remarks that even the 'new rich' in Hong Kong are far from homogeneous (p.128, notes 1–3). The well-rehearsed argument about Hong Kong is that it is 'an open society where individual merit is the main criteria for achievement', although the reality is that 'the distribution of power and material resources has never been in any way egalitarian, and economic development has continued to widen rather than narrow the gap between the rich and the poor' (p.99).

Chan's (2000) empirical research suggests that young middle-class professionals in Hong Kong in the 1990s favoured leisure activities such as cinema-going, eating out and shopping over television, with long working hours and the lack of home space given as the reasons. With the expansion of the middle classes in Hong Kong, leisure patterns continued to shift. An associated change was the increasingly important youth market segment that mushroomed since the 1990s, a pattern replicated across many Asian countries. The increasing trend of internationalization, China-Hong Kong co-productions, and pan-Asian production and circulation of media meant that young people could draw from an international 'image bank' through their consumption of popular mass media rather than only from the local culture (Chua 2000, p.16), a development which explains the decline in consumption of traditional media in Hong Kong from the mid-1990s.

As Hong Kong settled into a period of seeming stability in the late 1970s and early 1980s, the issue of reunification with China was substantiated by British Prime Minister Margaret Thatcher's visit to Beijing in 1984 to sign the Joint Declaration specifying the terms of the transfer of governance for the city. The social upheaval that followed was reflected in the mass emigration of Hong Kong residents before the handover; from 1984 to 1995, more than 500,000, out of a population of around 6 million, moved abroad, mostly to Australia, Canada, New

Zealand and the USA (Yahuda 1995). The disruption was felt most acutely by the professional, Western-educated baby boomers of post-war Hong Kong, who feared political and economic instability and could afford to emigrate (Siu 1996). Instead of political action, the professional class were more likely to choose emigration as a response to the handover (Salaff & Wong 1994). The sense of distance this particular generation felt towards China intensified after the events in Tiananmen Square on 4 June 1989, when the Chinese government clamped down on pro-democracy demonstrators. There were mass demonstrations in Hong Kong in June 1989 supporting those in Tiananmen Square. For those writing a 'macro-history' of Hong Kong, these events were confirmation of the threats to the stability and prosperity of the future (Cheung 2001, pp.566–7).

Substantial development in the political, economic and social spheres took place in Hong Kong from the mid-1990s. The most significant occurrence was the handover of sovereignty from Britain to China on 1 July 1997, an event preceded by years of expectation. In recognition of its autonomy, and as a result of negotiations between the British and Chinese governments, Hong Kong became a SAR within China after 1997, governed by Basic Law and a Chief Executive Officer (CEO). It was agreed that 'the socialist system and policies shall not be practised in the Hong Kong Special Administrative Region, and the previous capitalist system and way of life shall remain unchanged for 50 years' (Basic Law 1990, Chapter I, Article 5), in accordance with the principal of 'one country, two systems' first suggested by China's paramount leader Deng Xiaoping in the early 1980s. Shortly after this momentous event, a general recession, which became known as the Asian crisis, swept through the Asian economies in the late 1990s. Hong Kong was affected, although 'disaster was averted because the SAR government did the unexpected, and for many, the unthinkable: it intervened in the market' (Abbas 2001, p.622). The economy in Hong Kong recovered better than many of its Asian neighbours, but the downturn had a significant impact on the social and cultural lives of the population: 'as the recession began to bite, business slumped, the market tumbled and the tourists stayed away' (p.621). Economic difficulties were further compounded by several large-scale public health scares. The SARS (Severe Acute Respiratory Syndrome) epidemic of 2003 that spread from the region to many Asian countries and other continents severely hampered the economy, including the movie industry and other aspects of everyday life, with many public places in the city, like cinemas, deserted. The recession led to a sense of vulnerability for the population.

Since the handover, significant events in Hong Kong have demonstrated how the city attempts to understand its place within China's political, cultural and economic spheres. On 1 July 2003, one million residents took to the streets in protest against the proposed anti-subversion law (related to Article 23 of Basic Law). This was a result of dissatisfaction with a range of events and circumstances in the first few years of the SAR: the lack of progress towards universal suffrage in 2007 and 2008, the apparent incompetence of the first CEO, Tung Chee-hwa (who stepped down in 2005 and was replaced by Donald Tsang), the financial and planning difficulties associated with the West Kowloon Cultural District, the ongoing economic

downturn, and high suicide rates. The University of Hong Kong's Public Opinion Programme has been surveying the confidence in Hong Kong's future since
1994.[2] During 15–9 May 1997, the percentage of the 1,059 polled who reported
confidence in the city's future was 71.4 per cent. The percentage dropped to 67.1
per cent in December 1998 (sample size 530) and was 42.2 per cent in June 2003
(sample size 1,043) and 57.4 per cent in March 2013 (sample size 1,018).

The lack of confidence in Hong Kong by its own citizens does not reflect some
of the benefits of the closer economic ties developed since the handover. Since 1
January 2004 the Closer Economic Partnership Agreement (CEPA), a free trade
agreement between the Mainland and Hong Kong, has been in place, aiming to
make the SAR a springboard to doing business in China.[3] The agreement covers goods, services and the facilitation of trade and investment, and it has been
amended and supplemented continuously. By 2012 the PRC had become the most
important source of direct investment in Hong Kong (36.3 per cent of the total)
(Hong Kong Trade Development Council 2013). As part of CEPA, residents of
some Chinese cities have, since 2003, been allowed to visit Hong Kong on an
individual basis under the Individual Visit Scheme (IVS). In 2012 the number of
visitors from the Mainland increased by 24.2 per cent to 34.9 million, accounting
for 72 per cent of the city's total number of visitors and contributing to 60 per cent
of retail sales. Tourist spending has brought a much needed boost to the economy
since the SARS epidemic of 2003, but it has also driven up rents for commercial
premises.[4] In 2012 concerns were expressed over the expansion of the IVS to 4.1
million non-permanent residents of Shenzhen. The recent tenth year anniversary
of the IVS, with the scheme extending to 49 cities, prompted discussion in Hong
Kong about stopping further expansion of the scheme and the influx of mainland
visitors because of fear that the visitors would overwhelm the infrastructure of
the city.[5] An incident in 2012 escalated the resentment felt by Hong Kong citizens, exemplifying the post-handover tensions between the Mainland and Hong
Kong. A video posted on the Internet showing a Hong Kong passenger remon-
strating a young mainland visitor for spilling food on a subway train went viral. The
commuter could be seen shouting, 'This is Hong Kong!'. A Peking University
professor, Kong Qingdong, responding on television, called Hong Kong residents
'bastards', 'British running dogs', 'not human', and 'traitors'.[6]

Attempts to renationalize Hong Kong have included proposals to introduce
Chinese patriotism lessons in school, prevent mainland dissidents from entering the city and use pro-Beijing press in the ex-colony to attack individuals and
groups seen as subversive.[7] The proposed patriotism lessons led to a series of anti-
Mainland protests in Hong Kong in 2012, and the SAR government eventually
backed down from the plans. The 2012 election for CEO brought in Leung Chun-
ying with much controversy; most notably, Leung was rumoured to be a member
of the Chinese Communist Party, which should have precluded him from being
a candidate. Beijing's support for him was seen as part of its tactics to minimize
potential political threats (Chen & Yung 2012).

Later waves of post-1997 mainland migrants continued to cause concern and
resentment among Hong Kong citizens, who felt that the new immigrants drove

up property prices and should not have the same rights as established residents. The number of pregnant women coming to Hong Kong to give birth in order to attain citizenship for their children has increased, with 33,500 babies born in 2011 to Mainland-based parents (Chan 2012), putting a strain on public hospitals and schools in the city. There has also been an increase in 'mainland brides' from cross-border marriages who travel to Hong Kong on a one-way permit; many of these women are marginalized, live in the poorest housing and become dependent on welfare benefits (Luo 2011). In 2011 Hong Kong netizens organized several large-scale online protests that included a popular song posted on the Internet describing mainland Chinese as 'parasitic locusts'.[8] A shortage of baby formula in 2013 was attributed to hoarding by mainland tourists who feared tainted products at home. The tensions between the Mainland and Hong Kong can therefore be attributed to the fear of the 'other' and the threat of the destruction of the local way of life.

Instead of centering on the handover, my discussion frames the social and cultural transformations in Hong Kong against successive challenges to the city's self-understanding of its way of life as it adapted to each new condition (Abbas 1997). The post-war government endorsed a cultural discourse that constructed the ideal of social mobility and engendered a collective ethos in support of progress through commercial activities. The 1980s golden age encountered a crisis after the handover not as a result of political changes but because of economic, cultural and social development that challenged the discursive construction of collectivity. Meanwhile, post-handover Hong Kong continues to question the city's SAR identity and tries to reconcile its place in China's political, cultural and economic spheres.

The indigenization of local popular culture

The social and economic history of Hong Kong outlined above contextualizes the development of popular culture and, specifically, the rise of Cantonese mass media from the 1970s. The earliest Hong Kong film, *Zhuangzi Tests His Wife* (Li Minwei, 1913), was based on a Cantonese opera (Teo 1997; Zhang 2004). Before its occupation by the Japanese army in 1937, Shanghai had the main concentration of Chinese film-making activities, with many Hong Kong producers working with Shanghai-based studios. Under the shadow of the Second Sino-Japanese War (1937–45), Shanghai film directors and actors started to migrate to Hong Kong. These migrants from Shanghai and Hong Kong collaborated to make patriotic national defence movies, a practice that ended in 1941 when Hong Kong, like Shanghai, fell under the control of the Japanese army (Teo 1997; Zhang 2004). After the Second World War and the Communist Revolution, the centre of commercial Chinese film-making shifted to Hong Kong, though Mandarin and Cantonese productions remained separate.

In the early 1950s most Hong Kong-produced Mandarin films made little or no reference to the city itself, as many were produced for migrants from the Mainland and for export markets, especially Southeast Asia. The years between 1956 and

1965 were dominated by two competing studios in Hong Kong, MP & GI/Cathay[9] and Shaw Brothers Studio (Zhang 2004), the latter having been founded by Run Run Shaw in 1956. Shaw focused on costume dramas, historical dramas, *huang-mei diao*[10] and, later, martial arts films, effectively 'selling the "China Dream" to its diasporic Chinese audience' (Needham 2008, p.45), who at the time still had a stronger sense of affiliation with the Mainland than with their adopted home in Hong Kong. Conversely, Cathay was famous for musicals that celebrated urban modernity and youth culture, many of which were derivative of the Hollywood musical genre but were made specifically for the Chinese market. Gary Needham suggests that the musicals' setting in contemporary Hong Kong rather than China indicates that Cathay was 'given over to making Hong Kong the subject of Hong Kong cinema' (p.45), an early sign of the emergence of a strong local popular culture. Nevertheless, films from both studios were in Mandarin instead of the local Cantonese dialect, and they continued to cater for mainland immigrants in Hong Kong, who had a strong emotional attachment to China, and for overseas markets such as Taiwan.

The existing Cantonese cinema for the indigenous residents in Hong Kong was a regional industry with limited resources, with the Cantonese productions of the 1950s being made quickly and cheaply (Teo 1997). Cantonese opera films were particularly popular in the 1940s and 1950s. Production peaked in 1958, with 81 films made that year (Yu 1987). By the late 1960s, very few opera films were produced, as the genre could not compete with the popularity of Mandarin films, particularly those backed by major studios that boasted good production quality and appealed to young audiences (Yu 1987). The demise of the Cantonese opera film would precipitate a new form of 'indigenous' media in the 1970s that symbolized modernity. In the 1960s non-operatic Cantonese films also began to change. For example, films that reflected youth problems or the emerging interest in Western pop culture became popular. Many of the films of the 1950s and 1960s, whether in Mandarin or Cantonese, were didactic, with socially conscious messages (Teo 1997), signalling concerns about the social problems associated with a developing city.

Cantonese cinema briefly declined in the early 1970s as a result of the emergence of television. Nevertheless, the hiatus lasted only until 1973, when Chor Yuen's film *The House of 72 Tenants* (a co-production between the Shaw Brothers Studio and Television Broadcasts Limited [TVB]) came out, along with the appearance of the Hui brothers' comedy films shortly after.[11] Cantonese cinema soon overshadowed its Mandarin counterpart, and even the Mandarin studios, Shaw and Golden Harvest, began to make Cantonese features in the 1970s (Cheuk 1999). By the end of the decade, Cantonese was the predominant dialect used in Hong Kong-produced film (Teo 1997), a situation that remained until the more recent co-productions with China. Due to their increasing economic power and leisure time, the locally born generation had come of age to become the prime consumers of media and popular cultural products. The domination of Cantonese films, originally a regional cinema, over Mandarin films suggests the importance of a local cultural form, which has to be considered alongside the establishment of television in Hong Kong as another medium that was closely related to social and cultural development in the city.

The first television station was Rediffusion Cable, established in 1957. All of its programmes were initially in English, but from 1963 it diversified into different dialects, including Cantonese, in order to win over Chinese audiences. In 1973 Rediffusion became the free-to-view Rediffusion Television (RTV, then Asia Television [ATV] in 1982) in response to market competition (Cheuk 1999). The prime Cantonese channel, TVB Jade, was established in 1967 as the first local free (terrestrial) station.[12] The station purchased foreign programmes, but it also broadcast the first locally produced programmes, such as *Enjoy Yourself Tonight (EYT)*, the longstanding nightly variety show (1967–94),[13] which signalled television's importance as part of popular culture in Hong Kong. Television soon became a popular medium, with household ownership of television sets growing rapidly from 12.3 per cent in 1968 to 41.2 per cent in 1970 to 90 per cent in 1976 (Zhang 2004).

Commercial Television (CTV) was established in 1975 as a third channel. Its martial arts series *Legend of the Condors* generated the highest ratings (one million viewers) in 1976; TVB responded with more martial arts and soap opera series (Cheuk 1999). The TVB series *Hotel* made stars of Chow Yun-fat and Deborah Lee (b.1951) and described the rising middle class. In 1984 popular prime-time drama series were viewed by 50–55 per cent of the population (So 2005). Fierce competition between the three channels followed, especially in their drama productions, leading to the closure of CTV in 1978 (Cheuk 1999).

Popular drama series could be up to 100 episodes long, and they were consumed as daily family entertainment for several months. This led to the notion that television in the 1970s was the originator and magnifier of local identity and culture (Ma 1995). The virtual domination of TVB was seen to create a relatively homogeneous culture despite the existence of social divisions, although TVB would subsequently lose some of its market share to ATV. Costume dramas set in the remote past before the Communist regime avoided the problem of addressing national identities (Lilley 1993). Contemporary dramas, on the other hand, typically focused on individual or familial struggles to achieve material success, perpetuating the myth of the Hong Kong economic miracle that rewards those who work hard. Talent competitions and game shows were seen to be 'replete with very late capitalist images of prosperity: the manic compulsion to consume, economics as a game of chance, floating visual pleasures and impossible dreams of stardom' (Lilley 1993, p.268). The television stations also competed through the theme songs of the drama series, sung by popular singers and talent competition winners, a connection with pop music that I will turn to shortly.

The relatively small local population did not abandon cinema despite the rise in popularity of television, unlike the experience in many countries including the USA, UK and Japan. Conversely, as television in Hong Kong became more popular, it precipitated demand for Cantonese films by a growing middle class, engendering a close relationship between the two media (Cheuk 1999). Television initially utilized film talents, but by the end of the 1970s television was feeding the film industry with filmmakers and actors instead. The commercial success of film and local television in the 1980s could be attributed to the economic stability of Hong Kong and a demand for entertainment from the local population that benefited both indigenous media, accounting for the enduring, close relationship between film and television.

It can be argued that Cantonese television and cinema were aimed directly at the immediate sensibilities of the local population and were viewed by a large proportion of that population. Social trends, such as an emerging middle-class lifestyle, were often directly referred to in the content of both film and television. The Hong Kong film industry had distinctive production characteristics. A blockbuster in the mid-1990s usually cost HKD 50 million, of which the stars consumed at least a third (Bordwell 2000).[14] Film was a small and insular industry, and the informal pre-production process usually involved directors coming up with ideas and working with scriptwriters to produce a screenplay before directly approaching investors to secure financing. Producers and directors needed 'only to propose a specific project' (Bordwell 2000, p.120) with a synopsis, budget and cast list, and stars were ubiquitous. Generic conventions counted more than screenwriting skills, as screenplays were often written with a mass-production formula. In addition, films that became box office hits in Hong Kong spawned copycats of their types and genres, creating fads and cycles, which resulted in the highly self-referential nature of many local productions. Many of the filmmakers, cultural commentators and stars I interviewed belonged to the generation who had experienced this prolific and commercially strong period of the film industry. The 1980s were their formative years, which they often referred to as the 'Golden Age' of Hong Kong media.

In order to generate sufficient profit, it was necessary for Hong Kong productions to be exported to Taiwan, Southeast Asia and Chinese-speaking audiences beyond Asia. The most popular genres for export were action and comedy, and as a result it was relatively easy to sell homogeneous products to a variety of markets. In the 1980s and early 1990s, Hong Kong films dominated the export markets in Asia, to the extent that Lii Ding-Tzann (1998) argues that Hong Kong cinema was a 'marginal empire', and that through the practice of pre-sales, Hong Kong films yielded to the Asian markets rather than incorporating other cultures. The popular genres in Hong Kong were largely apolitical and eminently suitable for exporting to diverse cultures without any effort to be market-specific. Dubbing technology was widely used to overcome the problem of creating products for different linguistic groups, an issue for the film industry in the 1950s and 1960s. The apolitical nature and generic content of its films allowed Hong Kong cinema to accommodate foreign markets and also made these productions distinctive.

Homogeneity and convergence of production and consumption of cultural products, including films and television programmes, were common. Cantonese films of the 1970s and 1980s were often based on genres and conventions borrowed from television drama, with familiar characters and character types used in the higher-budget cinema environment. One character type first appearing in a 1970s television series was the stereotyped mainlander, *A Can* (*Chaan* is a common

Cantonese transliteration), an unsophisticated and socially awkward migrant from China who served as another assertion of Hong Kong's distinctive identity and, in turn, maintained and magnified local culture (Leung 1996; Lilley 1993; Ma 1995). A series of films in the 1990s entitled *Her Fatal Ways* (Chinese title *Biaojie, nihao ye!,* meaning 'Cousin, you are great!') features a female cousin from the Mainland as the main character. She is a staunch Communist Party member and part of the Public Security Bureau forced to solve crimes in Hong Kong. The cousin is in effect a female version of *A Can,* and her clumsy, backward ways generate numerous comedy moments.[15]

Further evidence that many films were culturally specific is found in the comedy films of Stephen Chow (b.1962), known for their *mou lei tou* (a Cantonese term meaning 'nonsense') humour. Teo writes with reference to Chow that 'much of the humour is vulgar . . . and based on a peculiar Cantonese argot which presupposes Hong Kong residents to fully enjoy the insinuations, slang and in-jokes' (1997, p.247). Sek Kei (1988, pp.18–20) calls these mainstream films 'the "common people" genre', regarding them as superficial, derisive or exaggerated, and asserts that while Hong Kong fiction cinema draws from changes in society, it is basically commercial and therefore unlikely to offer social critique in the majority of its films. Though few films offered direct social commentary, cinema remained a medium that was part of the everyday lives of the audiences. Radio Television Hong Kong (RTHK), however, a government station broadcast on the terrestrial channels, made many popular programmes that directly tackled social issues. The popularity of local cinema and television among Cantonese audiences indicates that their commercial entertainment nature was an important feature capable of articulating collectivity. The presupposition of a Cantonese mass audience for these media was the result of the cultural discourse of social unity, which inadvertently helped to suppress cultural and social differences.

Popular music similarly had an important but changing relationship with the cultural lives of audiences in Hong Kong. Cantonese opera was the indigenous 'popular' music before the 1960s, as seen in the success of opera films. Mandarin contemporary songs (*shidaiqu*) came to dominate the pop industry in the 1960s in a society with a mainly Cantonese population. *Shidaiqu* originated in Shanghai in the 1920s and was influenced by Western genres such as jazz. After 1949 Mandarin pop of this kind was banned by the Chinese government, which led to composers, lyricists and musicians migrating to Hong Kong and forging a new centre of production (Wong 2003). Young people in Hong Kong in the 1950s and 1960s also listened to Anglo-American pop; the Beatles' 1964 performance in the city caused a craze for male pop bands singing mostly in English. Subsequently, the indigenization of Hong Kong culture through the rise of the popularity of Cantonese media from the 1970s was seen in the domination of 'Cantopop' music sung in this local dialect (Lilley 1993) Cantopop benefited from the close relationships between the media, with songs having simultaneous exposure in different media products, including music videos on television and theme songs in television programmes and films. Theme songs circulated as music videos, trailers and clips for advance advertising, sometimes long before the shows were released. Cantonese pop was unique both in its musical style and in the development and operation of the industry in Hong Kong. Tim Brace describes the distinguishable style of Chinese pop music, referring to both Cantonese and Mandarin pop:

> Smooth, flowing melodies, which usually have no direct or obvious relationship with traditional Chinese melodic construction; a type of vocal production which was described . . . as the 'middle way' . . . between Western full, ringing vocal style and Chinese folksong style; lyrics emphasizing feelings of love; . . . an easy, dance beat background . . . which Americans might commonly associate with 'light' disco-inspired dance music, or with the popular music style commonly known as 'easy-listening'.
>
> (1991, p.47)

The practices of the pop industry in Hong Kong were well established, with a range of related merchandise, fan clubs and a public relations industry. There was also 'the phenomenon of "super-concerting" in which performing thirty or more consecutive concerts in rapid succession became the frenzied trend of mass Cantopop consumption' (Erni 2007, p.91). Cantopop attracted both mass and predominantly young audiences, leaving little alternative creative space. Companies affiliated with major multinational media conglomerates such as EMI and Polygram dominated the pop industry. There were many annual pop music awards shows staged by the main television and radio stations, including the RTHK Top Ten Gold Song Awards Presentation and Jade Solid Gold. Unlike films from Hong Kong, which were circulated internationally with subtitles, the assumed audiences of Cantopop and Mandopop (pop music sung in Mandarin) were Chinese speakers because the lyrics were not translated (Witzleben 1999). In the case of Cantopop, the home market in Hong Kong was substantial enough to sustain a commercially successful industry from the 1970s to the 1990s.

Despite the domination of love songs, Cantopop sometimes offered direct social commentary in its lyrics. An example involves the aforementioned television-turned-film and -pop star Sam Hui, who wrote and performed many songs reflecting the bittersweet reality of working-class life in the 1970s. Cantonese pop songs from the 1970s onwards were attuned to the values and sentiments of the second generation of refugees from China and reflected the social conditions of the period (Wong 2003). This close relationship between film, television and pop music was unique to Hong Kong, and the media shared the same target audience groups: the emerging middle class, an aspiring working class and young people. Television programmes and, sometimes, Cantopop song lyrics directly addressed these groups as a mass that assumed and maintained a homogeneous culture, in contrast to the diverse cultural and social groups that media products catered to in the past. However, the early 1990s saw the beginning of the decline of traditional media, which signalled social and cultural changes including the disintegration of the mass market for locally produced popular cultural products.

Changing mass media and media consumption from the early 1990s

From the 1990s, the consumption of locally produced media has declined, indicating that the cultural lives of the mass audiences have changed as a result of the specific social contexts of pre- and post-handover Hong Kong. The following discussion focuses on the consumption and production patterns of film and television. The next chapter will examine pop stardom in more detail, and Chapter 3 will focus on the printed press and advertising.

The 1980s were the peak of Hong Kong's film industry, with 200–300 films produced every year. Cantonese-language films from Hong Kong were not a limited phenomenon in a relatively small, local community; instead they circulated widely in established export markets. Since the mid-1990s the Hong Kong film industry has been in rapid decline: the 1988–96 annual average of 153 film productions in Hong Kong fell to 55 in 2005 (Cahiers du Cinema 2006) and to 53 in 2012.[16] From the 1980s to the mid-1990s, Hong Kong films dominated the local box office; local productions were the top selling titles with the exceptions of *ET* (Steven Spielberg) in 1982 and *Jurassic Park* (Steven Spielberg) in 1993 (*City Entertainment* 2002a). In 2012, however, only three local productions were among the top ten films at the box office, at numbers three, six and eight. This was partly due to the separate distribution of local and foreign films through much of the 1980s, a situation that benefited local productions. From the early 1980s onwards, mini-cinema complexes began to open, but with the lack of Hong Kong films to fill the mini-theatres, many chains were gradually forced to bring in more American products.

Hong Kong films have also lost much of their share of the regional markets in Korea, Taiwan and Southeast Asia since the mid-1990s. After the relaxation of import regulations in 1986, Taiwanese audiences gradually abandoned Chinese films for Hollywood productions. In 1999 Hong Kong films took 2.9 per cent of the Taiwanese box office and Hollywood films represented 96.7 per cent (Chiang n.d.). By 2012, Taiwan-produced films had increased their market share to 11.9 per cent, but only one local film was in a top ten dominated by imports from the USA (Cremin 2013). Export markets contributed to the domination of genre productions in Hong Kong cinema; therefore their subsequent decline in importance also affected the local film industry and the consumption patterns of domestic audiences. The trend of reduction in film production and box office receipts in the 1990s is shown in Table 1.1.

Given the rise in ticket prices over time, the figures show audiences deserting local cinema during this period. The decline was due to a number of factors. In the early 2000s, leisure activities such as surfing the Internet, web 2.0 (for example, blogs), social media, karaoke, and film and music downloading became increasingly popular, competing directly with cinema and other traditional media, including terrestrial television and Cantonese pop music. Chan (2000) reports that her survey of middle-class consumers in Hong Kong reveals that they 'are highly selective as to what films they see' (p.106) and that audiences saw local

Table 1 Number of local films produced and films with box office receipts of over HKD
10 million in the 1990s

	No. of films produced	No. of films with box office receipts over HKD 10 million
1990	120	30
1991	128	24
1992	160	32
1993	172	32
1994	137	27
1995	139	18
1996	98	23
1997	83	14
1998	84	9
1999	91	12

Source: Sze, M.H., n.d. *Crises and Opportunities for Hong Kong Cinema at the End of the Millennium.*
Unpublished Paper.

productions as 'rubbish' (pp.111–2), though they might watch them to kill time, socialize or for a laugh. When audiences no longer considered Hong Kong films to be of high quality, they became increasingly discerning when choosing to go to the cinema. Audiences preferred big-budget foreign films instead of local productions, at home as well as in theatres. In 2004 consumers gave the local movie industry a relatively low score of 59.3 out of 100 (University of Hong Kong 2005),[17] while over 80 per cent of more than 1,000 respondents could not name a local film they liked in that year.

The changing consumer culture in the city was a significant factor in the decline of Hong Kong's cinema industry. The suburbanization of film theatres in Hong Kong was manifested through the building of multiplex cinemas in consumption centres such as the new towns of Sha Tin and Tuen Mun. Cinema changed from a cheap neighbourhood leisure activity to entertainment consumption mainly for the young (Wong & McDonogh 2001a, 2001b), who were more inclined to consume films at new multiplex cinemas in urban centres and suburban malls that offered additional leisure choices like shopping and dining. Even though cinema-going, according to Chan (2000), remained a popular leisure activity, other youth-oriented leisure activities such as karaoke similarly offered opportunities for socializing and participation. David Bordwell's description of Hong Kong cinema sums up the direction of the industry: 'A local cinema definitely, but with fast-diminishing resources. A regional cinema for decades, but retreating before Hollywood's imperial advance. A diasporan cinema, chiefly on video' (2000, p.82).

In recent years, channels for the dissemination of feature films in Hong Kong have proliferated through the advent of cable television, satellite stations, video and VCD (video compact disc, a cheap form of reproduction), piracy and, finally, streaming and downloading. The ready availability of VCRs (video cassette recorders) began a longstanding and increasing trend of film viewing at home, creating competition with theatrical releases as early as 1990 (*City Entertainment* 1990).

Official VCD and DVD versions of films are released close to theatrical release dates and priced as low as possible because of the threat of piracy. Audiences can stay at home to watch domestic and foreign film products and television series that they buy, rent or download, often illegally, a practice that has become increasingly widespread since the early 2000s. In 2005 shops selling VCDs and DVDs were open 24 hours a day in areas such as Mongkok. However, on subsequent visits to this area in 2009 and 2012, the number of these shops had significantly decreased due to the popularity of downloading. The industry has failed to develop and promote legal methods of accessing paid movies online. Some viewers watch blockbuster Hollywood films at the theatres but prefer Hong Kong productions at home (Wong & McDonogh 2001a). Wong and McDonogh describe a diversification in the way Hong Kong films are viewed, involving specific and deliberate choices made by consumers according to their personal circumstances. In the early 2000s, renting a disc cost a few Hong Kong dollars, and a complete television drama series could be bought for HKD 100–300; feature film DVDs cost around HKD 60–120, and VCDs around HKD 20–50, depending on the age of the title. The average ticket price in 2002 was HKD 48.82 (US$ 6.26) (Screen Digest 2003), rising to HKD 85 (US$ 11) (AMC Festival Walk, Kowloon) and HKD 105 (US$ 13.5) (3D films, UA Cinema, Sha Tin) for evening screenings in 2013. Because local films are not considered a good value, audiences opt for less expensive options. NR, an assistant director and commercial producer, explained:

> Audiences are busy. They leave work at eight or nine [in the evening]. You spend time with your family and make dinner. Then you have to do other things on Saturday and Sunday. Young people are the only ones who go to the cinema and they will see anything as a group . . . Two tickets at the cinema cost HKD 120. A disc only costs HKD 80–90. Unless it's really original, why do you have to go [to the cinema] except for a big film, an event? Cinema is dead.
>
> (4 August 2005)

NR's comments focused on adult and family audiences. These views were supported by my own observations at the local multiplex in Hong Kong. Predominantly young audiences viewed films as a form of leisure activity. They often approached the box office and asked which film was being screened next, indicating that they were more concerned with convenience than making qualitative film choices. Their comments revealed that they had no specific idea of the films they wanted to see, partly supporting NR's observation. For the filmmakers, the crisis of local cinema might affect how they evaluate their own worth. Director Fruit Chan and independent filmmaker-programmer Jimmy Choi made these observations during my interview with them (24 August 2005):

> FRUIT CHAN: The audiences wait. Two or three times a year they go and watch a blockbuster . . . Otherwise they may find the films in the video shop later and borrow them. They don't think they've missed anything. Even the popularity of the video

shops is an insult to filmmakers . . . I feel that after a month the films are in the shops for HKD 10 or 15. They are not something to cherish. Art should be for appreciation. Now it's just a product; you make this today, it is useless rubbish tomorrow. It changes people's opinion about film.

JIMMY CHOI: It's a big problem. Several years ago, we had *Shaolin Soccer* (Stephen Chow, 2001) that took HKD 60 million at the box office. There are only a few big movies a year here.

LEUNG WING-FAI: Like Fruit Chan said, the audiences watch these films but it doesn't necessarily mean they go to the cinema the rest of the year.

JIMMY CHOI: Yes, that's right. It is explained by [the fact that] movie-going isn't an attraction any more. You can't reverse this trend. It's not about the lower quality of our films. No. Many people stay at home to use the Internet. There are too many leisure choices these days.

As a filmmaker who joined the film industry in the 1980s, Chan saw the decline in the popularity of locally produced films and the low costs associated with VCDs and DVDs as an indication that audiences perceived Hong Kong cinema to be of poor quality and to have low artistic values, and this lack of appreciation in turn personally affected how he saw his own work.

Typically, a strong market for local films is indicated by at least 50 per cent of total annual box office takings, a level Hong Kong films began to dip under after the mid-1990s as they lost share to foreign, mostly Hollywood, productions.[18] During the SARS epidemic, almost all the films released in the first half of 2003 grossed under HKD 10 million (Law 2004), yet another blow to an industry already in steep decline. The types of local films that were popular also shifted alongside the changing makeup and interests of audiences. *Infernal Affairs* (Andrew Lau & Mak Siu-fai), a trilogy spanning 2002–3, was an exemplar of the major blockbusters that emerged after the handover and a sign of the shift from an assembly-line mode of production towards high-budget, high-concept film-making. The series also signalled the emergence of Media Asia, a multimedia conglomerate set up by businessman Peter Lam, that adopted Hollywood-style management tactics, requiring completed scripts and detailed budget plans before shooting, allowing cross-media promotions to begin early in the process. *Infernal Affairs* moved away from the depiction of the working class that was the norm in the action films of the 1980s. The fact that *Infernal Affairs* competed successfully with Hollywood films could be attributed to the more affluent environment depicted. The film's cast, Tony Leung (b.1962) and Andy Lau (b.1961) and character actors Eric Tsang (b.1953) and Anthony Wong (b.1962), was able to attract a mass adult audience because they were well known from their early television and film work.[19] I (Leung 2009) examine Andy Lau's career elsewhere, using the *Infernal Affairs* trilogy as an exemplar of film-making in post-1997 Hong Kong, and I will return to him as a case study in Chapter 4.

Attempts to create blockbusters such as the *Infernal Affairs* trilogy paradoxically divided the industry further (Leung 2008a). Cinema audiences continued to wait for the occasional high-budget release, while many other productions, whether made with a high or low budget, failed at the theatres. The decline of the Hong Kong film industry can be linked to the changing leisure choices and more diverse lifestyles of its affluent consumers compared to the assumed homogeneous audiences of the 1970s and 1980s. In addition, the process of adjustment within the Hong Kong film industry indicated a step towards its becoming a regional cinema within China. Major blockbusters such as *Kung Fu Hustle* (Stephen Chow, 2004) were co-produced with the Mainland, a practice that has become the mainstay of the Hong Kong film industry.

The other dominant medium of the 1970s and into the 1980s in Hong Kong was television. With the growth of home entertainment and other leisure activities such as the Internet, karaoke and cable television, audiences have more choices than in the 1970s and 1980s, leading to fragmentation of the mass market for locally produced television. TVB used to produce 5,000 hours of local programming every year that was watched by two million viewers in Asia (Lilley 1993). The most popular programmes were drama series, *EYT* (the nightly magazine-format show that ran for over 30 years), the annual Miss Hong Kong Pageant, large-scale variety shows and TVB anniversary celebrations. In 1984, for instance, popular prime-time drama series were viewed by 50–5 per cent of the population, compared to 20–30 per cent in 2004 (So 2005). Joseph Chan Man from the Chinese University of Hong Kong suggests that local terrestrial television stations were a turn-off for young people and the better-educated middle class because 'TV productions . . . repeat the same stories, run nonsensical or bad storylines and have low production values' (cited in A. Lam 2005). The fall in quality of local television was recognized by media professionals, including production executive Shi Nansun, who stated:

> [TVB's] programming became stale because when you are the dominant player for too long, you start to think that people will watch whatever bullshit you produce. TVB had high standards at one time, and they had to, because they faced tough competition, but when the competition went down, so did the standards.
>
> (cited in Curtin 2007, p.111)

Chu Pui-hing, the Director of Broadcasting in Hong Kong, also warned that the local television market was saturated, with little room for expansion (A. Lam 2005). Increasingly, broadcasters in Hong Kong had to look to the Mainland and overseas for new markets. Star TV, Asia's first pancontinental satellite platform, was founded in 1991 by one of Hong Kong's richest businessmen, Li Ka-shing, and was bought and re-launched by Rupert Murdoch in 1994. The rapid growth of cable television, which began broadcasting in Hong Kong in 1995, and satellite television led partly to the decline in popularity of free-to-view television. As a result of the shrinking domestic market, TVBS (TVB Superstation) was set up in 1993 to compete with the cable, satellite and video-rental markets. During the 1980s and 1990s, TVB programmes and stars were popular with Chinese audiences in many parts of the world. However, TVBS increasingly faced stiff competition because of the growing sophistication of Mandarin-language television (Curtin 2007). Robert Chua (17 June 2009), one of my professional contacts and the originator of *EYT* and the Miss Hong Kong Pageants for TVB, thought that competition had caused the quality of local television to suffer as producers gave audiences whatever they wanted. He was particularly critical of game shows that used celebrities, especially skimpily dressed female starlets, to perform degrading acts for a laugh, and he called this type of broadcasting 'degratainment'.[20]

In an annual study of media use, it was shown that cable television users were more likely to be male, aged between 15 and 34, tertiary educated and have a higher income than viewers of TVB (So 2005). The average time spent watching television was 3.2 hours per day, and the average time spent on the Internet was comparatively high (1.9 hours daily), especially among the young, who tended to have higher Internet use (So 2005). In 2011, the Nielsen Media Index found that 85 per cent of residents in Hong Kong owned a desktop computer, 67 per cent owned a laptop, 62 per cent a smartphone and 35 per cent a tablet (with a further 22 per cent intending to acquire a tablet),[21] placing the new media in direct competition with traditional media such as television. Television was previously associated with immediacy and intimacy (Auslander 1999); the high number of popular live shows on terrestrial television in Hong Kong, such as the nightly *EYT,* was evidence of this. The discontinuation of this popular variety show in 1994 announced the passing of an era. It was resurrected as a weekly programme in 1997, and again between 2002 and 2004, without success. *EYT*'s original producer, Robert Chua (17 June 2009), described how the availability of specialist channels took viewers away from scheduled terrestrial programmes.

If television viewing was previously a communal experience, with the majority of the population watching the same programmes and drama series, the more diffused patterns of consumption from the 1990s onwards by diverse audience groups help to explain local television's lack of influence and overall decline. Lifestyle changes, including longer working hours, less leisure time, more entertainment alternatives, the rise of the youth market and the increasing importance of the Internet, account for diversified consumption patterns and the weakening appeal of terrestrial television.

Hong Kong's declining status as the capital of Chinese commercial television production paralleled the rise of Taiwan and China as media producers and co-producers. In Taiwan the end of martial law in 1987 led to a period of media privatization and liberalization during the 1990s (Curtin 2007). By the early 2000s, programmes made by China Television (CTV), set up initially by the Nationalist Party (KMT, Kuomintang or Guomindang), were shown during prime time on leading terrestrial stations in Hong Kong and China (Curtin 2007). Computer software was developed to aid cross-media promotion of recent CTV dramas to young, Internet savvy audiences (Curtin 2007). The markets for drama series have become increasingly competitive in Asia, with Japanese, Korean, PRC and Taiwanese producers all striving to increase production values and exportability. In contrast to the decline in locally produced television in Hong Kong, drama series from Mainland China and other Asian countries have increased in popularity.

Changes in the media industry in Hong Kong can therefore be mapped onto the city's political relationships with the Mainland and interpreted in relation to China as both a co-production partner and potential market. I (Leung 2008b) posit elsewhere that the rupture in the development of Hong Kong cinema coincided with the handover of Hong Kong back to China in 1997, the economic crisis in Asia, and the city's failure to remain the primary commercial centre in the region. CEPA, covering trade relations between China and Hong Kong, offered some hope of a commercial solution, but it also brought problems for media-production practices, as the Hong Kong media industry had to work within the defined limits of the Chinese government. The media industry's attempts to accommodate the Chinese production industry and market was another sign that the cultural power of Hong Kong was declining, giving way to other regional competitors, including and especially the Mainland. Increasingly, Hong Kong cinema moved towards being part of 'Greater Chinese cinema', with more and more mainland co-productions aimed at both markets. In contrast, Chinese film production was growing: 140 films were produced in 2003 (Barbieri 2004), increasing to 526 in 2010 (Italian Trade Commission 2011).[22] The Chinese market fully opened to Taiwan-produced films in mid-2011, following new regulations that gave the Taiwanese industry the same terms as Hong Kong films, in that the films were not subject to the quota on foreign films (Cremin 2013). The Taiwan film industry therefore became another potential partner and competitor of the ailing Hong Kong film sector. Hong Kong cinema's increasing reliance on co-productions with China reversed the previous power relationship in which the city's popular culture dominated the Chinese market (Gold 1993).[23] This reversal of previous power relations between Hong Kong and China was part of the city's re-sinicization process that has been ongoing since the 1990s (Ma 1999).

Cantonese pop music suffered a similar decline from the mid-1990s onwards, represented in the sales statistics of local pop albums (Table 1.2). The sales figures represented by the numbers of gold and platinum discs over the period 1977–2007 show the peak of the local music industry in the 1980s and early to mid-1990s. As an example of the kind of commercial success enjoyed by Cantopop stars, Jacky Cheung (b.1961) sold five million records globally and played 100 concerts during his world tour of 1995–6.[24] By contrast, there has been a lack of a mass market for the super-concerts of more recent younger singers. The recording industry has also been severely affected by illegal downloading; by the early 2000s many singers only managed to sell a few thousand copies of their CD albums. It is indicative that the IFPI (International Federation of the Phonographic Industry) Gold Disc Award was discontinued after 2008. The exact sales records of the top ten best sales releases in Cantonese and Mandarin are no longer disclosed by the IFPI. From 2011, the Federation has presented a Hong Kong Digital Music Award to the top-selling songs, although its website does not explain how the sales numbers

Table 1.2 Sales of gold, platinum and multi-platinum local pop albums (1977–2007)

Year	Gold Discs	Platinum Discs	Multi-Platinum Discs			Additional Notes
1977	16					
1988	23	62				Alan Tam (7 x platinum), Anita Mui (5 x platinum), Paula Tsui (5 x platinum), Jacky Cheung (4 x platinum, 1 x gold), Danny Chan (4 x platinum)
1997	37	24	Double 9	Triple 1	5x 1	Jacky Cheung (15 x platinum, 1xdouble, 1 x platinum), Sammi Cheng (3 x double, 2 x platinum, 1 x gold) Aaron Kwok (1 x double, 2 x platinum, 4 x gold) Leon Lai (2 x platinum, 2 x gold)
2000	1	5				The singers who achieved platinum sales included Cecilia Cheung,
2007	2					Nicholas Tse and Eason Chan

Source: IFPI website. Available: http://www.ifpihk.org (accessed 10 July 2013). The number of unit sales required is 15,000 for a Gold Disc and 30,000 for a Platinum Disc (Multi-Platinum = Multiples of 30,000). No figures were available for 1987.

are compiled. Meanwhile, EMI closed the operation of its Hong Kong branch in 2004, and many of its contracted singers struggled to find another record label.

With the economic growth of the Mainland, industry executives began to take into account the Mandarin pop market. Since the late 1990s, major Cantopop stars have been releasing Mandarin versions of their albums to cater for the Mainland and other Mandarin-speaking markets like Taiwan. Many Cantopop stars had released Mandarin songs before this, but the practice has become much more widespread since the 1990s. Mainland-produced television series and Mandopop have been increasingly consumed in the city from the late 1990s, as opposed to the previously dominant northward movement of Hong Kong cultural products (Gold 1993). This can be understood as a process of re-sinicization. Hong Kong stars' increasing involvement with Mandopop have helped make pop music from the city a global cultural force. Wai-chung Ho suggests that the local artists' appropriation of Mandopop demonstrates the globalization of Hong Kong's popular music, with a shift from its original domination by popular music from the West to an embrace of Asian territories, especially the Mainland (2003). It is particularly pertinent that from the late 1990s onwards there has been a trend of reclaiming 'Chineseness' through popular songs: *zhongguofeng* ('Chinese wind'). Although these kinds of songs, invoking traditional Chinese music through their melodies and lyrics, existed before the handover, the trend increased after 1997 (Chow & de Kloet 2011). Since these songs refer to an imagined community, a deterritorialized, cultural China (Lee & Huang 2002), *zhongguofeng* music interrogates and destabilizes Chineseness. The increasingly northward-looking careers of many of the multimedia stars in Hong Kong reflect the re-sinicization of the city and its mediasphere.

The rising political, economic and popular cultural power of China, together with the lingering recession of the early 2000s, has led to a sense of vulnerability for people in Hong Kong, a situation that confirms Abbas' prediction that 'the anticipated end of Hong Kong as the people knew it was the beginning of a profound concern with its historical and cultural specificity' (1996, p.7). This explains why the difficulties in catering for the Chinese markets are discussed among media professionals in relation to the diluting of the distinctiveness of popular culture in Hong Kong. The increasing power of China as a co-producer and potential market enter into debates about the Hong Kong media industry and contribute to the notion that a distinctive local culture has been disappearing since the handover. James Wong's (2003) thesis focused on the social-reflective function of Cantopop as it related to the rise of local television in the 1970s. It is understandable that, as one of the most prolific lyricists of Cantonese pop songs, Wong laments the decline of the music business and suggests that there was a shortage of creative talent in the 1990s to satisfy the demand for new songs. Rey Chow argues:

> As signs and codes, the [pop song] lyrics are intersemiotic with other signs such as those of fast food, mass communication, pocket novels, videos, karaoke, and so forth, in the sense that all such signs share a relation to post-colonial city culture, a relation that is legible only in its intersemioticity.
>
> (1998, pp.161–2)

Here, Chow refers to the interrelationships between the visual and verbal signs of the city, which have to be understood in their totality. The combination of these signs had existed before the emergence of post-1997 culture in Hong Kong due to the close relationships between media forms, although intersemioticity has become more difficult to discern since the mid-1990s because of a larger range of leisure activities. The main reason for the decline of the local pop industry was the emerging importance of a youth market that benefited from this wider range of leisure activities. The decline of a shared indigenous culture in the 2000s suggests that it could not cater for many of the emerging social groups and market segments such as the young and the increasingly affluent, who did not recognize the popular media intersemiotically.

Cinema, television and pop music in the 1980s and early 1990s were a central part of the locally produced popular culture that responded to social changes in the city, especially the emergence of a generation of consumers who were born and bred in Hong Kong. The decline in popularity of these media indicates a turning away by audiences and consumers, suggesting that these media have reduced cultural and social relevance. Economic factors include competition from foreign products, the shrinking local and Asian markets, the legal and illegal downloading of music and the rise in home entertainment formats such as VCD. In addition, the decline of indigenous media has resulted from the evolving leisure patterns in the changing social and cultural landscape of Hong Kong. The cultural and social lives of the mass consumers of Hong Kong media have changed; the youth market and (new) middle-class consumers prefer a wider variety of leisure activities and flexibility in their patterns of consumption, which domestic productions often fail to provide. The media industry has had to diversify and produce film, television programmes and pop music bound for several markets, especially China. These changes have challenged the distinctiveness of Hong Kong's indigenous media, which used to support the cultural discourse of a common social ethos.

Concluding remarks

Social and cultural developments in Hong Kong contextualize the unique history of the local media, especially the close relationships between the media and their popularity from the 1970s to the 1990s and their subsequent decline. Popular cultural products catering for diverse audience groups were superseded by the development of an indigenous Hong Kong popular culture from the 1970s onwards in response to the coming of age of a generation who were born and raised in the city. The emergence of a distinctive popular culture was the result of a demand for leisure from the post-war generation who enjoyed growing wealth. In the 1970s the economic development of the city led to the emergence of local popular mass culture geared toward a relatively homogeneous audience; television, Cantopop and, subsequently, cinema dominated the media landscape for two decades. In contrast, the difficulties facing the Hong Kong media industries since the mid-1990s are indicative of the changes in leisure activities, the reorganization of the everyday lives of consumers, the fragmentation of the market for media products, and the rising cultural importance of Mainland China as a media co-producer and market.

Not only has the range of leisure provisions increased, but audiences have also grown to think of themselves as discerning consumers. The earlier mass audiences of locally produced and focused television and films are no longer satisfied with lower production values, especially when compared to foreign imports. Television has also begun to lose middle-class and young audiences because of its perceived lack of quality. The increasing cultural power of Mainland China and the rise of Korea and Taiwan as producers of pop culture have de-centred Hong Kong's position in the Asian and global media landscape. The beginning of the 1980s also saw the emergence of a conscious anticipation of the 1997 handover that affected the social, political and personal lives of the residents throughout the transition period. The decline in previously popular elements of the mass media demonstrates the changing post-handover cultural and social contexts, in which diverse groups have resurfaced and China's cultural power threatens that of Hong Kong.

2　Multimedia stardom in Hong Kong

In this chapter I examine the historical development of multimedia stardom from early twentieth century Shanghai, 'a film-mad town' (Elley 1997), to Hong Kong, which became the centre of media production after 1949. I then detail the rise of a generation of Hong Kong stars connected to local television, including Chow Yun-fat, Leslie Cheung and Maggie Cheung, alongside the indigenization of popular culture in the 1970s and 1980s. I argue that the fluid movement of performers across different media is a central feature of multimedia stardom, and I describe how stardom has been affected by the decline of traditional media since the 1990s. I then describe Hong Kong stars' presence in the international cultural arena and as an increasingly visible part of the Greater Chinese mediasphere.

Early stardom in China and Hong Kong

The early days of cinema and film stardom in Hong Kong reflected the social values and cultural restrictions of the society and institutions in which they were made. The earliest Hong Kong film, *Zhuangzi Tests His Wife* (1913), featured the male director Li Minwei taking on the role of the wife because women were traditionally forbidden to appear in theatre, a custom that extended into early cinema (Teo 1997). This moral taboo led to the practice of male actors cross-dressing to play female characters. Shanghai was then the main Chinese-language film-producing city until the Japanese invasion of 1937. In the Shanghainese film industry of the 1930s, stars became studio trademarks when they were contracted for a monthly salary (Reynaud 1993), a practice not unlike that of the Hollywood studios of the 1930s and 1940s.[1] The first mainland Chinese female film star was Wang Hanlun (1903–78), who played a 'Westernized' secretary in *The Orphan Saves His Grandfather* (Zhang Shichuan, 1923). Early stars like Wang went on promotional tours that included performing songs on stage in order to garner support (Chang 1999). Over time, cultural restrictions and taboos surrounding female performers in China started to change, so that by the 1930s women began to appear in cinema, and several well-known female stars were produced, including Hu Die (1908–89), Li Lili (1915–2005) and Ruan Lingyu (1910–35). The Mingxing (Star) Film Company, established in Shanghai in 1922, opened one of the earliest training schools for stars (Farquhar & Zhang 2008). After the coming of sound to motion pictures, studios also recruited from song-and-dance troupes. Li Lili, for instance, studied Peking Opera when living in an orphanage, before working in song-and-dance ensembles and entering the film industry (Elley 1997).

Film stars were a central element of 1930s Shanghai, described as 'a film-mad town, with newspaper supplements devoted to movies, hordes of film magazines, get-rich-quick entrepreneurs, a star system of its own, scabrous gossip sheets, and glamorous premieres' (Elley 1997, p.127). The actress Ruan Lingyu committed suicide in 1935 at the age of 24, in what would become known as 'The New Woman Incident'. The suicide was apparently forced by news of scandals about her in the gossip press. Her last film was *New Woman* (Cai Chusheng, 1935), in which she played a writer who refuses to prostitute herself when her child falls ill; the writer becomes the victim of malicious gossip when her child dies, and as a result the writer kills herself. *New Woman* was inspired by the suicide of another young female star, Ai Xia (1912–34). The left-wing filmmaker Cai depicted the incident in the film in order to attack the tabloid press, who retaliated by hounding Ruan about her personal relationships (Reynaud 1993). Ruan's suicide note contained the words, 'Gossip is a frightening thing' (*Renyan kewei*).[2] The star's suicide prompted intense condemnation of the power of the tabloid press, including a rebuke from Lu Xun, a key writer of modern Chinese literature and one of the leaders of the 1919 May Fourth anti-imperialist cultural and political movement (Harris 1997). Ruan's life mirrored those of the suffering women she played on screen, and she was later the subject of Stanley Kwan's biopic, *Actress* (1991), starring Maggie Cheung. The case led to Berenice Reynaud's (1993) assertion that 'the combination of glamour and tragedy' (p.24) was a longstanding feature of Chinese female stardom.

Many Chinese-language film-production companies and associated film stars started to relocate to Hong Kong in the late 1930s. One of the most popular genres in Hong Kong in the 1940s and 1950s was the Mandarin musical that featured a new group of actresses known as 'the songstresses' (*genü*). They were divided into 'sweet' and 'sour' beauties, metaphors for good and bad girls, exemplified by Zhou Xuan (1920–57) and Bai Guang (1921–99), respectively (Reynaud 1993; Teo 1997). The songstress or 'Sing-Song' girl, a legacy from Shanghai's famous nightlife, 'is both performer and entertainer, a tamer and more cultured version of a street whore' (Teo 1997, p.29). These bittersweet women were products of a Shanghai film industry that exploited the stars' personal lives. The term songstress is derogatory in comparison to 'singer' (*geshou*), and the actresses were 'thought to be no better than prostitutes, they were often forced into the profession by unhappy circumstances – poor, raped, pregnant, exploited by cads, forbidden to marry for love' (Reynaud 1993, p.25). In line with 'the combination of glamour and tragedy' (p.24) of Chinese women stars was Zhou Xuan's personal life:

> She had a history of mental depression brought on by a broken marriage and subsequent affairs with men who turned out to be rogues and cheats. She spent her last years in a mental hospital in the Mainland where she died in 1957, aged thirty-nine.
>
> (Teo 1997, p.30)

Some later female stars showed more resilience and asserted themselves differently in public. A star from the 1940s, Li Lihua (b.1924), who made 158 films spanning four decades, defended her professionalism in an interview in 1997: 'People who are not in the profession think that we are loose and laid-back, that's not true at all' (cited in Chu 2000, p.177). The musical no longer exists as a popular genre in Hong Kong, and use of the term songstress is rare, having been replaced by *geshou* ('singer') and *gexing* ('singer star'). Nonetheless, a few insights can be gained from this description of early stardom. Multimedia stardom has had a long history in Chinese-language cinema, as shown by the close relationships between stage performance, songs, cinema and media commentaries. Moreover, the entertainment press existed alongside multimedia stardom and had a powerful presence in pre-war China. The social status of stars was traditionally low, especially for women, providing further evidence that stardom has to be understood through its social and cultural specificities.

The tradition of multimedia stardom continued in the 1950s and 1960s through the popularity of musicals. Mandarin musical films, many produced by Cathay Studio, became the vehicles for many female stars including Bai Guang, Lin Dai (1934–64) and Ge Lan (b.1933, also known as Grace Chang). The classic Shanghai and, later, Hong Kong stars such as Zhou Xuan and Ge Lan were also recording artistes.[3] Ge Lan is known for the musical *Mambo Girl* (Yi Wen, also known as Evan Yang, 1957), which features the theme song *I Love Cha Cha,* illustrating the influence of musical genres from the West during this time. Wang Tianlin's *The Wild Wild Rose* (1960) was a perfect showcase for Ge Lan as the protagonist Miss Deng, a popular night club singer and femme fatale with a heart of gold. The musical numbers supported the star's sultry and sexy image, with sophistication shown by foreign cultural references, such as the rendition of *Habanera* from the opera *Carmen* (by the French composer Georges Bizet). As one of the most successful Mandarin musicals of the era, *The Wild Wild Rose* illustrates how modernity was understood in Hong Kong, and it represents a collective desire of the inhabitants of the post-war city to imitate lifestyles gleaned from Western, especially American, pop culture. The musical genre, much produced by Cathay Studio, was based on the Hollywood model and infused by the 1930s Shanghai Sing-Song tradition, noted for its female entertainers. The Mandarin musicals of the 1950s and 1960s were eclectic; they were not simply about spectacle and catchy songs, but they also offered social drama in disguise.[4] The story of *The Wild Wild Rose* follows the tropes of a typical female-focused melodrama. In an altruistic act Miss Deng sells herself in order to help a former colleague and his impoverished family; however, she also seduces Hanhua (played by Zhang Yang, b.1930), an effete, classically trained musician-turned-nightclub-pianist who is already engaged. Hanhua betrays his fiancée to be with Miss Deng, who attempts to become a 'housewife'. When the two of them struggle to make a living, however, she has to resume her nightclub career. Miss Deng's ultimate sacrifice for love comes when Hanhua, consumed by jealousy, murders her. In Hong Kong cinema of the 1950s and 1960s, the familial sacrifices and economic struggles of the protagonists are typical tropes often weaved into the surface sheen of Westernized lifestyle and consumer culture.

Through their onscreen roles, stars such as Ge Lan embodied two social positions: the struggling, filial young woman and the middle-class aspirant. Hong Kong was not generally an affluent society, though it was rapidly changing in the 1950s. By the 1960s younger consumers began to create demands for popular culture, in particular films that made reference to the rise of consumer culture. Needham notes that 'fashion is one of the most important elements of the Hong Kong musical, not just in the costuming of the many female stars but the musical number where it occupies the main source of spectacle' (2008, p.51). Fashion was further related to consumer culture, change and modernity in 1960s Hong Kong as young adults began to come of age and out of the previous generation's poverty. Shaw Brothers and Cathay Studio both produced film magazines, *International Screen* and *Southern Screen,* that featured star profiles, new films, fashion shoots and beauty tips modelled by the actresses (Needham 2008)[5] and included advertisements for boutiques, hair products, perfumes and cosmetics. By comparison male leads of the time appeared weak, unconvincing and effete in comparison with their female counterparts. Examples included Zhang Yang and Peter Chen Hou (1931–70), who played leading men to female Mandarin musical stars (Teo 1997).

The biggest Mandarin studio, Shaw Brothers, established a Cantonese film unit in 1955 that began to use local talent, and subsequently its films became popular in Hong Kong as well as in Southeast Asia (HKFA 2003). In the 1960s and 1970s, Shaw Brothers had its own 'star-making system' (Fu 2000, p.45) utilizing a systematic drama training school that began in 1961. The school was divided into Cantonese and Mandarin units and offered classes in body movement, voice delivery, singing and dancing (HKFA 2003). Later, the same approach was transposed to the training of personnel for television at TVB. As Shaw Brothers moved into the production of martial arts films in the 1960s, male stars re-emerged, including Danny Lee (b.1952), Wang Yu (b.1943), Ti Lung (b.1946), Fu Sheng (1954–83), Gordon Liu (b.1955) and Lo Lieh (1939–2002). The martial arts films released by Shaw Brothers from the mid-1960s onwards, especially those directed by Zhang Che, were known for their depictions of violence and masculinity.

Cantonese opera performers were initially reluctant to act in Cantonese opera films, as these films were seen as lacking in prestige, although this soon changed as film overtook stage performance in popularity in the 1940s and 1950s (Latham 2000). Cantonese opera cinema in the 1950s and 1960s had its own associated stars. Yam Kim-fai (1912–89) and Pak Suet-sin (b.1926), known affectionately as *Yam-Pak*, were the most notable opera actresses. There are six key roles in Cantonese opera (Latham 2000). Yam played the *sheng* role, the chief male lead, and therefore she cross-dressed in almost all her screen roles, while Pak was the *dan,* the main female role. Yam died in 1989, aged 76, having made more than 300 films.

The 1960s saw the rise of two female stars who dominated the youth market, Josephine Siao Fong-fong (b.1947) and Connie Chan Po-chu (b.1946), both trained in the Cantonese opera tradition. Siao was a child star in the early 1950s and acted in literally hundreds of Cantonese and Mandarin films. At the height of her popularity,

Siao starred in a 1969 film about problem youth, *Teddy Girls* (Lung Kong), though she left Hong Kong to study in the USA in the same year.[6] The two stars were particularly able to cater for the female film-goers of the 1960s, including young students and factory workers in the newly industrialized city. 'Chan, as the girl next door, became the idol of lower-middle-class girls, while Siao, fashionably dressed and proficient in popular song and dance, attracted college girls' (Wong 2005, p.245).[7] The fans of Josephine Siao and Chan Po-chu were therefore divided into two groups, lower-middle-class women and college students, reflecting the existence of social strata while signalling the emergence of youth culture and increasing independence among the young generation.

Many of the melodramas of 1960s Hong Kong, including those starring Siao and Chan, were didactic about family responsibilities (Wong 2005) and were aimed at young audiences who were encouraged to become good citizens and contribute to the economic and social progress of the city. Such films were able to both entertain and provide a commentary on Hong Kong's social history through social drama. In *Teddy Girls* Siao plays Josephine, a rebellious girl from a broken home who ends up in a reform school after a fight in a nightclub. The didactic nature of the film was a response to increasing concerns about wayward youth, even though the protagonist is sympathetically characterized. At the end, Josephine avenges her mother's suicide, which she blames on her mother's lover. *Teddy Girls* is an example of the social concerns of the late 1960s, when youth problems and generational change were often referred to in the content of media products. Male Cantonese film stars of this period included Tsang Kong (b.1938), Tse Yin (b.1936) and Chu Kong (b.1941), many of whom continue to work in film and television today.[8]

The multimedia nature of stardom was therefore already in existence in the early days of Hong Kong cinema, as seen through the examples of both Mandarin (musical) and Cantonese (opera) films that featured lead actors who were also recording artistes. The entertainment press was also an active participant in stardom, as demonstrated by the tragic case of Ruan Lingyu. Female stars were employed to advertise fashion and beauty products through film magazines, reflecting the emerging consumer society in post-war Hong Kong. Stars such as Josephine Siao and Chan Po-chu catered for specific groups of audiences as they assumed different character traits associated with the newly affluent young consumers and the working class, respectively; as a result their screen roles often embodied the social concerns of the time. As the media in Hong Kong became more and more locally focused in the 1970s, the stars' existence also changed. The multimedia nature of stardom and the fluidity of stars' movement between media would become more pronounced with the advent of television and Cantonese pop music, creating a breed of local stars in the 1970s and 1980s.

Indigenous multimedia stars

When television broadcasting began in Hong Kong in the late 1960s and early 1970s, it co-opted the stars of Cantonese cinema (Chua, 17 June 2009). However, many Hong Kong stars who emerged since the 1970s started their career in television, usually in variety shows and drama series, before crossing over to cinema and, often, popular music and other media as well. Therefore, television can be seen to have played a key role in creating multimedia stardom in the city. The relatively well-defined avenues for entry into the media industry, such as beauty pageants, talent contests and television training programmes (rather than performing arts colleges), were all related to television. Apart from the beauty contests, these routes have usually been open to both men and women, and stardom is largely egalitarian in Hong Kong, as there is no specific academic qualification required.

Among 33 female stars who were active in 2003,[9] 12 had been beauty pageant contestants, 9 came from advertising or modelling, 6 had completed television acting classes or came from performing arts college, 3 were discovered through song contests and 3 were reported to have simply been 'discovered'. These avenues into the entertainment industry are well established. Many contestants from the Miss Hong Kong Pageant have become actresses, usually working for TVB and appearing in drama series. For Hong Kong actors, unlike in Hollywood, the appointment of agents, physical transformation and contacts come after performers already have a foot in the door.[10] Many of the entry routes into the entertainment industry have traditionally had a strong connection to local television, and I argue that this was a unique feature of multimedia stardom in Hong Kong. After its inception, TVB produced performers through its own training classes modelled on the Shaw Studio's drama school. Kam Kwok-leong, an actor-turned-filmmaker, describes the content of the TVB classes:

> The training class was very comprehensive and we learned acting theory, music, make-up, martial arts, the art of attack and defence, dance etc. It was rather like some of the classes in the present Academy [for] Performing Arts. The object was to give all-round training.
>
> (cited in HKIFF 1999, p.135)

Chow Yun-fat, Andy Lau, Tony Leung and Stephen Chow were all well-known graduates from the acting class who started their careers by working in television programmes, including prime-time drama series, for several years. Stephen Chow could not get into the acting school, but he joined the night classes (also put on by TVB) and then spent time working in children's television in the 1980s. Programmes such as the popular *EYT,* a live nightly variety show, provided on-the-job training for presenters and hosts.

It was common for television actors to cross over to film work after their stardom was established on the small screen. Tony Leung graduated from the TVB acting class in 1982, at the age of 20, and started working in film in 1985. His most prolific year was 1993, when he made ten films (*City Entertainment* 2002b; *City Entertainment* 2004). In the 1970s and 1980s, the average TVB prime-time drama series had 45–55 per cent of viewers (So 2005), and the stars became highly visible and familiar to television audiences. A series might run for two or three months and become a daily viewing habit for families.

Along with the popularity of television and Cantonese pop songs, many of which were theme songs from television programmes and films, came a new breed of stars who permeated the different mass media simultaneously. An early example of the kind of multimedia stardom created by television is TVB's first comedy-Cantopop programme, the *Hui Brothers Show* of 1971.[11] Sam Hui performed in a band, The Lotus, prior to his television and solo pop careers; The Lotus was one of the many male pop bands formed after the success of The Beatles' 1964 concert in Hong Kong.[12] Later, the Hui brothers (Michael, Sam and Ricky) also starred in blockbuster comedy films in the 1970s and 1980s (Lau 1998). Sam Hui's theme song for *The Private Eyes* (Michael Hui, 1976), *Half a Pound, Eight Taels,*[13] contains lyrics that reflect the bittersweet reality of working-class life in the 1970s and that were intended to resonate with listeners:

We're a team of workers

Running all over the streets until we get ulcers

This horrible boss gets mad all the time (crazy like a chicken) whether it's fair or not, he's always barking

Every time you ask for a raise, he pulls a horrible long face (it's just an act)

So you end up starving

(translation from Erni 2007, p.88)

The Hui brothers grew up in a government-built, low-income estate in Hong Kong, but Michael graduated from the University of Hong Kong, the city's most prestigious educational institution, with a degree in sociology. He soon used this unusual combination of intellectual and working-class background in the brothers' television comedy and social satirical films by developing 'the mean-spirited "little-men"' aspect of 'the *pak-dong* spirit', with *pak-dong* 'being the Cantonese expression for buddies, or partners' (Teo 1997, p.54). Michael, Sam and Ricky were all famed for their 'common man' image. Sam, who developed a successful pop career, utilized this image in his onscreen characters and in popular songs like *Half a Pound, Eight Taels.*

TVB and ATV held song contests and other talent competitions that became another route into multimedia stardom. Anita Mui (1963–2003), Leslie Cheung and Jacky Cheung were prominent stars who started by winning song contests and, while remaining primarily pop stars, were also able to build successful film careers. Singer-actors such as Mui and Jacky Cheung in the 1980s and 1990s anticipated the multi-faceted existence of stars like Miriam Yeung and Twins in the 1990s and 2000s. After winning a prize in a song contest staged by RTV in 1977, Leslie Cheung worked in television drama series for the station and soon embarked on parallel pop music and film careers. His early image was one of rebellious youth epitomized in his role as Yuddy, a handsome playboy, in Wong Kar-wai's *Days of Being Wild* (1990). The Chinese title of the film was *A Fei Zheng Zhuang,* the same title that was used for James Dean's *Rebel Without a*

Cause (Nicholas Ray, 1955). In 1989 Cheung 'retired' from the music business to focus on film, although he returned to music recording and touring from the mid-1990s onwards. He famously wore a long wig and dress (supplied by the French fashion designer Jean Paul Gaultier) during his series of 13 concerts entitled *Passion* at the Hong Kong Coliseum in 2000. Similarly, Cheung's later film roles became much more diverse and daring. Many were mature and complex characters, such as those in *Farewell My Concubine* (Chen Kaige, 1993) and *Happy Together* (Wong Kar-wai, 1997). *Farewell My Concubine* was particularly challenging, as Cheung had to master the stage skills necessary to play a homosexual Beijing opera *huadan*.[14] Cheung described himself as bisexual, and his long-term relationship with partner Daffy Tong Hok-tak was well known in the local media. Male homosexuality was only de-criminalized in 1991, but, despite homophobia in Hong Kong, Cheung's respected star status was largely unharmed by his decision to come out, and he was affectionately called *ge ge,* meaning 'older brother', in the media.

Beauty pageants, which had existed in Hong Kong since the 1940s, became another television-endorsed route to stardom when the terrestrial Chinese channels of TVB and ATV began to hold annual contests and broadcast other international competitions. One of the main annual beauty pageants, Miss Hong Kong, staged and broadcast by TVB since 1973, has generated stars such as Maggie Cheung and Michelle Reis (b.1970). Since its inception, the Miss Hong Kong Pageant has become a yearly mass-broadcast event, so these competitions can be seen to parallel the development of the indigenous media industry and contemporary female stardom in Hong Kong. More recently, some contestants from international Asian or Chinese pageants have also ended up in the Hong Kong media industry. The Miss Hong Kong Pageants were annual spectacles that used to be viewed by a large proportion of the population in the 1970s and 1980s. Rozanna Lilley describes many of the beauty contestants' subsequent careers in Hong Kong, particularly in the context of television work:

> Over five hundred female contract artists work at the two television stations, and many are former contestants. Around 5,000 women each year apply for ATV's Miss Asia Pageant and TVB's Miss Hongkong Pageant. The monetary rewards for winning either are there: a car, a flat for a year, clothes and free holidays. The real attraction, though, is that success in a pageant guarantees a contract in television, with the possibility of a career in film. As one ATV spokesman explained: 'We will audition girls after the pageant for jobs at the station. These include roles in dramatic programmes, comperes [sic] and singers'.

> (1993, pp.269)

Once they were signed up by a television company, actresses entering entertainment through beauty contests might attend acting classes, but many simply entered into the industry and were expected to learn on the job. The female stars who came from these contests were already familiar faces even before they developed careers elsewhere. The popularity and dominating influence of beauty pageants in the 40 years since their inception at TVB meant that there was a specific emphasis on the physical appearance of women stars in Hong Kong. The career trajectory of one beauty contest winner illustrates the importance of this traditional route for many women into the entertainment industry:[15]

> Winning the Miss Hong Kong Pageant, entering the entertainment business and marrying into a wealthy family are the dreams of many young girls but there are few successful examples. May Ng [b.1967] is one of the 'models'. In 1986, the 19-year-old was a three-time Miss Hong Kong, winning the runner-up, most photogenic and most talented prizes. She then signed up with TVB, became a singer . . . In 1993 she married . . . and left the entertainment world.

Though many film actors in Hong Kong came from television, the multimedia stars' preference for working in film was due to both greater prestige and financial rewards. Television work, especially in drama series, was seen as less prestigious and was reserved mostly for contracted actors, as salaries for these television performers were notoriously low. The figure given for 1991 was HKD 6–7,000 per month, with HKD 300 awarded for each acting appearance (Lilley 1993). Robert Chua, in an interview in June 2009, confirmed that salaries for television performers remained low, at less than HKD 12,000 per month, which made it impossible even to dress well. Chua also indicated that television stars typically earned extra income through public performances, outdoor events, openings and private parties; television stations effectively acted as managers, as they received commissions every time a staff performer made a public appearance. Performers therefore had to self-promote in the hope of gaining opportunities to supplement their meagre television salaries. At the same time, television acting remained a rite of passage and a training ground for many stars, with film being the more prestigious and lucrative medium.

David Bordwell (2000) states that stars claimed the biggest share of the film-production budget, more than the combined salaries of directors, producers and screenwriters. The estimated salary of leading actors and actresses in the 1980s and 1990s would be HKD several million per film. In the early 1980s, Sam Hui was paid HKD 2 million per film. In 1992, Jet Li was paid HKD 12 million per film, and a leading soft-porn actress, Veronica Yip (b.1966), was paid HKD 1 million (Zhang 2004).[16] In 2002, Stephen Chow received HKD 15 million per film (Chow 2005c). In 2005, Andy Lau, Tony Leung and Maggie Cheung were reportedly paid HKD 8–9 million per film (Chow 2005c). Jackie Chan's fee per film was reported to be Chinese Renminbi 45–50 (HKD 57–64) million and Chow Yun-fat's was Chinese Renminbi 30–35 (HKD 38–45) million in 2013 (November 2013 exchange rate).[17]

The lengthy production periods of long-running television drama series impacted a star's ability to participate in other projects. Most television productions in Hong Kong relied on large ensembles of actors and therefore offered less opportunity and accolade for leading stars when compared with film. Nevertheless, while the financial rewards were not as significant as for film work, television was the best medium for local stars to garner and build popularity with audiences; at their most successful, prime-time drama series might attract 70 per cent of viewers (So 2005). Levels of prestige also existed within the television broadcast industry, as making a programme for TVB was more prestigious than working for ATV due to the higher viewing figures of programmes broadcast by the former. The effect of this strong connection with local television was that many multimedia stars benefited from long periods of on-the-job training and were already familiar to audiences when they crossed media, even without substantive pre-entry training in acting or singing. This process was in effect a long ascendance to multimedia stardom. Despite the low salaries of television performers, it was a medium that could build a star's popularity with a large audience, and it remains a point of entry into the media industry.

In the 1980s and 1990s, the pop industry was an important facet of the local media, and many stars such as Andy Lau and Leslie Cheung went from television drama to simultaneous singing and film careers. Many popular singers emerged in the 1980s, among them the so-called Four Heavenly Kings of Cantopop, Jacky Cheung, Andy Lau, Leon Lai (b.1966) and Aaron Kwok (b.1965), who all had successful singing and acting careers. Cheung and Lai won television-sponsored singing contests, Lau came from TVB's acting class, and Kwok was in a TVB dancer training class.[18] All of them appeared in TVB drama series before focusing on their film careers.

The strong influence of television and cross-media promotion contributed to a mass market for Cantopop music. Cantopop singers typically released two albums or more a year; if the singers were also lead actors in films, they would often enjoy cross-marketing through the theme songs. Despite the decline of the musical as a popular film genre, theme songs from Hong Kong cinema, usually sung by the lead actors, benefited from simultaneous multimedia promotion, including radio airplay, music videos and karaoke. The theme songs were sometimes presented in the middle of the narrative like a music video with action sequences or montages, usually with lyrics that commented on the plotline. An example is Sally Yeh's (b.1961) theme song in John Woo's *The Killer* (1989). Sally Yeh was a popular singer and actress in the 1980s and 1990s. Yeh's career stalled after she married another singer-actor, George Lam (b.1947), in 1996, though her comeback albums and concerts since 2002 have been well received. Yeh was the female lead in *The Killer,* playing the nightclub singer Jenny, who nearly loses her sight after being caught in a shootout in a key scene at the beginning of the film. Yeh collected five platinum discs in 1989,[19] and this role came at the height of her pop stardom. The theme song begins as the eponymous killer-for-hire (Chow Yun-fat) receives a gun from his contact, goes to the nightclub, and walks past the poster of the singer outside the nightclub. He then sees Jenny performing:[20]

Another tear streams down my face

As my heart searches for you

Another night of despair

Another night of loneliness

I wait and hope for someone

Who will accept me as I am

Someone who will let me know

That he will always be there

So many dreams and hopes

Yet I am still so lonely

It is just a little dream

But enough for the future

The lyrics make reference to the promise that the lone hitman of the English title, John,[21] will soon be making to Jenny. As John walks through the nightclub to find his target, he listens to the song with a faint smile, as if the words were speaking to him. The sequence cross-cuts between the killer and the singer, with several close-ups on their faces, especially the eyes. After nearly blinding Jenny, John decides to do another 'hit' in order to make enough money for an operation to save her sight. It is this promise that occupies John for the rest of the narrative and that draws the two of them together in their futile dream of a shared future. The song acts as a refrain throughout the film, usually alongside the appearances of Jenny, including in a scene when John saves Jenny from street robbers and promises to return to her and fund the sight-saving operation. This scene is intercut with a flashback of the shooting and emphasizes the central motive of the protagonist. The song also provides a bridge into the next sequence that introduces the rogue cop played by Danny Lee. Sally Yeh's role in this film exploited the singer's stardom and popularity, and the theme song emphasizes the film's central emotional motif and supports the other lead actors, who carry the weight of the dramatic performance.

Radio was another multimedia avenue for pop stardom in the 1980s. The popular singer Sandy Lam (b.1966) started her career as a radio DJ. Vivian Chow (b.1967) joined RTHK as a DJ in 1987 after winning TVB's New Talent Singing Awards. She performed in radio drama series before developing a parallel film career, but she was best known as a singer throughout the 1990s. Many foreign pop songs, usually from the USA, Britain and Japan, were transformed into Cantonese cover versions. Similarly, Hong Kong singers often issued their albums in Mandarin (and occasionally in other languages) in order to capture different markets. At the height of his popularity in 1988, Alan Tam released seven albums, two of which were in Mandarin and one in Japanese.[22] He also held a longstanding record for performing 38 consecutive concerts at the Hong Kong Coliseum in 1989, which equated to a total of 475,000 available seats. Footage of the stars' concerts was typically circulated as VCDs, DVDs and karaoke. The mass market for local pop music in the 1980s and 1990s was also reflected by the high sales figures in Hong Kong for many of the singers. Jacky Cheung's five-time platinum record in 1997 demonstrated the mass interest in some of the city's most popular stars, representing 150,000 units sold in a city with a population of six million.[23]

The strong influence of television, a prolific production system, an accessible mass market and the fluidity of popular stars' presence in a range of media were unique features of stardom in Hong Kong in the 1980s and part of the 1990s. As Brian Hu observes:

> The fluidity of personnel between media is accepted, and even encouraged, by the media. (This is not the case in Hollywood, where a crossover artist is approached with scepticism, or in Bollywood, where actors dance but their songs are almost always overdubbed by playback singers who are then the ones who become concert and album stars.)
>
> (2006, p.410)

Hu cites the Anglo-American examples of David Bowie, Prince, Madonna and Whitney Houston, whose film roles were often met with negative critical reception; their film careers were at best marginal to their pop stardom.

I argue that the generation of indigenous stars in Hong Kong who began to emerge in the 1970s reveals several specific features of multimedia stardom that existing star studies fail to capture. First, the film-centric approach to star studies in the West needs to be qualified in view of the unique and longstanding multimedia nature of stardom in Hong Kong. Media stars' extra-screen presence as celebrity is a central characteristic of their existence, while in the literature film stars are seen to mainly 'organise the [film] market and act back upon the "quality" of the films they are in' (Dyer 1979, p.11). As film actors in Hong Kong are unlikely to be film stars exclusively, so any discussion of stardom also necessitates investigation of other media practices. At the height of the media industry's success in the 1980s and early 1990s, there was a reverence for stars who succeeded, often simultaneously, in film, television and pop music. Second, the generation of stars from the 1980s was central in the indigenization of local popular culture at a time when media such as television created daily opportunities for these public figures to become familiar faces to mass audiences. The influence of local television as the main avenue for the circulation of stardom and a prominent source of film actors and pop singers is evident in relation to this generation of multimedia stars. Third, the fluidity of stars' multimedia existence was unique, especially compared to other media industries like that in the USA. Media products and their stars in Hong Kong benefited from cross-media promotion to mass audiences.

While I have sketched out the specific conditions for multimedia stardom in Hong Kong, television as the training ground for many stars has been of declining importance since the 1990s because of the diversification of leisure activities and the contraction of the more traditional media, as detailed in Chapter 1. The nature of multimedia stardom has therefore been changing since the mid-1990s, an issue to be explored next.

Changing stardom from the 1990s

The changes in the Hong Kong media industry and in residents' choices of lei-sure activity since the mid-1990s, detailed in the previous chapter, have affected the characteristics of multimedia stardom. In the following discussion, I examine multimedia stardom since the 1990s, including new stars who have had career trajectories different from the 1980s generation and crossover stars who worked in Hollywood before their re-immigration to the Chinese-language mediasphere.

The generation of stars who emerged in the 1980s established themselves through television, especially via drama training and series, beauty pageants and song contests. However, some of these traditional entry routes to stardom in Hong Kong lost their importance with the declining popularity of local television. Like other major television events, beauty pageants were less popular in the early 2000s than they had been in previous decades, an indication of the changing nature of mass viewing habits and the lack of interest shown by local audiences and poten-tial contestants. A magazine report suggested that the 'quality' of contestants had fallen, and the programme producers now had difficulties persuading women of Chinese origin from abroad to participate because they did not want to face media pressure and possible scandals.[24] In 2012, the Miss Hong Kong contest introduced public voting in an attempt to raise interest.[25]

With the contraction of Hong Kong cinema since the mid-1990s, the previous generation of stars had to choose between either maintaining a shrinking screen presence or pursuing other opportunities. As assistant director NR explained:

> The actors are very pragmatic. They have busy schedules. Since the market has been bad in recent years, they may [give up film] for television drama series that are fairly good earners. They are paid HKD 20,000 per episode of soap opera. A series of 40 episodes would give them around HKD 1 million.
> (4 August 2005)

Some of these actors, like Carina Lau (b.1965) and Anita Yuen (b.1971), chose to focus on television work, reversing the previous trend. The expansion of the mainland television production industry and its market generated extra demand for these actors, and the increasing presence of Hong Kong stars in the mainland Chinese mediascape reflected the process of re-sinicization. The contraction of the Hong Kong film industry seen in the 1990s therefore partially broke down the traditionally strong interrelationships between local television, film and stardom. The relative importance of routes of entry other than television, including mod-elling and advertising, has increased in recent years. Commercial work, most commonly in advertising, arguably requires only a recognizable image and fame, and so it has increasingly become the most profitable facet of the stars' existence, an issue that will be discussed in Chapter 3.

Film stardom seemed to have peaked in Hong Kong around the mid-1990s. In 1993, the Chinese New Year releases included films fronted by Sam Hui, Leslie Cheung, Jackie Chan, Stephen Chow and Jet Li, all popular stars at the time.[26]

Many of these stars, who emerged in the 1970s and 1980s, remained popular through the early 2000s, as revealed by quantitative research such as the Hong Kong Entertainment Poll 2004 (Chow 2005b; University of Hong Kong 2005).[27] The ten most liked local film actors were as follows:

1 Chow Yun-fat
2 Andy Lau
3 Tony Leung Chiu-wai
4 Maggie Cheung
5 Jackie Chan
6 Anthony Wong
7 Stephen Chow
8 Sammi Cheng (b.1972)
9 Miriam Yeung
10 Cecilia Cheung

All of the top seven except Jackie Chan, who was also the oldest, came from or were connected to local television and started working in the entertainment industry in the 1970s or 1980s. Only in the eighth, ninth and tenth positions did younger stars appear: Sammi Cheng, Miriam Yeung and Cecilia Cheung were all singer-actresses who had their starts in the mid- to late 1990s. It appears that in the early 2000s few new performers were able to capture the interest of the local population as well as stars from the previous generation. As a further example, much of the success of the blockbuster film *Infernal Affairs* was attributed to the two main leads, Tony Leung and Andy Lau. In another poll conducted in 2005 of 'Favourite Actor' and 'Favourite Actress', Leslie Cheung and Maggie Cheung, who both started their careers in the 1980s, were the favourites out of the top 20 actors and actresses respectively,[28] with only Sammi Cheng being included from the mid-1990s generation. *Cold War* (Sunny Luk and Longman Leung), the top-grossing Hong Kong film in 2012 and also the only Chinese-language film in the top ten box office hits of the year, starred Tony Leung Kar-fai (b.1958), Aaron Kwok and Andy Lau, all from the 1980s generation.[29]

The Hong Kong Entertainment Poll 2004 (University of Hong Kong 2005) also studied the most liked singers or groups. The top ten were:

1 Jacky Cheung
2 Hacken Lee (b.1967)
3 Andy Lau (featured in both charts)
4 Kelly Chan (b.1972)
5 Joey Yung (b.1980)
6 Sammi Cheng (featured in both charts)
7 Jay Chou (b.1979)
8 Leo Ku (b.1972)
9 Miriam Yeung (featured in both charts)
10 Twins

The differences between the respective charts for film and pop music are useful in the current consideration of the characteristics of multimedia stardom. Only three stars, Andy Lau, Sammi Cheng and Miriam Yeung, appeared in both lists. Even though Tony Leung and Anthony Wong had released albums, the top seven film stars, with the exception of Andy Lau, were all actors who had focused on careers in film. However, all of the pop stars in the second list had also acted in film and/ or television. Television and song contests featured strongly in the backgrounds of these pop stars. Jacky Cheung, Hacken Lee, Joey Yung, Sammi Cheng and Miriam Yeung competed in song contests; Andy Lau came from TVB acting classes; Leo Ku started as a presenter on pop music shows for TVB; Kelly Chan and the two members of Twins were models. Jacky Cheung, Hacken Lee and Andy Lau began their careers in the 1980s. The pop stars from the fourth to the ninth positions all started in the 1990s, while Twins formed in 2001.[30]

To some extent the comparison between these two charts demonstrates that stars from earlier generations were still very much revered in Hong Kong in 2004, while younger singers from the 1990s were more accepted in the pop music world than they were in relation to film acting. Pop music remained largely a leisure pursuit for younger audiences who were more open to the new generation of singers. Similar trends of career entry through song contests and the popularity of the younger generation of stars can be uncovered by examining the results of the 2012 IFPI Hong Kong Top Sales Music Awards. The top ten local artistes were G.E.M. (Tang Zhi-kei, b.1991), Twins, Ivana Wong (b.1979), Leo Ku, Denise Ho (b.1977), Joey Yung, Alfred Hui (b.1988), Miriam Yeung, Andy Lau, Lung Kim-sheng (b.1944) and Mui Shet-sze (b.1946). Tang's career began in 2006 when she was only 16, following a singing competition. Ivana Wong also won a competition in 2000 and signed with Universal Music in 2004. Denise Ho won the New Talent Singing Awards in 1996, but her career was slow to become established. Ho also had a parallel film career; in 2012 she won the Golden Horse Award's Best Actress for *Life Without Principle* (Johnnie To, 2011). Alfred Hui participated in a TVB singing contest in 2009, and his music success has been a recent phenomenon.

The career trajectories of Faye Wong (b.1969), a singer most active in the 1990s, and Sam Hui demonstrate the longstanding popularity of the earlier generations of pop stars and further illustrate the changes in pop music stardom. Faye Wong was born in Beijing. She moved to Hong Kong in the 1980s and signed a contract with Cinepoly Records, a subsidiary of Polygram, in 1989. Her first three records, released under the stage name Shirley Wong (Wang Jingwen), quickly became platinum albums. However, Wong was 'criticized for coming across as too much of a bumpkin – that is, as a mainlander in need of refinement'; Cinepoly hired a style consultant to reinvent her as a modern 'Hong Kong woman' (Fung & Curtin 2002, p.270), and in 1991 she went to New York 'to discover herself'. Upon returning to Hong Kong, she released an album, *Coming Home,* that included a hit song, *The Woman Who Easily Gets Hurt*.[31] She reverted back to her original name, Faye Wong (Wang Fei). The name she used initially, Jingwen, denotes a quiet and calm personality, while the new name Fei rhymes with the word for the wife of a prince or imperial concubine, suggesting her status as, or aspiration to be, a diva.[32]

In *Coming Home,* Wong no longer sang love ballads but instead asserted an image of independence, choosing songs to cover that were edgier and less mainstream, including some by Icelandic singer Björk and the Scottish alternative rock band The Cocteau Twins, artistes that were largely unfamiliar to Hong Kong audiences. With her newfound image she often criticized the media and market pressures explicitly; her song *Please Myself* (1994) contains the line '[I sing] only to please myself and not the market'. Faye Wong reportedly said,

> Realistically, we who work in the entertainment industry often have to use phony emotions. [A singing] idol is in itself a fake image, but many people make a big deal of idols. When there is a need for a certain image demanded by the fans, the entertainer must portray that image and become that fake person.[33]

Wong's criticism of the media suggests that it is the fans who demand changeable 'phony' and 'fake' media images. Wong's comments illustrate what Lawrence Grossberg calls 'a logic of authentic inauthenticity': 'the only possible claim to authenticity is derived from the knowledge and admission of your inauthenticity' (1993, pp.205–6). This might explain why Wong gradually distanced herself from the Hong Kong entertainment world and instead embedded herself among a group of rock musicians in her native Beijing.[34] Instead of being a commercial risk, this newfound image attracted advertising contracts for a range of products, including Virgin Atlantic Airways, Motorola, and Pepsi. After establishing herself as a Cantopop singer, Wong began to record mainly in Mandarin in the mid-1990s.[35] Wong's acting career has been sporadic compared to other Hong Kong singers. Hu (2006) argues that Faye Wong plays herself in *Chungking Express* (Wong Kar-wai, 1994); even the character she plays is simply called Faye. Her dreamy presence in the film is accentuated by the use of her hit song *Dream Person,* a cover version of *Dreams* by the Irish band The Cranberries. Hu (2006) also suggests that there are intertextual references to other music videos and a KTV (Karaoke TV) aesthetic in the film.

This examination of the career of Faye Wong highlights several features of the 1990s generation of multimedia stars. Wong had to establish herself as a modern Hong Kong singer by changing her image, stage name and the kind of music she produced. After she had conquered the Cantonese pop world, she seemed content to focus on the Mandopop market, and she occasionally appeared in commercials, television and film. Wong's career was multimedia but footloose, a sign of the more general decline of the Hong Kong media industry as opposed to the rise of pop and rock in Mainland China. Wong was an early example of Hong Kong-based stars who would turn to the mainland market in the process of re-sinicization.

The market for Hong Kong media products became increasingly fragmented over time. The inclusion in the 2012 IFPI Top Sales Music Awards of Cantonese

opera stars Lung Kim-sheng and Mui Shet-sze is evidence of a fragmented popular music market that included an older generation of audiences. Both Lung and
Mui debuted in the 1960s, and the pair has had a successful comeback career
since the mid-2000s. This appearance in the Awards coincided with the release
of their collaboration on the Cantonese opera *Long Qing Shi Yi Ban Shi Ji* in 2012.
This older audience group also ensured the continued success of the early
generation of singers that included Andy Lau and Jacky Cheung. The other two
Heavenly Kings, Leon Lai and Aaron Kwok, also continued their multimedia
work, with Kwok starring in the aforementioned film *Cold War*. Low sales figures of CD albums, especially for the new generation of pop singers, were mainly
attributable to illegal downloading. A veteran television and commercial producer
(Chua, 17 June 2009) commented that pop stars made more money through
performances than album sales, especially in Mainland China, where singers
were paid more than in Hong Kong for their concerts and appearances at public
events. The appeal of the previous generation of stars was often demonstrated by
the ticket sales of their concerts. Hacken Lee and Alan Tam, both popular singers
in the 1980s and 1990s, joined forces for a series of concerts in 2003; tickets for
the 12 concerts quickly sold out. Eason Chan (b.1974), in comparison, did not
sell out any of his six concerts despite winning a series of awards in the same year.[36]
Andy Lau continued to perform in Hong Kong and on world tours, as well as at
a series of concerts in China in 2007, 2009, 2011 and 2013. Many of the previous generation of pop stars, including Sam Hui, Jenny Tseng (b.1953) and Sally
Yeh, have performed comeback concerts since the early 2000s with a high level
of commercial success.

Sam Hui's comeback concerts in 2004 generated great excitement among
adults ordinarily considered above the age of pop star fandom. He has since performed concert tours in Hong Kong, Mainland China and North America. Hui's
success demonstrates the strength of the mass market in the 1970s and 1980s,
to the extent that the local critic Tao Jie (2004, pp.17–9) suggests that this was
a form of 'revenge' by the middle-aged against a predominantly youth-oriented
pop culture. Hui's performances in 2004 boasted ten changes of outfit and several
special guests, including Vivian Chow, who had not made a concert appearance
for many years.[37] One of Hui's costumes was a red, white and blue suit that referenced the cheap nylon bags used by many migrants for heavy loads, nick-named
in Hong Kong 'the poor man's LV (Louis Vuitton)' (see Figure 2.1). The bespoke
suit by a local designer illustrated Sam Hui's common man persona and proximity
to the ordinary people, an element of his early stardom employed to address his
middle-aged fans 30 years on.

The enduring popularity of Cantopop singers from the earlier period was
explained by media professional Cheung Tung-joe, who began his career in the
1970s:

> During the last few years, the recording industry has been bad due to BT [Bit
> Torrent downloading] and other problems. Yet, Sam Hui managed to put
> on over 20 shows. These earlier stars really had talent and skills in singing

Figure 2.1 Sam Hui on stage in 2004 wearing a red, white and blue suit.

Source: Eastweek, 12 June 2004, p.50. Reproduced with kind permission.

and writing. We all remember the classic songs of Beyond,[38] Anita Mui and Leslie Cheung because the singing talent, the melodies and lyrics worked together as a whole. The new singers have poor skills and their companies try to promote them quickly.

(29 July 2005)

Cheung sets out some of the key debates that form the subjects of Chapters 3–5. The commercial success of the comeback albums and concerts of the previous generation of pop stars illustrates the strength of the mass market for indigenous media as well as its subsequent fragmentation. The performance and skills of this generation of pop stars would become the main elements of the discursive construction of their enduring stardom, and the older audience group would consider these stars as representatives of 'a golden age'.

With the decline of the film, television and pop music industries in Hong Kong since the late 1990s, many stars turned to mainland television drama series, and pop singers like Faye Wong focused on Mandarin-speaking audiences. By the 2000s, stars in Hong Kong needed to look to the Mainland and international markets for their continued existence. Filmmakers and actors leaving Hong Kong for Hollywood in the 1990s, such as John Woo, Chow Yun-fat, Jet Li and Jackie Chan[39] marked the beginning of the decline of Hong Kong cinema. Stars like Tony Leung and Maggie Cheung had either gone to work abroad or garnered a degree of fame through the international distribution of their films; both went on to make the international hit film *Hero* (2003) with mainland director Zhang Yimou. Andy Lau also managed to develop the Chinese and Western markets, with films such as *House of Flying Daggers* (Zhang Yimou, 2004). Stephen Chow, with *Kung Fu Hustle,* left behind his 'Hong Kong style' *mou lei tou* humour and local sensibilities to please his American investors, Sony Columbia;[40] his locally focused comedy was tamed in favour of more universal, cartoon-like physical gags (Leung 2008b) in an attempt to appeal to a wider market.

Celebrity culture, which returned to China following the post-1978 economic reforms, was initially influenced by the culture industries already operating in Hong Kong and Taiwan (Jeffreys & Edwards, 2010). Factors that influenced the subsequent growth of Chinese celebrity culture included a market economy, the liberalization of media and the commercialization of popular culture. Elaine Jeffreys and Louise Edwards describe celebrity culture in China as heterogeneous, in that famous people could come from different walks of life. These two scholars assert that this is indicative of the rise of importance in the public sphere of 'ordinary' people, often self-made rather than promoted by the State, and represents an element of Chinese celebrity culture that distinguishes it from that in the West and, more importantly, from the Hong Kong mediasphere. Chapters 4 and 5 will examine the salient characteristics of multimedia stardom in Hong Kong that challenge this distinction. It is important to note at this point that many Hong Kong stars have been more and more active in China since the handover while also maintaining an international presence.

Chow Yun-fat's career illustrates the place of Hong Kong popular culture in the Greater China and global popular culture nexus. He is an exemplar of the re-immigration of several stars who moved from Hong Kong to Hollywood in the 1990s but have since been engaged in transnational Chinese productions, taking advantage of the increasingly integrated film industries of the Mainland, Hong Kong and the Asian region and Hollywood's interest in diverse international markets. While in Hollywood, Chow was employed mainly for generic Asian roles, with no distinction drawn between 'Asian American males' and non-US, 'Asian men' (Stringer 2003). The limitation of his American career trajectory follows the typical history of Asian American actors in Hollywood, seen through examples like that of star Anna May Wong (1905–61), who was active in the 1920s and battled against stereotypes in Hollywood. She had to move to Europe in the late 1920s in search of better opportunities (Bergfelder 2004; Quan 2004; Wang 2008).

Chow Yun-fat's star status in the West was closely associated with the action genre, most notably John Woo's seminal *A Better Tomorrow 1* and *2* and the aforementioned *The Killer*. These films were mainstream hits in Hong Kong that became reconstructed as cult films in the West (Mendik & Mathijs 2007) within their own subgenre known as 'heroic bloodshed', featuring gun play, violence, male melodrama, unique performance styles and sentimental moral undertones. Chow's initial star persona in the USA, at the height of the migration of other Hong Kong film talents, was almost exclusively connected to cool killer and gangster roles, even though his career in his native city had included a variety of roles, typical of a generation of television-turned-film stars, in genre films including comedies, romance and action. Like his predecessor Jackie Chan, who made several failed attempts to conquer Hollywood before being accepted, Chow's US career was a reinvention and Americanization of his star image for mainstream consumption. Chow's image in Hollywood films indiscriminately conflates Chineseness and Asian-ness, with little specific focus on character origin and back-story. Chow is the almost silent hitman character, John Lee, fresh off the boat from China in *Replacement Killers* (Antoine Fuqua, 1998); a bent cop, Nick Chen, associated with Chinese gangsters in *The Corrupter* (James Foley, 1999); a Siamese king (*Anna and the King,* Andy Tennant, 1999); a mysterious, nameless Tibetan or Shaolin monk (*Bulletproof Monk,* Paul Hunter, 2003); and Captain Sao Feng, a pirate lord of the South China Sea (*Pirates of the Caribbean: At World's End,* Gore Verbinski, 2007). The names of these characters, or the lack of a name for the 'bulletproof' monk, betray the blandness of some of these roles (Leung n.d.). The employment of Chow Yun-fat's star status as a floating signifier of Asianness in Hollywood mainstream productions illustrates how foreign stars are often like other migrant workers 'looking for a new career in a different market' (Lo 2005, p.132).The foreign stars also provide the multi-ethnic casting needed by the American film industry to cater for its ethnically diverse internal and international markets (Xu 2008).

Chow's re-immigration and re-sinicization began with the high-budget co-production *Crouching Tiger, Hidden Dragon* (Ang Lee, 2000) and continued with his recent Chinese-language films, most of which were mainland productions, including *Curse of the Golden Flower* (Zhang Yimou, 2006), *Confucius* (Hu Mei, 2010) and *Let the Bullets Fly* (Jiang Wen, 2010). Like many of his re-immigrant counterparts, Chow Yun-fat bypassed the Hong Kong film industry on his return to Asia and participated in high-budget Chinese blockbusters. Assuming the role of Confucius in a biopic of the Chinese philosopher, Chow transformed from a local Hong Kong hero (more about that in Chapter 5) to one of the founding moral pillars of Chinese culture. Chow's recent career is indicative of the extent of the re-sinicization of Hong Kong stars in the Greater Chinese mediasphere.

Other signs indicated that Hong Kong stars and their films and pop music in the Asian export markets they had previously dominated were being replaced by stars and products from other media industries in the region. Film and television co-productions with China had to incorporate mainland actors, many of whom had become familiar faces to audiences in Hong Kong through television drama series. Edward Lam (2005) points out that the new Hong Kong stars no longer had the glamour of the 1980s generation and were being overtaken by stars from Taiwan and Mainland China. This also had to do with the restructuring of the local, regional and international media markets, and, in turn, Hong Kong audiences' changing relationship with local popular culture, as well as the older generation's apparent irreverence for young stars.

Although stars from abroad, especially those from Taiwan, were also present in the 1980s and 1990s, such as Brigitte Lin Ching-hsia (b.1954) and Sylvia Chang, they tended to be absorbed into the media industry in Hong Kong because of the opportunities offered there. By the early 2000s, the casts for many film productions reflected the lack of new Hong Kong stars with box office clout and the increasing presence of actors from other Asian countries who were imported for specific productions. Woody Tsung, chief executive of the Hong Kong, Kowloon and New Territories Motion Picture Industry Association, suggests that Media Asia's summer blockbuster in 2005, *Initial D* (Andrew Lau & Alan Mak), 'is a typical example of what the local productions will look like. This film has a strong cast and it is adapted from a popular Japanese comic. Action and special effects will dominate the screen' while 'other genres, such as sitcom and drama, which were popular in the past and can be produced at a lower cost, are less likely to attract investment' (cited in Chow 2005a). *Initial D*'s main protagonists were played by Taiwanese pop singer Jay Chou and Japanese actress Anne Suzuki.[41] In the same report cited by Chow (2005a), John Chong, executive director of Media Asia, pointed out that the company would focus on big-budget films and Asian star casts because they had international appeal and would guarantee at least one other foreign market, therefore providing a degree of security against a weak local market. Since the late 1990s, a 'Korean wave' (known as *hallyu*) has spread across many Asian territories, including Hong Kong, with commercially successful South Korean stars, soaps, films and pop music challenging the markets for local media products.

Multimedia stars in Hong Kong were familiar faces to local consumers, and they dominated the mediascape of the 1980s and early 1990s. The continual popularity of this generation of stars demonstrates the strength of their cultural influence since the indigenization of local culture, especially for fans whose formative years coincided with this period of popular media history. The strength of the indigenous media of the 1980s and early 1990s was associated with home-grown stars who remained popular by quantitative measures. Stars who focused on film acting dominated cinema, which catered for audiences of a wider range of age groups, while the new generation of singers were accepted more for their music than their film work, likely because the pop industry attracted younger consumers. The lack of interest in terrestrial television and locally produced cinema in Hong Kong since the early 2000s was related to changes in lifestyle. In response to these trends, many of the earlier generation of stars had to adjust their positions in the Hong Kong entertainment industry by going abroad, reverting to television or trying to enter the Chinese market in a process of re-sinicization. Even stars who had gone to Hollywood in the mid-1990s returned to act in Chinese blockbusters produced or co-produced by and in the Mainland. From the 1990s, social and cultural developments in Hong Kong led to changing fortunes for the media industries and consequently affected the practices of local multimedia stardom, such as the increasing need to cater for the youth and mainland markets.

Concluding remarks

In this chapter I have provided a brief historical overview of stardom in Chinese-language mass media, showing its interrelationship to the distinctive social and cultural contexts. For example, post-war Hong Kong cinema saw the emergence of stars who were often symbols for modernity and economic development. The indigenization of Hong Kong culture occurred throughout the 1970s and 1980s, when the popularity of television, cinema and pop music was high due to the increasingly affluent lifestyle of post-war generations. Many of these cultural forms did not directly address social and political changes, but they formed an important part of the cultural lives of the citizens. This generation of indigenous multimedia stars became associated with a strong local popular culture that addressed a mass market.

Hong Kong stars have always traversed different media, as seen through actors participating in musicals or Cantonese opera and martial arts films. From the 1970s the creation and maintenance of multimedia stardom became closely related to the popularity of local television and cinema. Popular stars came from television training classes and beauty contests, acted in long-running drama series and became familiar faces to audiences, while singing competitions generated singer-actors. Many lead actors in television drama series crossed over to film and Cantopop careers, while theme songs from television and films, often sung by the main leads, were circulated widely as music videos and in radio airplay. The popularity of these media during the 1970s and 1980s and the resulting rise of multimedia stardom led to continued reverence for the previous generation of stars, demonstrated by the enthusiastic reception of their comeback albums and concerts since the early 2000s. Television is generally seen as lacking in auratic distance from viewers (Evans & Hesmondhalgh 2005) because it is highly accessible. Television celebrities therefore may engender sympathetic identification by the audiences. In Hong Kong, the close relationship between television, film and Cantopop, especially in the 1970s and 1980s, capitalized on this familiarity with mass audiences. As stars crossed between media, this familiarity was employed in the building of their popularity, a process which benefited from the closeness between media, another unique feature of the entertainment industry in Hong Kong.

Signs have appeared since 2000 to indicate that Hong Kong cinema, television, pop music and the means of creation and maintenance of stardom have changed. Although stars from the 1980s and early 1990s, especially those focusing on film, are still able to capture some audience attention, new cultural and leisure activities are crowding the entertainment market. The importance of the youth market and the rise of China's cultural power have challenged the media industry to diversify. Arguably, it is the lack of audience familiarity with television-generated stars since the mid-1990s that is responsible for these changes in multimedia stardom.

Many of the most popular film stars are from the 1980s generation, while the film work of pop singers from the 1990s and 2000s is less recognized by young consumers. In the meantime, even stars who had crossover success in the American film industry have re-immigrated into the Greater Chinese mediasphere as the cultural power of the PRC rises in importance.

3 Image

As the traditional media of film, television and pop music in Hong Kong began to experience varying degrees of decline during and after the 1990s, the circulation of 'stardom as image' became an important facet of existence for many performers, because a reliance on any one medium was becoming increasingly economically unviable. As a result, audiences were far more likely to have been exposed to images of multimedia stars in the printed press, advertising or online than to have actually seen or heard their professional work in films or music. In this chapter I draw from a spectrum of media to describe image-making as a set of practices related to multimedia stardom in Hong Kong. I also discuss the discourse about the new breed of stars known as idols, especially their perceived reliance on image-making and their association with the youth market. I examine how some actors in Hong Kong have responded to criticisms of star image-making and then turn to a case study of Miriam Yeung.

Critiques of star creation

In star studies literature, terms such as persona and image are often used in a confused fashion; while some writers use one or the other, others treat them interchangeably. The visual image of the star is a facet of persona,[1] though the term 'image' is increasingly used to refer to a set of characteristics associated with the star, combining individual performances with personal biography, publicity and media exposure (Lovell 2003). The importance of this conceptualization of image is that it points to the fact that stars are more than their individual performances, as they openly have an image, persona and personality (King 2003). In English, the word 'personality' is also used as a noun to refer to an individual, as in the term 'media personality', which suggests a celebrity known for his or her personality (Boorstin 1961). Geoffrey Blowers (1991, pp.259–60) suggests that 'personality' (*gexing*) also means 'individuality' among Cantonese speakers in Hong Kong. For Cantonese speakers, there is no separate word for persona. The Chinese term for image is *xingxiang*. Many of my interviewees also used the terms 'personality' and 'character' interchangeably in their discussion of stars. In this discussion, the notion of personality is used to refer to a facet of a star's image, while persona is employed in the senses adopted by existing star studies.

In existing literature, stars and celebrities have been conceptualized in a variety of ways. Stars may be called pseudo-events and they are 'a new category of human emptiness' (Boorstin 1961, p.49), famous for being famous and lacking meaning even though they appear meaningful (pp.6–12). Chris Rojek's (2001) typology categorizes celebrity as ascribed, achieved or attributed. 'Ascribed' celebrity refers to lineage and bloodline, such as that associated with the British royal family. Ascribed celebrity does not exist in Hong Kong, though many wealthy families are known for their business empires, and entrepreneurs and their relatives often attain celebrity status through familial connections. Rojek states, 'In contrast, *achieved* celebrity derives from the perceived accomplishments of the individual in open competition' (2001, p.18, original emphasis). In contrast, 'attributed' celebrities are not defined by any special talents or skills they possess but by their representation as exceptional individuals by cultural intermediaries. Rojek calls attributed celebrity 'celetoid', refiguring this type of celebrity as a media-generated, compressed, concentrated form that is remarkably similar to Daniel Boorstin's (1961) categorization of celebrities and pseudo-events. In my discussion of stars in Hong Kong, the tension between achieved celebrity and celebrities, or celetoids, forms the subject of this and the next chapter, as the two extremes of these dichotomized notions are examined through stars' existence as image and in their performance (and other work).

Dyer suggests that criticism of stars as the manufactured products of film companies is nothing new: 'No aspect of the media can be more obviously attended by hype than the production of stars; there is nothing sophisticated about knowing they are manufactured and promoted' (1991, p.135), a view that explains concerns over media power in contemporary society. Walter Benjamin's (1936) *The Work of Art in the Age of Mechanical Reproduction* provides a seminal framework for considering image production and the creation of stars in modern society. In the modern technical age, mass-produced, aura-less commodities such as films move away from an original artistic presence, a process which also applies to film stars; as Benjamin states, 'The cult of the movie star, fostered by the money of the film industry, preserves not the unique aura of the person but the "spell of the personality", the phony spell of a commodity' (1936, p.224). Film stars are present in a medium that is divorced from the original work of art (acting), and there exist two layers of reproduction: the rendering of the person as character on screen and the star personality circulated for consumption in other media, most notably the printed press. Both performance and image are commodities of the media industries, although the image is considered separate and distinct from artistic work.

The star system is particularly prone to the criticism that the industry's manipulation involves an enormous amount of money, time and energy spent on the building up of star images through publicity, promotion, fan clubs and other means (Dyer 1979). Manipulation to achieve stardom raises social-ethical concerns, especially when stars are discursively constructed as empty images with no substance beneath their superficial differences (Dyer 1979). This manipulation thesis also leads to criticism of stars for their lack of talent, even though talent is a historically and culturally specific term based on subjective value judgements (p.17). An example of this kind of criticism is Cheung Tung-joe's (29 July 2005) assertion that earlier stars had the talent and skills to create memorable songs, while new singers are simply products of promotion. In the manipulation thesis, stars are commodities, a view that raises anxiety about the passivity and objectification of individuals in contemporary culture.

Conflicts within the discourse of multimedia stardom arise from stars' assigned role as 'talented performers', despite their public existence as the subjects of celebrity news articles and advertising campaigns consumed as images. Star biographies fill entertainment news, opening their 'ordinary' lives to public scrutiny via a simplified and accelerated format in which the milestones of their private existence – romance, infidelity, marriage, divorce, illness and parenting – are much reported and commented on (King 2003). There is a contradiction between the notion of stars existing as extraordinary people with qualities that make them different from others and as ordinary people who can be imagined as individuals in society (Ellis 1997). Dyer (1979) observes that stars have changed from being gods and goddesses to mere mortals, but the expectation of their being both exceptional and ordinary continues. As the media are now saturated with stars' presence, the often contradictory nature of reportage can only suggest that there is no one true self associated with the individual stars.

Stars as commodities divorced from their real selves can be understood through Jean Baudrillard's (1981) notion of simulacra, an idea that extends and refigures Benjamin's (1936) critique of the mechanical reproduction of art because Baudrillard considers 'art', central in Benjamin's theorization, to be expunged from the contemporary process of image generation. Baudrillard defines simulation as 'the generation by models of a real without origin or reality: a hyperreal' and 'the desert of the real itself' (1981, p.166). With the increase in channels of communication and the range of media in contemporary societies such as Hong Kong, stars seem all the more visible. Behind the individuals as commodities are the original referents and values, such as artistic talent and extraordinariness, but in Baudrillard's (1981) notion of simulacra, these are the values that are absent or lost in the manipulation and generation of stars as images for consumption.

As I discuss in the Introduction, stars in Hong Kong often took on or were assigned by others the role of model individuals, as in Francesco Alberoni's notion of the powerless elite (2007). So any shift from traditional media towards image-making must also have an impact on how the stars are seen as model individuals:

> Even while the notion of the individual is assailed on all sides, it is a necessary fiction for the reproduction of the kind of society we live in. Stars articulate these ideas of personhood, in large measure shoring up the notion of the individual but also at times registering the doubts and anxieties attendant on it.
>
> (Dyer 1986, p.10)

In the sections that follow, I examine the changing practices and discourse of multimedia stardom in Hong Kong since the mid-1990s and demonstrate how they have been shaped by the specific cultural and social contexts outlined in Chapter 1. Through a focus on advertising, media corporations, and newspaper and magazine publishing, my analysis examines the significance of the multimedia star image and the challenges posed by contemporary image-making to stars' role as model individuals.

The production of media image in Hong Kong

Stardom in Hong Kong changed after the mid-1990s as the media environment transformed, demonstrated by a decrease in popularity of the traditional media of pop music, film and television and the proliferation of means to circulate news about stars. Newspaper and magazine publications in Hong Kong underwent radical transformation in the 1990s, and the printed press became a major avenue for the circulation of stars' images, directly impacting the production and consumption of stardom. Figures in 2004 showed that 71 per cent of the population read a daily newspaper, and 56 per cent of those sales were for the two majors, *Oriental Daily* and *Apple Daily* (33 per cent and 23 per cent readership, respectively). Both are mass-market newspapers with large entertainment news sections (So 2005). Since the mid-1990s, newspaper publication has become increasingly market driven, with editorial content declining due to ownership by wealthy profit-seeking investors. The watershed in Hong Kong came in 1995 when Jimmy Lai, a local business tycoon and founder of Next Media, established *Apple.* This mass-market newspaper initiated the tabloid trend for mainly image-based features, short and simple news items, a colourful design and graphic layout, and an abundance of photographs, prevailing over editorial and other written content. *Apple Daily* has been described as 'well known for its brazen, sensational news coverage . . . Legitimate political and social topics have been supplanted . . . by sex, sensational crimes, the rise and fall of celebrities, scandalous paparazzi investigations, rumors, and even sham news' (Lo 2005, p.29). Paparazzi, a term originating from the Italian film *La Dolce Vita* (Federico Fellini, 1960), now refers to freelance photographers who pursue celebrities in order to photograph them. *Apple* initiated a series of price wars in its first few years that led to the closure of several rival publications.

The newspaper sector experienced a second major change in the early 2000s with the launch of free newspapers: *Metro* in 2002; *Headline Daily* and *AM730* in 2005; and *The Standard,* one of the main English-language papers in Hong Kong, in 2007. As a result of these competitors, average circulation per day for *Apple Daily* was 227,751 in the latter half of 2012, down from 343,302 for the same period in 2004.[2] The average daily circulation between 1 January and 31 March 2013 of the main free papers was 854,120 for *Headline Daily* and 401,776 for *AM730*, while *Metro* issued 380,265 copies.[3] Jimmy Lai launched *Sharp Daily* in 2011, which had a circulation of 573,967 in the first three months of 2013. The availability of free dailies threatened the survival of paid newspapers, several of which, including *Oriental Daily,* responded by reducing their price. Most of these free papers follow the practice of mass-market newspapers like *Apple* and offer an abundance of entertainment news with little editorial content, a practice that attracts advertisers (Asia Sentinel 2011).

In 2004, 32 per cent of the population read weekly magazines dominated by infotainment and entertainment stories; *Next* and *Sudden Weekly* had the highest circulations in Hong Kong, with readership of 10 and 8 per cent of the population, respectively (So 2005). *Next,* containing both entertainment and general society news, began in 1991 and had doubled in size by 1995 due to the growth in its number of advertising pages (Ha 1998). Its audited circulation from 1 July to 31 December 2012 was 86,463 per issue (compared to 153,459 a decade earlier); the circulation of *Sudden Weekly* for the same period was 119,672 copies per issue.[4]

I witnessed entertainment news reporting first hand in Hong Kong. The opening of *Eros* (Wong Kar-wai, Michelangelo Antonioni, Steven Soderbergh, 2005), an omnibus of three short films, on 13 May 2005 was an event sponsored by the fashion label Fendi. The affair appeared to have little to do with the films, but it was the place to be seen for the attendees, who were predominantly stars, those engaged in public relations and local celebrities. About 20 newspaper reporters were present, and a similar number of photographers and camera staff were poised to take pictures of the famous. These images of the night were to be seen in the major newspapers and weekly magazines over the following days. The only director in attendance, Wong Kar-wai, refused to be interviewed by journalists. The experience exemplified the practice of entertainment reportage in that the main focus of the evening was about a commodity (a fashion brand) and the circulation of fame as image. In the course of our conversation earlier that day, Flora Wu, then gossip columnist of the *South China Morning Post* (*SCMP,* one of the two main English-language dailies), who let me shadow her during the opening, distinguished herself from the other entertainment news reporters:

Leung Wing-Fai (LWF):	Is your job easier than writers from *Apple* or *Next?*
Flora Wu (FW):	Yes, it is actually. I have more respect than the press. I don't really have to stay behind the red tape that the press have to stand behind. They know I'm not going to write something totally ridiculous or untrue.
LWF:	That's the nature of the *[South China Morning] Post,* as opposed to the local entertainment press?
FW:	Yes. It's very conservative. Our editor reads what I write and approves the stories.

(13 May 2005)

Wu asserted the quality of *SCMP* as opposed to the other, chiefly Chinese-language, press. The distinction she made between paparazzi and her own practice was based on the idea that, although much gossip news might be false, she as a journalist from the main English-language newspaper in Hong Kong, would not write anything 'ridiculous or untrue'. My interviewees, including those who produced media commodities, distinguished themselves from other producers who might be involved in the manufacturing of 'untruths'. This experience illustrates how the mass media, even in the opinion of those involved in its production, were known to circulate image without reality while at the same time presuming the existence of underlying truths.

My discussion in Chapter 2 of The New Woman Incident of the 1930s indicates the longstanding practice of tabloid journalism. The entertainment press in Hong Kong rose to dominance out of the competitive, crowded field of magazine and newspaper publication of the mid-1990s, and paparazzi journalism became the prevailing practice. Ruan Jihong's 2003 article charts the changes in the Hong Kong press, and particularly the tabloidization of newspapers, during the 1990s and suggests that the use of the paparazzi had a negative impact on the relationship between stars and the press, which in turn affected the way in which entertainment news was reported and written. Ruan (2003) describes how entertainment news in the 1970s focused on television stars and local films, and there was no specialist entertainment supplement in the main daily papers. For instance, the daily newspaper *Ming Pao* had separate columns on opera, cinema and television news. Entertainment journalists had good relationships with stars, to the extent that they might construct 'news' by incorporating into their stories promotional materials from television stations and record and film companies (Ruan 2003). The watershed came in 1995 with the publication of *Apple Daily,* which included at least three pages of entertainment coverage. *Oriental Daily* and *Sing Pao* soon followed, increasing their entertainment content in order to compete. By 2000, *Apple* published eight pages of entertainment news, while most of the high-circulation newspapers were each employing 50 to 80 journalists and paparazzi to follow the stars. Ruan (2003) criticized the new breed of entertainment editors and journalists for their lack of professional standards, and even their 'corruption' (p.138). Since the friendly relationships between stars and individual journalists had broken down, it became impossible to generate exclusive stories. Instead the entertainment press aimed to discover sensational stories and scandals and to publish revealing photographs of the stars caught unawares, often damaging their 'official' image (pp.126–38). The entertainment news reports of the personal lives and behaviour of unsuspecting stars therefore revealed the fact that the stars, their agents and management companies manipulated the official image presented to the media.

Stars lack full control over what is reported in the news, and their condemnation of the intrusive entertainment press is often expressed through the mediasphere itself. The singer-actor Eason Chan's father was a high-ranking civil servant at the Housing Department who received a seven-year custodial sentence for bribery in 2003. In December 2003, on a key date during his father's trial, Chan gave a performance that was described thus: 'With bulging eyes and tense movements, the singer cut a disturbingly menacing presence as he launched into *Lies,* a track lambasting a "deceitful" mass media which "trades with fervour millions of lies/ as brains are numbed and fried"' (Tsui 2005, p.8).

Many sensational news stories illustrate how the circulation of scandals in the printed press might discredit the stars' image. Ari Adut (2009) suggests that scandals arise when private transgressions become public. In 1991 a court hearing that became known as the 'Miss ABC' case 'revealed an active trade between pimps pressuring hopeful starlets and wealthy customers' (Lilley 1993, p.269). The newspapers were saturated with details of the evidence given by five actresses and beauty contestants who testified against businessman Chin Chi-ming, who blackmailed them for sex. Rozanna Lilley (1993) criticizes the press coverage of the case as evidence of voyeurism and double standards towards women. In November 2002 *Eastweek* published a topless photograph of the star Carina Lau taken when she was kidnapped many years ago. Much of the press and many stars united in condemning the magazine.

The Hong Kong media's fascination with sex scandals was epitomized by the Edison Chen incident in 2008. As mentioned in the Introduction, the scandal concerned the illegal distribution over the Internet of private photographs of the young star Chen and several other female celebrities and models who were his sexual partners. In an article in *Time Magazine,* Edison Chen is cited as describing Cantopop as 'No sex. No Drugs. Maybe a little rock 'n' roll' (Corliss 2001); this case therefore shocked the general public. There was much media criticism of both Chen and the female stars, though the public remained fascinated. The subsequent trial in February 2009 had to take place in Chen's native Canada, as he had received death threats in Hong Kong. There was public outrage at the 'disgusting images' and an expectation that the government would stop their circulation. The careers of all the stars involved were negatively affected, but the way the media reacted to the female 'victims', as they were known, was markedly different from the way they treated Chen (*Eastweek* Entertainment Editorial 2009). While Edison Chen was described as *jiannan,* a 'vulgar man', the responses to the female victims were diverse and often contradictory, depending on how they managed their public appearance. Although they were all seen to have been exploited by Edison Chen, the more they appeared as authentic (that is, consistent in their private and public lives) and conforming to the heterosexual ideal, the more positively the public seemed to respond to them. One of the stars involved, Bobo Chan (b.1979), had already left the entertainment industry by the time the photographs were exposed. She was engaged to be married, but the ceremony was postponed due to the scandal. Being protected by her new fiancé seemed to earn her sympathy. Another of the celebrities, Rachel Ngan (b.1983), had left modelling and become an undergraduate law student at City University; she received relatively little negative response in the media and Internet discussion forums because she was seen to be living a 'healthy' life.

The female stars and models involved also included singer-actresses Gillian Chung and Cecilia Cheung. When the scandal broke, Chung's appearances in public and on a television programme generated hundreds of complaints to TELA (Television and Entertainment Licensing Authority). The negative responses were related to and exacerbated by her previously promoted *yunü* ('virginal young woman') image. Derogatory terms commonly used in sexual innuendos were directed at Chung by fans. She was accused of hypocrisy because she had publicly spoken out against pre-marital sex at the same time that she was photographed by or with Chen. Chung waited a full year before returning to filming and advertising. Cecilia Cheung married in 2006 and became a mother in 2007, and she seemed to receive comparatively more support in the opinions expressed on Internet forums and in the printed press. Her husband is actor-singer Nicholas Tse, whose parents are the well-known actors Patrick Tse (b.1936) and Deborah Lee. She repeatedly talked about how her family had supported her and how she would repent and write in a diary every day to show her son when he grew up. Public opinion also appeared supportive after an interview on a cable channel in February 2009 during which she became distraught several times and accused Chen of hypocrisy, thereby casting herself in a more positive light.

Media attention focused on how the male partners of the female victims responded; the women who were supported by families and partners, and therefore stayed within the realm of heterosexual monogamy, were portrayed as victims who deserved sympathy from the media and the public. The media scandal was a result of a breakdown between the public-private interface. No matter how successful their professional lives were, these women were not viewed by the media discourse and in debates in online public forums as centred and knowable subjects in their own right. The way they were assessed in the media (including the press, the Internet and inter-media commentaries) depended on whether they failed to uphold the heterosexual family ideal; those who were supported by their families appeared authentic. The incident was regarded as an aberration, and the female stars were treated as victims of the vulgar, sex-mad Chen. In the photo scandal, sex outside of marriage was not the central issue; rather it was consistency between the public and private realms that mattered.

Once the Edison Chen scandal became public, online discussion soon turned to debate about the public and private lives of the celebrities involved and about Internet use, freedom of speech and government intervention. The Hong Kong police arrested nine people in connection with the case, urged owners of major websites to delete the images, and requested local websites and BBS (bulletin board system) management firms to submit information about their clients. The Chinese police arrested and imprisoned several people involved in manufacturing CDs of the images. Despite these efforts to censor and crackdown on the distribution of the images, there was no stopping the photographs from appearing on the Internet or public discussion of the scandal. As the Hong Kong police tried to crack down on the uploading of new photographs, the online discussion criticized their perceived heavy-handed approach. While the Internet helped to circulate the images and paradoxically condemned the scandalous contents, some mainland Chinese netizens suggested that 'mass voyeurism' might be a form of democracy:

> One poster [on the Tianya forum] said it proved Mainland-style politics are better than the democracy of Hong Kong and the UK. 'Britain has democracy but the biggest selling newspapers there are tabloids, which report all the private matters of the royal family. The US has democracy, but its Internet is filled with the Paris Hilton sex video. We have more democracy than Hong Kong'.

> (Watts 2008)

The Internet was therefore full of contradictory claims as talk of the scandal became a discussion on the power of the masses. In both China and Hong Kong, the images were circulated and consumed freely through blogs, Flickr, emails and digital memory devices. The speed and distance with which media discourse travelled (especially through the Internet) were unprecedented, and news of the scandal spread widely among the Chinese diaspora, as far afield as North America and Australia. There was little space for the stars to assert consistency between the private and public when the latter was now open to literally millions. If scandal symbolizes the breakdown between the public and personal lives of stars, then this case demonstrates that the public (the people) have now become involved in the mediating process.

The dominance of paparazzi journalism and the decline of the traditional media formats of television, film and pop music illustrate the widening distance between stars as actors and singers and their presence in the entertainment news. This disjuncture between performance and image, together with the commercial necessity for many young idols to diversify and participate in producing different cultural products, exaggerated the multimedia nature of stardom in Hong Kong beginning in the mid-1990s. Many younger stars participated in a variety of media in order to increase their income, as markets for individual media, particularly film and to some extent television and the recording industry, had gone into decline. Although media such as television might not be the stars' top choice, the decline of the film industry might lead them to opt for the steady income of a television series. The local writer and scholar Sze Man-hung summed up the new media landscape:

> Film used to be the main medium. The situation has reversed. The [stars] use the songs from the commercials to sell CDs, then the movies. To be blunt, films are now only a marketing tool. In the 1970s television was really important. Newspapers and magazines are now the stars' daily bread.
>
> (4 March 2005)

What Sze describes is the rise in importance and prominence of advertising in the printed press; the new media landscape of advertising, promotion, infotainment (free) press, Internet and cross-platform mobile media indicates a consumer society in which the traditional mass media are no longer central.

The shifting practice of multimedia stardom can be further characterized by the mid-1990s emergence of large entertainment conglomerates in Hong Kong, which are also involved in the press and advertising. One of the most powerful media corporations, the Emperor Entertainment Group (EEG), has increased its multimedia investment since it was formally established in 1999.[5] EEG's interests include Emperor Motion Pictures, a production-distribution branch that released several international blockbusters involving Jackie Chan, including *Chinese Zodiac* (also known as *CZ12,* Jackie Chan, 2012). Of equal importance is EEG's music branch, which has contracts with many young multimedia stars based in Hong Kong. The corporation also covers artiste management, television production (in Hong Kong and Mainland China), event management and a publishing franchise, business arms that the company fully utilizes to promote its contracted artistes. Furthermore, its publishing branch prints the *Hong Kong Daily News* (*Sun Pao*) and *Oriental Sunday,* both mass newspapers; *Weekend Weekly,* an infotainment magazine; and *New Monday,* a teen magazine launched in 2000.

Multimedia stars contracted by corporations work across media forms that include films, Cantonese and Mandarin pop music, television drama series, advertising, concerts and public appearances, all promoted through inter-media commentaries. In addition, many young multimedia stars are produced in an attempt to capture the recently emerged teen market. The pervasive presence of these stars can be seen through the example of Charlene Choi (b.1982) and Gillian Chung, members of the girl band Twins, who together or individually appeared in 11 out of a total of 63 films produced in Hong Kong in 2004. In their first year after signing with the Emperor Group in 2001, Twins issued three records, made four films, eight commercials and a television series, published a photograph album, and performed thirty-five concerts and made thirty public appearances.[6] They became the most profitable group that year under Emperor Group management. The popularity of Twins was affected by the Edison Chen scandal, but Choi and Chung (after her comeback) continued as actresses and solo singers.

The selling of images, most notably in commercial advertising, has become a highly profitable activity for stars in Hong Kong, overtaking products such as films, television appearances and pop records. Stars are regularly employed to promote products on television and in magazines and newspapers. Headline stories of entertainment magazines often detail stars' love affairs, break-ups, divorces and other scandals. Star features discuss their income from different assignments, films, concert performances or advertising, as well as the value of the properties they own. Female stars appear prominently in advertising, especially in campaigns for slimming products, beauty treatments and cosmetics, while male stars are employed to front advertising campaigns for lifestyle products like Pepsi, mobile phones and gym memberships. In one issue of *Next* (1 April 2004), out of 102 advertisements (in a total of 147 pages), 26 were fronted by a star or celebrity. In comparison to the 1980s and early 1990s, newer stars are more likely to be engaged in using their public image to promote material goods and to be seen as models of consumer culture, rather than participating in more traditional entertainment products like widely seen and heard films or pop albums. The strong link between stars and fashion is suggested by the covers and feature stories of a range of glossy magazines; the Hong Kong editions of international fashion magazines, especially the key titles, *Cosmopolitan, Marie Claire* and *Elle,* often employ stars on their covers.

Hong Kong had been the regional advertising capital in Asia since the 1980s, with the largest number of multinational regional headquarters, especially American multinational advertising agencies (Ha 1998; Pae et al. 2007). With the increasing importance of the Chinese-speaking market to multinational companies, many advertising agencies have based their Greater Chinese market operations in Hong Kong, with branch offices in Mainland China and Taiwan (Ha 1998). Advertising spending has risen in line with the tabloidization of the printed press and the continual growth of the consumer market. In the first quarter of 2012, spending on advertising was 14 per cent higher than in the preceding year, rising to HKD 8.78 billion, with the top three advertisers dominated by skincare and cosmetics companies (CFO Innovation Asia Staff 2012). The most significant year-on-year increase in spending was by Samsung, chiefly on its mobile phone and tablet products. The relatively new interactive and mobile platforms reported growth that was expected to continue. The more the advertising industry expands, the higher the budgets of their campaigns and the better their ability to recruit stars as spokespersons.

Robert Chua (17 June 2009) explained that commercial contracts for stars were initially for the right to the performance for perpetuity. Beginning in the late 1980s and early 1990s, stars signed contracts specifying a period of only months or one or two years, after which they would be paid royalties if the companies wished to continue using their image or performance. The revenue from advertising has given the stars more income and power than ever before. Along with the growth of the advertising market in Hong Kong, the rapid economic development of Mainland China has also increased the demand for star-led commercials for consumer goods. The advertising market in the Mainland has been valuable for many stars, as they are paid more than for similar assignments in Hong Kong. Tony Leung was reportedly paid US\$ 1.3 million in endorsement fees for commercials aimed at the Chinese market.[7] Because commercials typically take only one or two days of shooting, they are often the most profitable facet of many stars' work.

This disjuncture between the selling of an image and the work of art (after Benjamin 1936), such as onscreen performance and singing, by stars is exemplified by the manufacturing of young stars by media corporations, a practice common in Hong Kong since the mid-1990s. This development is also partly the result of the fragmentation of a media market in Hong Kong in which teenage stars are created to capture a particular target market. The young stars are susceptible to criticism about their lack of talent and skills, especially by the middle-aged who perceive the new generation of stars as commodities without original reality, a deficit exacerbated by their over-exposure in the press and advertising, resulting in comments such as these by producer-director Jeff Lau:

Jeff Lau:	The earlier generations of stars such as those from the Shaw Studio were much more mysterious. Now the stars don't have any sense of mystery. It's related to today's technology. You get the information quickly in the media.
Leung Wing-Fai:	I was told that previously stars would only come out dressed up. You saw them occasionally when their films were released.
Jeff Lau:	Yes. You'd imagine that their personal lives were the same as their screen roles.

(3 August 2005)

Earlier stars remained at a distance from their audiences, rather than being readily available, corporation-endorsed, packaged media products reproduced repeatedly in the printed press, in advertising and on the Internet. According to

Lau, the less transparent the manufacturing process of the stars' image was and the less the public knew about the stars, the more the public had to guess who the stars truly were. When the public and private personae of a star are revealed to be incongruent, perhaps by a media scandal, the star is discursively constructed as lacking in authenticity. This was evident in the Edison Chen scandal through the difference in treatment of the male perpetrator and female victims by the media. Nonetheless, the new breed of multimedia stars continues the distinctive practice of fluid media-crossing and prolific production, similar to their predecessors. Therefore, criticisms of younger stars' ordinariness, engendered by their pervasive presence in the printed press and advertising, exemplify hostility towards contemporary image-making, a discursive response to the recent changes in the media industries in Hong Kong, an issue to be discussed next.

Contemporary idols and clawback

The rise of market-driven journalism, media corporations and the advertising industry since the 1990s has led to much debate about the new breed of multimedia stars in Hong Kong. Bede Cheng, a programmer at the HKFA and the HKIFF, explained that image-making and advertising have overtaken traditional media, so that the latter are now only a small part of the multimedia existence of teen idols:

> A lot of new stars, especially the girls, are from the advertising industry. A lot of them cross over as singers. Being a pop star is the easiest way to become famous, then the fans are attracted to them. They are not called stars but idols. Their CDs don't sell. The media corporations use the images of the idols to sell [other products].
>
> (3 January 2005)

Cheng's emphasis on the differences between old and new generations of stars in Hong Kong rests on his use of the term 'idol'. 'Idol' (*ouxiang* in Chinese) is defined as:

1   An image or representation of a god or divinity used as an object of worship; a false god
2   A person who or thing which is the object of extreme or excessive devotion
3   An image or representation of a person or thing; a likeness, an imitation; a counterfeit, a sham; an imposter, a pretender
4   An image without substance; a reflection, a phantom; a false mental image or conception; a false or misleading notion; a fallacy
5   A fantasy, a fancy

> (*Shorter Oxford English Dictionary* 2007, 6e)

The word is from the Latin *idolum,* meaning image. Cheng's focus was on the new stars as images that are false and 'without substance' and that attract blind admiration, usually by younger fans. The manipulation by media corporations to create ever younger pop idols was evidenced by the Emperor Group's 15-year contract with Isabella Leong (b.1988) in 2001 when she was only 13 years old and still in Form One (first year) of secondary school.[8] Soon after, she was employed in advertising, released pop albums and acted in films.

Cheng's use of the term idol to refer specifically to the new generation of stars emphasizes their reliance on surface image as simulacra. The circulation of Hong Kong stars' images in the printed press and through advertising, in connection with activities of multimedia corporations, has overtaken the importance of their involvement in the more traditional media, a situation that raises two main issues. First, while the multimedia idols are over-exposed in the entertainment press, as well as in public spaces such as advertising in public transportation, bus shelters and hoardings, the declining traditional media means there is less direct consumption of their films and pop albums. Second, multimedia stardom has changed from the practice of the 1980s, when stars diversified but focused on one medium (for instance, pop music), to the newer practice of young idols simultaneously engaging in several facets of the media industries, most notably as image. The young idols have nevertheless continued to rely on the close relationships between the different media. The changing practices have led to comments such as this one from Jacky Cheung, a popular star from the previous generation:

All these new stars are not singers. Some were introduced to me as models. I thought, 'Why did a record company sign up a model?' There are some who make commercials. Another one is about to make a film. Perhaps there are different methods and things have changed now, but record companies should be about cutting records. Now that seems to be only secondary.[9]

Although the new breed of multimedia stars is more focused on image-making, the distinctive practices of the media industries in Hong Kong founded on inter-media circulation of image and fame have continued. New idols are nevertheless conceived as ephemeral celetoids, and their public existence is made up of pseudo-events manufactured by media corporations, signifying the breakdown of the mass market. Cheung Tung-joe stated:

You only have these fans [of young idols] going to see a film. A film costs HKD 10 million, so you need an audience of several million to break even. That requires a collective sense of value. These management companies now want to maximize profits in the shortest time . . . That's the worst thing in Hong Kong. There's no desire to build the fundamental skills of the young. Lots of singers quickly disappear.

(29 July 2005)

Cheung suggests that the ephemeral nature and lack of skills of these stars make them disposable commodities reliant on heavy promotion by the media corporations, while a collective sense of values is neglected. In other words, the young stars are commercially sold as image without original qualities and are further articulated to the decline of collective values. The local writer and playwright, Edward Lam, presented a similar view:

> Corporations would promote those common looking people to encourage identification by teenagers. In Hong Kong, it's hard to say which [star] will survive the test of time and stay in people's memory. The entertainment industry today is only about consumption. So you buy, consume and discard. We human beings have changed. We were more active before; now we are passive.
>
> (3 August 2005)

The association of contemporary stars with consumer goods suggests that their worth has decreased, even though previous stars and their films were equally about consumption. For commentators such as Lam, the target audiences of young idols are teenagers and young adults, and the 'ordinariness' of contemporary stars explains why they are qualitatively different from the previous generation. Nevertheless, many from the 1980s, such as Andy Lau, Tony Leung and Chow Yun-fat, were also 'ordinary' Hong Kong born-and-bred stars. Bede Cheng went on to imply that the new generation of stars is associated with anxiety about social changes in the city, a view which supports Edward Lam's nostalgia for the 'more active society' and Cheung Tung-joe's idea of a 'collective sense of value':

> A lot of parents are absent parents who do not spend much time with their children. They are busy making money and so on. So, they dish out cash for the kids to spend to compensate. Adolescents everywhere need people to look up to. If there is no one immediately around them, they will look up to these idols.
>
> (3 January 2005)

The younger generation's media experience of downloading, Internet use, mobile gaming and so forth differs from the collective television viewing, film-going and super-concerting of the 1980s. The success of young idols, a result of the fragmentation of the media market, is not recognized by those commentators who experienced the mass media economy. Anxieties towards the young stem from the rise of the cultural and consumer power of the 'children of affluence' (Chua 2000, p.13). Bede Cheng's assertion specifically refers to this young generation's consumption of idols as a significant cultural shift from their parents' generation. Cheng sees the youth consumer market as a sign of social breakdown, implying that young people identify with new stars as role models because parents, while providing their children with material wealth, fail to be role models.

In Hong Kong in the early 2000s, after traditional media had been in decline for some time, discussion of manipulation in star creation was rife among media professionals and commentators, especially those who had worked in and witnessed the development of the industry since the 1980s. Although stars had always arguably been 'manufactured' and relied on the selling of their image, the production of stardom in Hong Kong since the mid-1990s, overwhelmingly centred in printed media and advertising, and connected to the growth of corporations and the rise of the Internet, has served as a prime example of Baudrillard's conceptualization of simulation. Multimedia stars are commodified and sold as images in the pervasive production, circulation and consumption of gossip and commercials. The commentaries cited in this chapter are therefore related to anxieties about the commodification of these individuals as image-products. For older adults not interested in the new breed of stars, the changes in the media landscape suggest that the younger generation in Hong Kong worships only packaged, manufactured idols created through heavy promotion by corporations that conceal the fact that the idols are 'pretty faces with no artistic value'. Contemporary stardom is part of a wider cultural change seen by my expert witnesses as representing the decoupling of referents (performance skills) and images (as recognizable faces for the selling of products), a view that resonates with Baudrillard's (1981) idea of simulacra without origins and referents. The fragmentation of the media markets means that the mass consumption of pop culture seen in the 1980s has disappeared, so the newer generation of young idols are also seen as signs of social breakdown resulting from changing family life and the disappearance of a collective spirit. The Edison Chen scandal exemplified the contemporary means of image circulation and the inconsistency between stars' public image and private existence, while the media and netizens continued to search for the authenticity of those involved. Meanwhile, the middle-aged have continued to assign collective values to the previous generation of stars, seeking especially for missing personal qualities behind the simulacra.

Few stars in Hong Kong would be able to operate without a presence in the press to maintain their fame and promote their films, television programmes and other media products. Sylvia Chang, an actress originally from Taiwan, has lived and worked in Hong Kong since the 1970s. She diversified into directing, producing and scriptwriting, and has made nearly a hundred films altogether. She also established a small production house in 1998 that managed two younger actresses, Angelica Lee Sinje and Rene Liu (b.1970), originally from Malaysia and Taiwan, respectively. When asked what stardom was, Chang explained that she wanted to be known as a filmmaker instead:

> [Being a star is] only a profession. I'm a filmmaker. Stars and actors are all under the category of filmmaker. Sometimes it depends a little on our image to make people remember us. Other than that, just like other professions you must have certain skills to survive.
>
> (7 July 2005)

She was also critical of the practices of the paparazzi:

Leung: You think that paparazzi, *gouzaidui*,[10] are a necessary part of
Wing-Fai: being in this profession?

Sylvia: Yes. [Sighs.] Paparazzi exist for a reason, in a specific space.
Chang: A lot of brainless people like to read gossip press. They allow paparazzi
     to exist . . . The newspapers would say, 'We have fewer and fewer film
     sets to visit and report. If we don't do stars' juicy news, what can we
     do?'

The young multimedia idols are regarded by an earlier generation of media professionals as an indication of the loss of artistic skills behind the star image. These professionals also show a concern for a perceived cultural decline, of which paparazzi journalism is both a sign and a by-product. Chang imagined the readers of entertainment news as brainless people, and she therefore wanted to be known not as a star but as a filmmaker. By criticizing the practice of paparazzi journalism, Chang asserted artistic skills that have been under threat in a mediated world full of simulacra. Although her company also had an artiste management branch, Chang asserted the difference between her and other management companies by stating that, 'I can see that lots of companies would use a lot of money to boost [the stars' popularity]. I don't think that's a lasting method' (7 July 2005).

This practice of counter-argument against the paparazzi and multimedia corporations by stars may be understood through the notion of clawback. Clawback as ideological containment originally comes from John Fiske and John Hartley's (1978) discussion of the control of disruptive elements in news reporting. John Fiske developed the concept as 'a structure of reporting that works to claw back potentially deviant or disruptive events into the dominant value system' (1987, p.288). As part of this practice of clawback, news producers arrogate personality traits such as reliability or credibility in support of their objectivity:

> Clawback . . . is the process by which potentially disruptive events are mediated into the dominant value system without losing their authenticity. This authenticity guarantees the 'truth' of the interpretation that this mediating involves and thus allows, paradoxically, that which has been interpreted to present itself as objective . . . Hand in glove with objectivity go authenticity and immediacy.
>
> (Fiske 1987, p.289)

The attempts at clawback by the stars are not to support a dominant ideology in this instance but rather to counter-argue against criticisms and re-inject the missing referents – professional skills – behind the simulacra. The counter-attack on the entertainment press was evident in an interview with another actress, Lee Sinje, who talked about the paparazzi in ways very similar to Sylvia Chang:[11]

Leung: In media commentaries, idols are criticized for their lack of
Wing-Fai.   singing and acting skills . . . Do you feel you're different?
Lee Sinje: I'm not a Hong Kong person. [Laughs.] Yes. Hong Kong is a city
       made with money. There's a lot of pressure in everyday life because
       it's a very materialistic place. Most people judge others by their
       appearance, the material goods they possess and how much money

they have. You don't read many articles in the newspapers about how much internal value someone has but it's all about how big her chest is and what shoes she wears. Many singers have less skill, compared with those in China or Taiwan.

(6 June 2005)

In the interview, Lee set up a contrast between herself and other Hong Kong artistes who rely much more on their appearance, illustrating how some actors in Hong Kong use clawback to assert their credibility in the face of criticism of stars being commodities sold on the basis of surface image. This strategy to re-inject realness and referentiality can be seen as a means to 'convince us of the reality of the social' (Baudrillard 1981, p.179). Paparazzi originated in the West and are not unique to Hong Kong, yet stars who were not born and raised in the city, including Sylvia Chang and Lee Sinje, used the rise of the practice of paparazzi journalism to critique Hong Kong culture. Their foreign origins were used in their commentaries to assert objectivity as observers of the media world in the city.

In this section I have presented comments from two stars who identified themselves as filmmakers and actors and asserted their skills by insisting on finding substance beneath the image, in contrast to the practice of the paparazzi. The 'rise' of the multimedia idols is considered by the middle-aged to signal social breakdown and the end of collective values, but these actors identified themselves as outsiders in Hong Kong society and attempted to claw back credibility as individuals. A star born and raised in Hong Kong, Miriam Yeung, will serve as a case study to strengthen these arguments.

Miriam Yeung: An idol and a star

Miriam Yeung Chin-Wah emerged in the 1990s and became one of the most commercially successful singers and actresses in Hong Kong. Yeung's career exemplifies the development of the media industry and the practices and discourse of multimedia stardom in Hong Kong. Like many of the other multimedia stars in Hong Kong, Miriam Yeung was discovered in a talent contest. While studying nursing, Yeung entered TVB's New Talent Singing Awards in 1995 and came in third. Yeung started out mainly as a pop singer, and her subsequent diversification into different media was typical for Cantopop stars. Emblematic of the practice in Hong Kong's pop industry, she was prolific, producing 22 albums between 1996 and 2005. She was contracted to Capital Artists (1996–2001), Cinepoly Records (2001–3) and Gold Label (2003–6) before switching to AMusic in 2007. Yeung's career is further proof that the multimedia presence of young idols is not an entirely new phenomenon, although her career paralleled the decline of local film and pop music.

Yeung embarked on a film career utilizing her pop stardom. She made two films in 1998, *The Group* (Alfred Cheung) and *Rumble Ages* (James Yuen Sai-sang), which did not fare well at the box office. It was not until 2001 that she became commercially successful as a screen actress through *Feel 100% 2* (Joe Ma) and

Dummy Mommy, Without a Baby (Joe Ma & Mak Kai-gwong). Yeung then made *Love Undercover* (Joe Ma, 2002), *Dry Wood, Fierce Fire* (Wilson Ip Wai-shun, 2002), *Love Undercover 2: Love Mission* (Joe Ma, 2003), *Dumplings* (Fruit Chan, 2004), *Drink Drank Drunk* (Derek Yee, 2005), *Hooked on You* (Law Wing-cheong, 2007), *Love in a Puff* (Pang Ho-cheung, 2010) and *Love in the Buff* (Pang Ho-cheung 2012), among others, and most of Yeung's films can be considered 'star vehicles'.[12] Yeung remained a pop star, released records, and was involved in advertising, concerts, television appearances and other engagements, conforming to the typical cross-media practice of pop idols in Hong Kong. Since her marriage in 2011 and the birth of a son the following year, Yeung's output has decreased considerably.

Increasingly, pop album releases in Hong Kong have been marketed on different platforms reflecting the leisure choices of young consumers: mobile phone technology, downloads, ringtones, karaoke and music videos. Popular singers such as Miriam Yeung have been employed by large corporations to endorse cross-marketing targeted at this consumer group. In a magazine feature around the time of the release of the 2005 album *Single*, Yeung talked about how she wanted a more feminine image that would make her look more like 'models in foreign fashion magazines', and discussed some of the designers she liked.[13] She also discussed her previously released albums and how she deliberated on changes to her image through the choice of songs, therefore demonstrating openness about image-making. In this sense, the connection between star image, fashion and consumer culture was a continuation from the 1960s film magazines produced by Shaw and Cathay Studios, explored in Chapter 2, which featured star profiles, new films, fashion and beauty advertisements modelled by the actresses. However, the practice of employing stars to cross-market fashion, cosmetics and consumer products became more pronounced and geared towards the youth market segment during the 1990s.

After several cameo roles, Yeung was the lead star in almost all of her subsequent productions. These films, from *Dummy Mommy, Without a Baby* onwards, were mostly comedies. The financial difficulties facing the Hong Kong film industry since the late 1990s had pushed it towards homogenization, and comedy was a consistently popular genre. Yeung's film career was constrained by the decline of the film industry, and the roles she found were mainly in commercial popular genres. Yeung's appeal remained very much in the Chinese and Southeast Asian markets among the more traditional audiences of Hong Kong stars. Product placement had also become a common practice in Hong Kong.[14] In *Drink Drank Drunk*, a romantic comedy, Yeung plays a bar waitress who can drink a copious amount of alcohol without getting drunk. She meets a Chinese French chef, Michael (Daniel Wu, b.1974), who is the complete opposite and gets drunk after a few sips of wine. The brands of the main sponsors are clearly visible throughout the film. Prime Credit (a financial company) lends the funds to Michael to open up his dream French restaurant, and Budweiser beer is prominently placed through the entire film, as seen in Figure 3.1

Despite her conscious decision to develop her image, Miriam Yeung is mostly known in Hong Kong media as a *sha dajie* (literally, 'silly old sister'); the term, used in Cantonese, refers to a woman who is a little mad and clumsy and lacks

Figure 3.1 A still from the romantic comedy Drink Drank Drunk (Derek Yee, 2005) demonstrating the practice of product placement. Reproduced with kind permission from Film Unlimited Production Co. Ltd.

subtlety, but is harmless enough. Yeung is usually represented in the media as an ordinary girl-next-door. Most of her screen roles have been in the romantic comedy genre, in which she has been paired with young male actors, supporting this image. *Dummy Mommy, Without a Baby,* the film that first hinted at a commercially successful film career for Yeung, saw her in the role of the OL (Office Lady),[15] Kuen, who pretends to be pregnant when threatened with dismissal; her employer cannot sack her because of employment regulations that protect pregnant women. She is helped by her best friend (Niki Chow, b.1979) and an unsuspecting boss (Edison Chen) in her battle with the female executive who wants to sack her. The ending is predictably happy; although Kuen's lies have been found out, her boss forgives her and even promotes her to an executive position, and there is even a hint of romance between Kuen and the male boss. Yeung's acting skills, like those of many young stars, have often been criticized in the local media, and she is frequently assumed to play herself and rely on her image:[16]

Miriam Yeung is a dream. I am not saying that Yeung is an idol for thousands. It is the opposite; Yeung's miraculous rise comes from her closeness to the audiences . . . Miriam Yeung is different. She emphasizes her own ordinariness, and that she is not beautiful but friendly and approachable. Ordinary women can see their experiences reflected in Yeung.

The above film review centres on Yeung's lack of acting skills (related to her comedienne image) and her closeness to the audience (ordinariness). Yeung's screen image has been highly consistent, with her other media appearances, such as in advertisements, further perpetuating her healthy, wholesome image. Edward Lam (2005) criticizes stars like Miriam Yeung, whose film roles seem to be all about maintaining a healthy image so advertisers will continue to use them, leaving their acting skills to stagnate as a result. This is taken as evidence that Yeung has no skills; that is, the actress plays herself as a commoner. However, in interviews Miriam Yeung has distanced herself from the character types she tends to play, drawing attention in particular to her hard work. In this regard, Yeung's comments are comparable to the practice of clawback by Sylvia Chang and Lee Sinje. Here is an example of Yeung's denial that she is her onscreen character and stereotyped image in the press:[17]

It is all down to the script. Everyone thinks I am only playing myself. Sadly that silly woman is closer to what you assume is me. In reality I only played a role [every time I made a film]. For every film I carefully analysed the role but I didn't know no one noticed.

Yeung was therefore aware that she was being typecast. She has also asserted diligence against the criticism of her lack of ability. In an interview, Rowena Chan, Yeung's then media relations manager at Gold Label, stressed the star's professionalism and career choices, distancing Yeung from the stereotypical image of the girl-next-door:

Rowena Chan (RC):	Of course, she doesn't want to be typecast. For an actress she likes to try different things. For investors and directors that is her selling point.
Leung Wing-Fai (LWF):	Her roles are often from the grassroots.[18] Does she consider herself part of the working class?
RC:	Her mum worked for a bank. Her dad is a teacher. So hers is a middle-class family. No matter what the role demands, Miriam still spends time preparing for them.
LWF:	How does she choose the roles? Has she got the final say?
RC:	The company will analyse them for her: whether the role can be a breakthrough, whether the script allows for expression . . . She is not just an actor: singing, touring concerts . . . she does a lot of different kinds of work, so time is important. For Miriam, recording is always more important than film.

(23 August 2005)

Chan was trying to project that Miriam Yeung, despite being stereotyped as a young idol who could not act, was in fact serious about her acting. Even her onscreen ordinariness was a little removed from her middle-class background. Additionally, management companies have to consider their investors, and Chan therefore acknowledged that Yeung's comedienne image was a commercial advantage. Time and financial rewards are also important pragmatic considerations for Yeung as a multimedia star, and she has always been more of a singer than an actress, as her management company stressed. Yeung's serious approach to acting and her commercial appeal was confirmed by Fruit Chan, who used Yeung to play a woman in her 40s in his 2004 film *Dumplings*. The film is a horror story in which Yeung's character is an ex-starlet who eats dumplings made with human embryos in order to stay young. In my interview with Chan, he stated: 'I can't say I was 100 per cent satisfied [with Yeung's performance] but I feel it's the right casting. In Hong Kong those who could play this role and help [the film] commercially were hard to find' (24 August 2005). Yeung turned 30 in 2004, and her choice to take the role in *Dumplings* seemed to be a strategic move away from her young-idol career up to that point. Fruit Chan commented that even though Miriam Yeung was not the ideal choice for the role, her popularity could help the film commercially. Recognition for her acting ability came when she was named Best Actress at the 32nd Hong Kong Film Awards (2013) for her role in *Love in the Buff*.

By the mid-2000s, Yeung had achieved a level of commercial success in Hong Kong and was starting to move away from being a young idol into work that might help to prolong her career. Like many of her counterparts, Yeung tried to enter the mainland pop and film markets by releasing Mandarin records for Chinese audiences and performing concerts in China. The case study of Miriam Yeung and the cross-marketing of her music and films through telecommunications and other advertising campaigns provide evidence of the commodification of young stars as image, a particularly prominent feature of multimedia stardom in Hong Kong since the 1990s. Many advertising campaigns have positioned the singer in such a way as to capture the youth market. Yeung and her manager have practised clawback to assert professionalism and work ethic against the criticism that the star lacks acting skills. In the early 2000s, Yeung was at a turning point in her career. It was necessary for her to stay ahead of her successful career, and therefore she needed to diversify through distancing herself from the *sha dajie* image.

Nevertheless, her management company was open about the commercial nature of her stardom, and it was evident that Yeung had to exploit her image and consider the competing demands of multimedia work. The past decade has seen Yeung focusing more on the mainland market and achieving greater recognition for her acting skills. Miriam Yeung's career exemplifies the distinctive practices of image-making in Hong Kong that capitalize on the interconnectedness of the different media, though Yeung and her management company attempted to reconcile the commodification of the star image as simulacra and commercial considerations by asserting her hard work and skills as a professional singer-actor.

Concluding remarks

In a shift since the 1990s, Hong Kong stars' existence as image commodities has become the most commercially profitable facet of their multimedia careers, rather than their work in film, television and music recording. The mass market economy that the media industries relied on in the 1980s had fragmented. As a result of technology, popular journalism, the prominence of the advertising industry and the rise of privately owned media corporations, multimedia stars are more widely seen than ever before.

Benjamin's (1936) thesis of the absence of original authenticity in mass media products provides a starting point for the discussion of star image-making. Baudrillard's (1981) notion of simulacra extends Benjamin's critique, as 'art' in the earlier theorization is now expunged entirely from the process of the creation of images. Discourse about the commodification of individuals as images for sale therefore must address the relationships between the changing practices of multimedia stardom and anxieties about the disappearance of original qualities among the stars in contemporary Hong Kong. Comparisons between the two generations of stars (those from the 1980s and early 1990s and the young idols who have emerged since) represent a failure to accept the de-centring of more traditional media forms and the disintegration of a mass media culture. Many young idols are promoted by media corporations who produce a range of media products, and cross-marketing is employed to increase the popularity of both the products and their contract artistes, leading to the charge of manipulation by industry professionals to create young stars without original qualities.

In constructing the discourse about stardom, the interviewees, mostly media professionals who were already active in the 1980s, have continued to cling to the importance of the earlier generation of stars, while viewing the young idols as empty images. New stars are considered to be lacking in performance skills and to provide evidence of the breakdown of a society with collective values. The Edison Chen scandal was a case in point. While the images were circulated mostly through the newer formats of the Internet and social media, the expectation of coherence between a star's public persona and private life as a sign of authenticity, especially for the women involved, followed the pattern of media scandals in the Chinese-language press from the early twentieth century. Baudrillard pessimistically declares that 'it is always a false problem to want to restore the truth beneath the simulacrum' (1981, p.182), though he predicts 'a collective demand for *signs* of power' (p.180, original emphasis). The practice of distinguishing themselves from others who are said to be responsible for the production and consumption of idols would appear to be a cultural strategy for both media professionals and the stars themselves. In response to critiques of their human emptiness, actors assert their professional skills and shun paparazzi journalism, thus sharing some of the same values as their critics. Miriam Yeung, one of the prime targets for criticism against young idols, also stressed her serious attitude towards work. Through diversifying her work and the type of roles she played on screen, Yeung transformed from being a young idol to a more mature, professional star, even though the cross-marketing of her music, films and product endorsements continued to exploit her image and target young consumers.

In order to survive commercially, stars in Hong Kong since the late 1990s could no longer rely on traditional media that had lost the mass market support enjoyed in the 1980s and early 1990s. In response to this specific context, my industry contacts criticized the imagined others as producers and consumers of simulacra despite the fact that the circulation of star image also utilized the distinctive set-up of the media industry in Hong Kong, namely the interconnectedness of the different media. Critics of multimedia stardom in the early 2000s and the stars themselves, including those from a younger generation, have participated in a practice of clawback by emphasizing the referents behind the simulacra in order to regain credibility. These referents are performance skills and the ability to represent an essentialist, collective notion of society. In the next two chapters I will examine performance and work, two elements that have been cited as the missing referents to star image. Through a discussion of a distinctive history and understanding of performance and the relationship between work and stardom, I will demonstrate the importance of the persistent phenomenon of multimedia stardom in Hong Kong.

4   Performance

For a new generation of multimedia stars, the production of image and fame through advertising and the entertainment press has become the most profitable elements of their existence, while traditional performances in film, television and pop music have declined. In this chapter I examine the distinctive practices and discourse of performance in relation to multimedia stars, and explain their significance with reference to the notion of work as understood through the specific social and cultural contexts in Hong Kong. I will then discuss the case of Andy Lau, an enduring star who emerged in the 1980s.

Performance and the Hong Kong media industries

The cross-media nature of stardom in Hong Kong has had a long existence that uniquely influences how performance is understood. My discussion deploys the term performance with this context in mind in order to provide a wider focus that goes beyond acting (impersonation) to incorporate singing, dance and other stage crafts associated with multimedia stardom. This wider view challenges the mainstay of star studies that focuses on the screen performance of film stars as the privileged expression of star image (Dyer 1979), although this may well be the case with Hollywood studio pictures. My discussion argues for a different conceptualization of performance in Hong Kong, and I start from a consideration of the notion of performance in star studies. In the West, the concept of performance is intrinsically linked to the theatre. The origin of screen acting can be contextualized through theatrical performance, and certain types of performance relate to theatrical genres such as vaudeville, music hall and melodrama. During the silent era, performance was marked by exaggerated facial expressions and gestures, made necessary by the lack of verbal communication. The opposite of these types of acting styles of exaggeration and emphasis is the repertoire-Broadway method where 'the performer should be hidden behind the character s/he constructs and in no way play him/herself' (Dyer 1979, p.140), which became the predominant form of acting in Hollywood studio productions.

Using the terminology of contemporary Hollywood, good performance is a combination of repertoire-Broadway and Method acting, with respected actors giving naturalistic portrayals of characters, often through in-depth psychological analysis and bodily transformation. Their off-stage presence, however, makes stars less able to hide behind different protagonists, a skill that has become the benchmark of good acting in the West. Audiences today are aware of the valorised acting style, but at the same time they recognize the gap between stars and characters, particularly because of publicity that points to the fact that they are witnessing Method acting (Geraghty 2000). Some stars under-perform, relying only on their image, while others may become known as Method actors. Therefore, assessment of performance or acting skill is based on aesthetic judgement, subject to the particular discourse in time and culture; both the stars' image and performance are known to their audiences and influence the discourse of performance. Even though some stars are revered for their acting ability, their off-screen media presence and fame are also important elements of stardom, often overriding their performances, and only a few stars have 'graduated' to be seen as serious performers. To make sense of the discourse surrounding stars and performance, Christine Geraghty (2000) attempts to place stars into three categories: 'celebrity', 'professional' and 'performer'. A celebrity is a person whose private life is better known than their work; the reputation of professionals is 'associated with work and the public element of the star duality rather than the private life of the celebrity' (p.187); a performer is associated with their work only, and the emphasis is on the public rather than private persona. All three characteristics are applicable, to a greater or lesser extent, to many contemporary stars in Hong Kong. What Geraghty highlights in her classification are the relationships between image, performance, and stars as workers, the subject of the preceding and the current chapters.

Performance is further affected by a range of industrial conventions, especially related to the kinds of film production. The privileging of Method acting is not universal. In the Hong Kong context, commercial mass film production, the multimedia nature of stardom, and the training received by most stars has contributed to practices and a discourse of performance that should be understood differently to those of the West. The dominant genres of comedy and action in Hong Kong do not support naturalistic acting, and so a more appropriate understanding of the notion of 'good acting' is needed. In the day-to-day operation of the Hong Kong film industry, it would be hard to find evidence of the use of Method acting, given the time constraints of commercial film production, with most Hong Kong movies written, shot, and edited in three to five months. The number of projects (film-related or otherwise) that stars worked on could also be a factor in acting style; for example, Maggie Cheung made up to ten films a year in the 1980s and worked on as many as five at the same time. In mainstream Hong Kong cinema, therefore, few actors had time to prepare thoroughly for each film, and the Hollywood benchmark of Method acting was rarely employed. Film-making in the 1980s and early 1990s was characterized by post-dubbing (re-recording the dialogue, sometimes in other languages for different markets), which meant that actors did not have to worry about precise delivery of the script. The above film-production practices are objective evidence that stars in the 1980s and 1990s were not necessarily better actors than subsequent generations of stars in Hong Kong.

Much of the casting of main actors in Hong Kong films depends not on the ability of actors to perform specific roles, but rather on the stars' image and schedule, as an assistant director, NR, stated:

> The main cast should be the producer's decision. The director and I will make suggestions. You need to consider the actors' image. For those above the line,[1] the salary is high. For the supporting cast, you may get actors who are completely different from your suggestions. In Hong Kong, it all depends on their schedules.
>
> (4 August 2005)

Formal casting is seldom practised in the relatively insular entertainment world since the producers and directors already know most of the stars and lead actors. The most important considerations for many filmmakers and multimedia stars in Hong Kong are not suitability for the role or ability to act but time schedule, rewards and image. In some cases, better performances might be produced by lesser-known actors rather than stars. In contrast to stars, experienced performers (usually older actors) in Hong Kong have a category of their own, *jincao yanyuan* (literally 'gold leaf actors'), which expresses skill and endurance and is similar to the term 'character actors'. They rarely play leads in either television or film work. The director Wai Ka-fai spoke about the difficulties of working with star-actors that stem from their multimedia nature:

Wai Ka-Fai (W):	As a director, of course I prefer that the actors focus on the film but I have to accept the fact that the stars cross media. If they are popular as singers, they cross over to film. If they are good in films, they cross over to pop. That's how the sector is.
Leung Wing-Fai:	What are the effects on you as a director?
W:	On set there may be lots of fans for the idol-actors.[2] For a director, of course it's good to have a full time actor but I feel [that] you can't generalize that idol style is necessarily bad. Some cross-media artistes may not be really good at acting but they have their attraction and charisma from the stage [pop music] to contribute to the film. That could be an advantage.

(24 April 2006)

Wai Ka-fai distinguished between actors and stars (or idol actors) and suggested that it may sometimes be worthwhile to accept poorer acting skills in exchange for what the stars' off-screen presence can contribute to the film. Although multimedia stars are unlikely to be the best actors, they can help films commercially and are central to the promotion of the productions, as in the practice of cross-marketing discussed in the previous chapter.

Alan Lovell asserts that the 'disjunction between stars and acting ability is frequently observed. But is it an accurate observation? The majority of stars have a background in acting' (2003, p.262). Conversely, Hong Kong stars tend not to have formal acting training but are instead exemplars of multimedia practices. Because of the unique nature of their stardom, the local discourse of good performance differs from the Hollywood standard of Method acting. The close relationship between theatre and screen acting, seen in some countries like the UK, did not exist in the Hong Kong media industry even though performance training was available, most notably in the acting classes run by the television stations. A critic and playwright connected to the theatre in Hong Kong, Edward Lam, suggested that there was little performing arts training, and hence the media industry only produced stars:

> As we do not have literary masterpieces in Cantonese, acting here is superficial. Hong Kong's role is more about producing stars rather than actors because there is no theatre industry. It only has media industries, and film and television companies train actors. The classes are very functional and basic: martial arts, Chinese and Western dance. The training is only for one year, so it limits further development. These graduates become our mainstream, cheap labour.
>
> (3 August 2005)

Lam asserted a reverence for the stage acting of what he called 'masterpieces of theatre plays' above performances in popular media, even though there is little evidence that modern theatre has had much influence on the discourse of performance in Hong Kong. According to Lam, television and film actors are 'cheap labour'. Institutions like the Academy for Performing Arts (APA), formed in 1985 and the main acting school in Hong Kong, have supplied relatively few graduates to the media industries. It was only in 2002 that the APA started a course called 'Acting in Front of Camera' to give students some experience and knowledge of screen acting.

The distinctive characteristics of commercial cinema in Hong Kong mean that most stars have come from television drama series, beauty pageants, singing contests and, more recently, modelling, instead of from theatrical training. Many pick up performance skills simply through learning on the job. Robert Chua (17 June 2009), the creator of the popular nightly *EYT* variety programme, maintained that live shows such as *EYT* were common in the early days of local television and were responsible for training presenters and hosts to improvise, memorize, and deliver scripts and information. While attempting to establish itself, television also attempted to replicate the intimacy and immediacy of theatre, and by doing so problematized the relationship between live and recorded media:

> Distinctions need to derive from careful consideration of how the relationship between the live and the mediatized is articulated in particular cases, not from

a set of assumptions that constructs the relation between live and mediatized representations *a priori* as a relation of essential opposition.

(Auslander 1999, p.54, original emphasis)

Live television performance might be contrasted with the recorded and scripted shows that subsequently became more common in Hong Kong, in which present-ers were typically aided by teleprompters with five- to ten-minute scripts to read out, a practice which contributed to an unnaturalness of delivery. In addition, the ontological characteristics of the production and consumption of early television changed because of a reduction in live broadcasts and more diffused viewing hab-its. For instance, instead of tuning into the main evening news at a particular time, audiences today may watch 24-hour satellite or cable news channels or read the headlines on the Internet whenever they wish. As these media choices are more or less constantly available, 'liveness' has become less of an attraction, and television compères lack opportunities to learn to perform live under pressure. Performers trained in television are particularly prone to using a style of acting that focuses on the surface, such as facial expressions that look good in close-ups, as television pre-senters and actors are more accustomed to a frontal orientation towards the viewers. In the 1980s, popular genres in Hong Kong cinema like comedy fully utilized tele-visual aesthetics, including exaggerated facial expressions and body movements. In the 1980s and early 1990s, when the industry was prolific, on-the-job opportunities were plentiful for stars to cross into film. Familiarity from local television enhanced stars' auras for their audiences, which, together with iconic roles in television or film and popular theme songs, cemented their multimedia stardom.

During a seminar on the star Andy Lau,[3] critic Bryan Chang discussed a 'Hong Kong style of acting', an idea advanced by local critics that refers to the way that performers trained in television rely on a type of acting that focuses on the sur-face. The differences between performance in Mainland China and Hong Kong were also part of the discussion; the critic Keeto stated that mainland actors were classically trained and used formal acting techniques, while Hong Kong actors often came from television with only basic training and so tended to use their own personalities.[4] Directors in Hong Kong also commonly used the stars' personali-ties by basing characters and roles on them. The trend of China-Hong Kong co-productions in the last 15 years has highlighted the contrast in performance styles between mainland Chinese and Hong Kong stars. Li Cheuk-to agrees that 'Cantonese acting stresses naturalness' and 'immediacy', and 'lines are more col-loquial [and] weeping seems more convincing' (cited in Chu 2003, p.72). This kind of assessment of the acting style in Hong Kong asserts that the lack of formal-ness in screen acting is not a weakness but is simply different; the stars' performances are spontaneous, interactive and natural. Stars in the context of the media industry in Hong Kong have developed a unique style as performers, often due to their tele-vision training. This style was initially ignored when the assumption of Method acting as an industry standard began to influence debates in the city.

Since stardom focuses our attention on the individual, scholarly studies of popular music in the West are often predicated on discussions of authorship and performance. Even when the same song is sung by different singers, it is the song *'performed by a specific artist'* (Ahonen 2007, p.1, original emphasis) and the artist's image and aura that make the product unique and original. Singer-songwriters and rock bands tend to write their own music and lyrics and play instruments, especially the guitar. Within the rock tradition, authentic performers are capable of playing an instrument, performing live and recording their own music, and their music should be about 'individual expression'; rock's 'other' is pop, which does not share the rock ideology of authenticity (Auslander 1999, pp.62–79, 85).

Pop musicians in Hong Kong also have their own specific tradition of multi-faceted performance. The description of Cantonese pop as 'easy listening' (Brace 1991, p.47) suggests a homogeneous kind of musical genre aimed at the mass market. The rock traditions that are often part of the youth culture narrative in the West are distinctly lacking in Hong Kong because of the dominance of the commercial pop industry. Pop stars from Hong Kong usually do not create their own songs, which are written by a few well-known composers and lyricists. This follows the tradition of Chinese opera, in which singers are idolized for their renditions of pre-existing compositions (Witzleben 1999). It also explains the practice of covering Anglo-American and Japanese pop songs, and the lyricists' work known as 'text-setting' (*tian ci*). The lyrics, nevertheless, are usually written for specific singers or as television and film theme songs that comment on the storylines. Instead of the tradition of a musician as the sole creator of every aspect of a song, Chinese pop songs are produced by separate individuals to be performed by a singer who is expected to express the sentiments contained in the song, much like an actor following a script. As a result, even though some of these pop stars might be proficient in playing musical instruments, it is rare for them to do so in live performance and even more unusual in recording. The voice, and therefore the singer, is emphasized in Cantopop above all.

The Western star epitomizes the Romantic notion of the single originating artist and individual author. Music is made collectively, usually involving a producer, sound engineer, backing band and so forth (Brackett 2000), but the singer is commonly expected to be the song's emotional source, and music stardom is closely associated with the singer's voice, body, public image and biography. The notion of the musical auteur who expresses personal vision and authenticity was particularly pertinent in the construction of the stardom of singers such as Bob Dylan, Brian Wilson and Neil Young as talented individuals. In contrast, the Chinese and, later, Hong Kong traditions of pop stardom have been about the relative separation of the creative process and the performer. In this tradition, pop stars are entertainers enjoyed for performances that focus on the star's voice and the expression of collective sentiments, usually written by others. The specific discourse on performance skills in Hong Kong, given the distinctive practices of the media industries and the cross-media nature of stars and skills-training, is explored next.

Discourse of performance and multimedia stardom

Unlike the close relationship between the stage and other performance arts in countries such as Britain and China, Hong Kong film and television do not boast a strong link with live modern theatre, as it is not a popular cultural activity. David Jiang, then Dean of the APA, confirmed the differences between performance training in China and Hong Kong and offered a negative assessment of young actors, 'In China, there is the Beijing Film Institute. They have an acting department that specially trains actors. Many stars [in Hong Kong] do not have any training, especially the young ones. They are just lucky enough' (21 February 2005). Cheung Tat-ming, a graduate of the APA who worked on stage and as a character actor in television and film, offered a similar view on performance arts in Hong Kong:[5]

> Theatre is different from cinema in that it is free from commercial considerations, like politics and investors. The film industry is competitive, and it is all about pretty faces. Beauty contestants may no longer be popular next year. The commercial society is cruel . . . but theatre work is immediate and magical. It moves the audience while film acting can be about using eye drops, editing and camera work.

Artificiality and reliance on stars' images (pretty faces and their ephemeral existence) are familiar themes from the discussion in the previous chapter. Cheung Tat-ming's views conform to the longstanding assumption that theatre and television are opposites, the latter being mediatized and lacking immediacy, while theatrical performance is valorised as truer than the media (Auslander 1999). The privileging of stage performance in Cheung's comments is intriguing because modern theatre has largely been a minority interest in Hong Kong. The main traditional Chinese theatrical practice is opera in a variety of dialects, although Peking and Cantonese opera are the most well known in Hong Kong. However, it would be essentialist to consider concepts of performance in Hong Kong today to have derived directly from Chinese opera, because the influence of Western theatre has co-existed with Chinese opera in China and Hong Kong for well over a century. In the 1930s and 1940s in Hong Kong, Cantonese stars were first and foremost opera performers, and their film stardom was secondary. Cantonese opera films became particularly popular in the 1940s and 1950s, though the genre had almost completely ceased by the mid-1960s (Zhang 2004). Therefore, as a traditional art form, Cantonese opera in stage performance or on film has also been a minority interest in Hong Kong. Nevertheless, two interconnected influences of Chinese opera, namely performance training and multi-faceted skills, are relevant to the discourse of performance and stardom in Hong Kong.

Chinese opera actors in Hong Kong are famed for the long and arduous training they have to endure, and they are therefore well respected and valorised. Surviving opera stars might remain respected entertainers today, but the fame and adoration associated with opera stardom is disproportionate to Cantonese opera's overall economic status and commercial value since opera films have not been produced for a long time (Latham 2000). Stardom associated with Cantonese opera has continued to be circulated from the 1990s through fanzines, videotapes, CDs, VCDs, karaoke, and dedicated websites, instead of through live performance. The editor of *Cantonese Opera Monthly* reported that he took some 13,000 photographs in the first nine months of the publication to satisfy the fans' demand for visual representation of the stars (Latham 2000). The photographs published in the magazine also perpetuated the idea of the glamorous lifestyle of the stars by depicting luxury apartments, expensive cars and the attendance of stars at showbiz parties, even though in actuality few Cantonese opera performers still earned large sums of money since public interest in paying to see the traditional practice had long since declined.

The most vocal supporters of Cantonese opera have been from previous generations of film and television stars. Connie Chan Po-chu, the popular actress from the 1960s and student of the Cantonese opera star Yam Kim-fai, performed in a play entitled *Yam-Pak,*[6] *A Sentimental Story,* which ran for 100 shows in 1999 and was resurrected in 2005 in a 37-show run at the APA. Chan hoped to attract new talent to the dying craft of opera, saying 'this form of art is a part of Guangdong [Cantonese] culture' (cited in Sun 2005). Another well-known advocate for Cantonese opera was Lisa Wang (b.1947), who went from a successful television and pop career in the 1970s to becoming a performer and champion of Cantonese opera. Wang was also instrumental in saving the New Light Theatre, an important venue for opera performances, from demolition in 2005. That the theatre needed saving is indicative of the disjuncture between the discourse and the material history of the opera arts. The discourse of stardom connected to Cantonese opera is very much alive although few performances are widely staged or seen; the legacy of opera is therefore based more in a concept of performance related to the possession of a combination of stage skills acquired through lengthy training. Although opera's multi-talented performers remain among the most revered stars, the art form is no longer active or highly popular in contemporary Hong Kong.

The martial arts genre maintains one of the strongest links between opera and cinema. The *wuxia* ('swordplay') films produced during the post-war period were frequently based on modern martial arts novels, and the popular genre demanded action by both male and female performers. Kung fu movies, beginning in the 1970s, also relied on the skill of actors and martial arts directors such as Jackie Chan and Sammo Hung (b.1952). Both were trained at the same Peking Opera school when they were children, and they dominated the martial arts genre for over 30 years. Many Hong Kong martial arts directors and choreographers had a similar theatrical background. Their reliance on these hard-earned skills was demonstrated by the reverence for the success of Jackie Chan. One of the most renowned martial arts stars, Chan started out as a stuntman in the 1970s before embarking on a successful film career. The actor 'is now comfortably ensconced as an "elder brother", if not a father figure, within Hong Kong's movie culture, a member of the older generation' (Fore 2001, p.136). Jackie Chan has always traded on the authenticity of his martial arts, as can be seen in the publicity for *Rumble in the Bronx* (Stanley Tong, 1995): 'No Fear. No Stuntman. No Equal' (Hunt 2003, p.41). This claim to authentic martial arts has been longstanding in Cantonese cinema; Kwan Tak-hing (1905–96), the actor who played Cantonese martial artist and folk hero Wong Fei-hung in over 70 films between 1949 and

1970 was also trained in Peking Opera (Rodriguez 1997). Producer Bey Logan (6 January 2005), who specializes in co-productions and action films, relates that many female stars who act in the martial arts genre are trained as dancers, and it is their physical capability that the producers look for. In opera, the notion of performance is multi-faceted; a skilled actor should be an all-round performer, proficient with music, costume, make-up, gesture and movement techniques that 'can only be acquired slowly' (Ward 1979, p.20). They should excel in *sheng, se, yi* ('the voice, make-up and stage crafts'). Performance ability, therefore, is a concept that encompasses different art forms, most notably in singing, acting and physical abilities. Barbara Ward goes on to discuss the notion of 'total theatre' with 'a procession of simultaneous sounds, actions, words, colours' that is not the Western concept of opera, play or ballet, 'but all three together with music-hall and acrobatics too' (p.21). Hong Kong filmmakers often acknowledge the influence of martial arts action on their work. The director Tsui Hark states:

> [In opera,] you see somersaults and flips and fights and it's very visual and then at a high point before the climax it stops for tension or suspense and then it goes on and they do a fantastic demonstration . . . When we structure something by building up and then holding it back for suspense, that's the influence of Peking Opera.
>
> (cited in Hwang 1998, p.18)

The opera tradition provides a historical context for the unique evolution of performance in Hong Kong, especially in relation to the importance of training and multiple skills. The influences of the performance tradition were manifested in the cross-media presence of many stars in Hong Kong, and this multimedia practice developed further in the 1970s when many stars crossed from television to film and sang popular theme songs associated with both media.

I previously examined how Cantopop stars are first and foremost performers known for their voices rather than for individual creative talents. Lip-synching, a practice sometimes used in television programme recording and 'live' perfor-mances, is therefore generally considered to be a sign of the singers' inauthenticity. Moreover, the stage performances of these stars in super-concerts are all about spectacle,[7] featuring extraordinary sets, expensive handmade costumes denoting role changes, carefully choreographed dance routines supported by dance troupes, and stage-lighting effects. Music criticism in the local printed press assesses the singers, looking in particular at whether they can reach a pitch, sing in tune, remember the lyrics, manage a vocal range, follow the beat, and do a dance rou-tine, usually all at the same time, a feat which arguably is more about practice and skills than the creativity and individual expression extolled in the rock ideology of authenticity.

In a magazine article about Anita Mui's concert series in 2002, her fitness level in being able to dance and sing for two and a half hours was duly noted,[8] as were the high costs of the bespoke costumes by Christian Dior and local designers, the stage set, and even the amount of necessary insurance (Li 2002). She was supported not only by dance troupes but also by a team of young singers. Mui pulled a muscle that necessitated physiotherapy after each show, but 'she was so professional that audiences would not notice her back problem', according to the feature article (Li 2002). The multi-faceted nature of music performance in Cantonese pop allows concert performances to be regarded as texts which include sounds, words and images that are open to audience interpretation. The visual display of Cantopop, stemming from its original link to television, film and music videos, is an important element, reflected in the unique spectacular nature of pop performance that encompasses multiple skills. This characteristic of Cantopop supports my argument that there is a specific discourse of performance in Hong Kong constructed on the stars' voice, body and skills, but not on their creativity.

The practice of traditional Chinese theatre (opera) is based on performance as a multi-skilled craft, and opera-associated stardom is predicated on the hard work and long endurance necessitated by the lengthy performance-skills training. There is little evidence that performance in Hong Kong is modelled on Western theatrical performance, as most actors are not formally trained. However, actors and playwrights connected with the theatre – along with opera, another minority activity in Hong Kong – privilege the authenticity of stage acting in their comments about performance. The association of multi-faceted skills with opera is a trope to articulate performance in the popular media to hard work and, ultimately, to demonstrate reverence for stars who endure long periods of training, such as the international martial arts star Jackie Chan, whose skills came from Peking Opera training.

If hard work and endurance are revered in the discourse of performance, performance skills may be perceived to be accumulative through life experience and achieved by those with a strong work ethic, while the young and beautiful are prone to negative discursive constructions that present them as people without skills who are seen to 'play themselves' (Lovell 2003, p.263) or are 'just lucky' (David Jiang, 21 February 2005). The distinction between impersonation and personification is of particular relevance to my discussion; the former refers to acting and impersonating roles and characters, while the latter places the stars' image in the foreground, over and above different onscreen characters that the stars may play. In personification, differences between the fictional roles and the stars' real lives are often minimal, and stars are said to 'play themselves' and rely on their off-screen image (Geraghty 2000, pp.185–6; McDonald 1998). Actresses are more likely to be talked about in terms of their physical attractiveness while their acting is ignored. Character actors from Hong Kong may also emphasize life experience as a prerequisite for good performance when they talk about their acting methods, as exemplified here by two experienced actors:

Leung Wing-Fai: How do you prepare for a character?
Lam Suet (b.1964):   I don't. Most characters are basically about life experience. [I simply] follow the script. You just experience life in order to play these characters.

        . . .

Lau Ching-Wan (b.1964):   When we started, we worked in television for a long time or there are actors like [Lam] Suet who has a lot of life experience. New actors lack life experience and opportunities to try different kinds of acting.

(26 April 2008)

The notion of good acting as a result of life experience and learning is discussed by media professionals in Hong Kong as a way of distinguishing themselves from the new generation of actors who lack life experience because of their youth, while training opportunities have been less abundant due to the decline of the film sector since the 1990s. For instance, Edward Lam commented that it was no longer possible to produce actors or stars, in comparison to 'the 1970s, when after the advent of the TVB classes that trained *yi yuan* ("staff artistes"), graduates like Tony Leung, Andy Lau, Chow Yun-fat and Stephen Chow negotiated the long road to film stardom' (3 August 2005). Lam further suggested that a material difference between the two generations of actors is that new stars often fall by the wayside as there are fewer opportunities for development. Nevertheless, those who succeed by being young and beautiful in each generation are equally susceptible to criticism of their lack of skills, a fact recognized by the actor-director Lam Tze-chung (b.1976):

Lam Tze-Chung (LTC):   Even for Tony Leung, Stephen Chow, Andy Lau and Simon

Leung Wing-Fai: Yam (b.1955), their performance was not so good during the first decade or so. They were more concerned about their image than the lives of the roles. You mean their image as idols?

Ltc: Yes, image. Tony Leung has his own 'pose'. Stephen Chow has his trademark smile.

(25 April 2006)

Lam asserted that while image has always affected how stars are viewed on screen at the beginning of their careers, the members of each generation of actors are capable of acquiring skills through long-term, on-the-job training. Singers who turn their hands to acting are similarly judged for their lack of experience and skills. Furthermore, media commentaries perpetuate a notion that, except for actors already trained in performing, acting skills have to come from life experience and hard work. Experience might well improve performance, but youth, associated with physical attractiveness, is also an asset for popular stars. Thus there is a tension between the demands for both accumulated skills and youthful appearance in a media industry that has traditionally relied on the commercial appeal of stars. The constraints of the media industry, such as the temporary nature of stardom, are to blame for new stars' lack of opportunities to receive the training needed to achieve the same level of skill as performers of the previous generation.

This view, that acting requires life experience and that young, attractive actors cannot impersonate roles but always act as themselves, is echoed by the director Riley Ip:

> As a director it's hard to teach them to act. You can only try to make use of their real characteristics. They have limited experience . . . Very experienced actors know how to use method acting but young people have to be told what to do.
>
> (cited in Youngs 2003, p.23)

Despite the lack of evidence that Western teaching and styles of acting are central to performance in Hong Kong, some filmmakers and actors, including Riley Ip, refer to Method acting. The discourse of performance in Hong Kong emphasizes accumulated skills learned over time through hard work, while young stars are unable to acquire such skills because they lack experience. Given the connection of female stars to beauty contests, appearance and youth, they might be more susceptible to criticism of their lack of skills than their male counterparts. Cecilia Cheung won Best Actress at the 2004 Hong Kong Film Awards for her role in *Lost in Time* (Derek Yee, 2003). In a melodramatic storyline, the young character she played has to look after the son left behind by her dead fiancé. Commentators noted that Cheung gave such a good performance because she was able to draw from her troubled personal background. She was regarded as performing herself: 'Cecilia Cheung is particularly good at acting the kind of woman who gets abused because that's like her real life. Cheung has to support a family of a dozen people. She's playing herself in *Lost in Time*' (Bede Cheng, 3 January 2005).

Those connected with the theatre in Hong Kong often extol the performance skills of stage actors but denigrate film and television drama, even though the latter had been the main training ground for local stars. Chinese theatre (opera) is a minority interest in Hong Kong, but the notion of performance has its origins partly in this traditional art form, as demonstrated by the reverence for the multiple skills and lengthy training involved. The importance of multiple skills is seen in the fluidity of the cross-media movements of singers and actors and in the spectacular concerts that showcase their skills. Conversely, young actors have difficulty gaining life experience as they have not had the opportunity to acquire popularity over a long period of time or experience the on-the-job training that television used to provide. Young stars are therefore seen as lacking skills; even when their performances receive critical acclaim, they are often thought to be 'playing themselves'. Young female stars are particularly prone to the criticism that they are reliant on beauty and youth. The focus on acquiring skills over a long period of time by many of the media professionals means that the success of an individual (in this case, the star) is articulated to personal effort and diligence. Therefore, the criticisms targeted at young stars for their lack of skills could be a discursive response to the changing practice of multimedia stardom, in which work might no longer be labour in the traditional sense and stars' success therefore appears arbitrary.

Hong Kong stars, work and success

Performance as work is an under-researched aspect of star studies. The discourse on performance labour is an indication of the hierarchies in film production and artistic merit, with stars elite amongst actors (McDonald 1998). At the same time, Paul McDonald inadvertently points out that there is a large pool of jobbing actors who do not reach star status; stars are therefore successful individuals who are socially mobile among groups of entertainers. Stars are 'examples of the way people live their relation to production in capitalist society', so their work serves to illustrate 'more general ideas in society about what a person is, and stars are major definers of these ideas' (Dyer 1986, p.6). There is also a distinction between the star as labour and the star as capital, and image can be seen as separable from the performer (McDonald 2000). This kind of distinction is based on the traditional conception of labour as the production of material goods, but the image is also an end product of creative work that is becoming ever more important in contemporary visual culture. This development is part of the shift towards the production of immaterial goods in contemporary culture, which engenders particular anxiety about the loss of traditional work, as Jeremy Rifkin states: 'From the beginning, civilization has been structured, in large part, around the concept of work . . . Now, for the first time, human labor is being systematically eliminated from the production process' (1995, p.3). When the production of stardom relies on the stars' image as intangible 'capital' instead of on the making of cultural products, the existence of stars destabilizes the meanings of human labour.

The tension between the many potential roles of a star – as worker, performer and image – challenges traditional conceptions of labour. There has been a blurring of the definitions of stars and celebrity as a result of the existence of many media 'personalities' who are not connected to performances, and the shift towards the domination of the star image in contemporary culture thereby reflects changing notions of work in consumer society. Multimedia stars in Hong Kong have traditionally worked by transforming themselves into media products (films, pop music and television), but they increasingly labour by promoting other commodities through their image and fame. As a result, traditional labour through the production of consumer goods seems divorced from their existence. Meanwhile, stars' wealthy lifestyles, frequently reported in the printed press, exemplify the consumer economy, so in the commercial exploitation of multimedia stardom, success may be seen as arbitrary and problematic without much evidence of traditional work (performance).

One of the general themes in the discourse of stardom is success, identified by Dyer as 'getting to the top' (1979, pp.42–3), alluding to the myth of the American dream that suggests open opportunity for all. Status is a dynamic concept, standing between the social structure and the individual (Marshall 1977). Status emphasizes the position in the social structure, while the role refers to the persona who occupies the position. Therefore, individuals who have achieved the role of a successful star serve to explain the social structure giving rise to that position. As many stars are known to have come from humble backgrounds, their consumption and excess 'presented the trappings of stardom as material pleasures which could be legitimately aspired to and possibly achieved by one and all' (McDonald 2000, p.32). The success myth of stars is in fact contradictory: they are ordinary people who are also special; they may have lucky breaks, but hard work and professionalism are also necessary for stardom (Dyer 1979). Anxiety about the rise of stars is therefore also about social mobility achieved not by hard work but as something fortuitous, where 'there is no longer a pattern for the way up. Success has become an accidental and irrational event' (Leo Lowenthal, cited in Dyer 1979, p.23).

Lowenthal's assertion that stars' success is achieved through luck rather than by working within a meritocratic structure assumes that stars' career trajectories can be mapped onto the social structure. The increasingly overt presence of stars in celebrity news and their existence as image that has overtaken their importance as performers has raised anxiety about accidental success. Stars appear even more 'frivolous' due to the lack of evidence of work, if work is defined by the production of cultural commodities as material goods. As Hong Kong stars' productive activity has shifted towards advertising that relies on image and fame and away from traditional media like films and television programmes, they can be perceived to be 'idols of consumption' who lead lives of conspicuous consumption that seem to be 'all play and no work' (McDonald 1998, pp.194–5).[9]

Can stars in Hong Kong justify their success like any other workers? Are they worthy of the material wealth that some of them possess? Discourse about multimedia stardom in the city is often centred around work and success; critiques of the new stars are about their seeming lack of a strong work ethic, while the older generation of stars are seen to have justified their success and achievement by their longstanding effort. Cheung Tung-joe, a producer, director and actor since the 1970s, summarized the criticisms directed at young stars:

> It's not possible in Hollywood [to make several films at the same time]. Even big stars put in every effort for a film for six or eight weeks. [Film-making] should be your work; it represents your success or failure. There are no actors [in Hong Kong now]. After becoming a little popular, stars would promote products in advertising campaigns in order to make money. Some of them say, 'I don't have time. I only have ten days in which to make this film'. They do not respect their work.
>
> (29 January 2005)

Cheung commented on the effort that actors should expend to make a film. Because they are exploited for maximum profit, young stars have such hectic schedules that they lack the concentration necessary for any sort of real performance, and film productions have to work around them. Nevertheless, there is little evidence that the previous generation of stars did not have the same kind of hectic schedules. According to Cheung, acting should be 'work; it represents [one's] success or failure', but many contemporary stars are seen to lack interest in the quality of the films and to act merely to earn money. Cheung therefore articulated performance to both work and justification for success. Nevertheless, he did not acknowledge that the 'work' of contemporary multimedia stars has diversified beyond acting.

With no clear progression path to achievement in the entertainment industry, the success of many stars might seem to have come by chance rather than effort; 'Working in the film industry is still seen as an alternative career, for those without much education' (Zhang 1998, p.30). The government-endorsed collective ethos, the 'Hong Kong dream', depends on a meritocratic society with the possibility of mobility open to all, so material success is not automatically celebrated but requires justification through a strong work ethic. Multimedia stardom, because it does not rely on received conceptions of work and material production, further focuses general mistrust and hostility towards a mass media that rewards those who have not worked hard. This hostility is often contextualized in the examinations of changes in Hong Kong society and mobility offered by cultural commentators such as Edward Lam:

Edward Lam (L):	The formation of our middle class is incomplete. In terms of income or lifestyle, they may be middle class [but] their ideology is still very working class.
Leung Wing-Fai (Lwf):	Class is not only determined by income.
L:	In Hong Kong, most stars have never gone to college. In the UK lots of actors have intellectual and middle class backgrounds . . . In this society the status has to come from climbing from the bottom, which is the essence of people's lives. All the soap operas are about this myth.
Lwf:	If you work hard, you can succeed?
L:	You call that an ideal! Stephen Chow, for instance, perpetuates this myth in *Shaolin Soccer* . . . There's a fear of poverty. There are fewer and fewer stars who have quality; they are chosen by people who don't have an eye for good judgement.

(3 August 2005)

Lam examined the notion of social status in Hong Kong and found that since stars are generally not highly educated or from the recently emerged middle-class, they can only reflect the achievement of material success by climbing the social ladder. The television programmes and pop music that the stars produce often support the same ideology about material success. According to Lam, the stars do not have any special qualities that might justify their success, and their careers compound the concern of many in Hong Kong about social mobility and the associated anxiety regarding the security of their newfound wealth.

If respected stars are multi-skilled performers who worked hard, then the discourse about young stars, constructed as unskilled celebrities because of their focus on the selling of image, casts them as 'frivolous' people who cannot justify their success. Without educational achievement, young, attractive stars, often referred to as idols, might be seen to have entered the industry by sheer luck and therefore have to prove their worth in other ways, for instance through diligence in their acquisition of skills. In a society that has only recently and gradually prospered, the Hong Kong dream is about the received ideology of materialist success through labour. The shift in work towards immaterial production, exemplified by the later iterations of multimedia stardom, contradicts more traditional values about work ethic and personal rewards. The above commentaries on the essential and dominant ideology about work and success in Hong Kong came from media professionals and critics who saw themselves as able to stand outside of 'society'. Thereby they inadvertently challenged the very existence of the dominant ideology that they seemed to suggest. These ideas about stars have arisen from changes in stardom-related practices, namely the decline of the traditional labour of acting and singing, while the shift from the importance of performances to image-making has conjured up anxiety about the basis of the Hong Kong dream as a central myth for the population. In the next section, I present a case study of a multimedia star who emerged in the 1980s and summarize the key points in this chapter.

The enduring multimedia star: Andy Lau

Andy Lau Tak-wah graduated from TVB's training class in 1981 and acted in television drama series. Lau became popular through television series such as *The Emissary* (1982) and a period drama, *The Duke of Mount Deer* (1984). His image as a young rebel came from early roles such as the young street punk he played in the episode 'See You on the Other Side' (1981) of the RTHK series *Hong Kong Hong Kong.* In many of these roles, the actor wore a sleeveless T-shirt showing a tattooed arm, which became a defining feature of the physical appearance of young gangsters on screen. Lau soon became a film actor and embarked on a singing career that began in 1984. His acclaimed early roles included a Vietnamese refugee in *Boat People* in 1982, although he also played numerous melodramatic roles that depended on his television soap-opera-idol image. Lau also acted in many popular genre films, playing gangsters and young anti-heroes, roles which referenced his early television work. One of his most successful portrayals was in the hit production *Moment of Romance* (Benny Chan, 1990), a gangster romance in which Lau played a sentimental delinquent. In 1991 he founded his own production company, Teamwork, later renamed Focus. The star's film career dipped during the mid-1990s but was rejuvenated by *A True Mob Story* (Wong Jing, 1998) and collaborations with the producer and director Johnnie To. The series of successful collaborations between To and Lau included *Running Out of Time* (1999), *Needing You* (with Wai Ka-fai, 2000), *Fulltime Killer* (with Wai Ka-fai, 2001), *Love on a Diet* (Wai Ka-fai, 2001), *Running on Karma* (with Wai Ka-fai, 2003), *Yesterday Once More* (2004) and *Blind Detective* (2013).

The seminal crime thriller *Fulltime Killer* transformed Lau's image overnight, from young gangster to cool assassin in hot pursuit of the 'number one hitman' in Asia, although the local critic Kozo states that the film is self-referential and that Andy Lau's performance emphasized 'his own pop star image' (Kozo 2001).

Lau's long acting career and enduring popularity can be attributed to the strong partnership with the Johnnie To–Wai Ka-fai team that allowed him to gradually shed his young-idol image. Lau won the Best Actor Award at the Hong Kong Film Awards for *Running Out of Time, Running on Karma*[10] and *A Simple Life* (Ann Hui, 2012). Johnnie To therefore helped to redefine Andy Lau as a 'serious' actor. With the decline of the film industry, Lau reinvented himself as an elder of Hong Kong cinema and attempted to broaden into art cinema and the Chinese market, following the pattern of re-sinicization set by other stars. Lau acted in films such as *House of Flying Daggers* (Zhang Yimou, 2004) and *A World Without Thieves* (Feng Xiaogang, 2004) in collaboration with mainland directors and *The Warlords* (Peter Chan, 2007) and *Detective Dee and the Mystery of the Phantom Flame* (Tsui Hark, 2010) with Hong Kong-based directors co-producing in China. *A World without Thieves* was a box office success, consolidating the star's popularity in Mainland China. *Detective Dee* was released around the National Day holidays and was number six in a list of the top ten highest-grossing films in China in 2010 (Screen Daily Staff 2011). By the early 2000s, Lau's acting credentials had been confirmed by the winning of acting awards. He was such a familiar face in the Hong Kong media by then that he did not need to be seen to be recognized, as attested by his voiceover in *McDull: Prince de la Bun* (Toe Yuen, 2004) and in numerous cameos where he played 'himself', most famously as the future CEO of Hong Kong in *Golden Chicken 2* (Samson Chiu, 2003).[11] His star status in China was further affirmed by cameos in two Chinese state-endorsed epics: *The Founding of a Republic* (Huang Jianxin & Han Sanping, 2009) and *The Founding of a Party* (Huang Jianxin & Han Sanping, 2011), celebrating the beginning of the People's Republic and the Communist Party, respectively. Lau is an exemplar of a star of the earlier generation; he has had a long and popular acting and singing careers, crossed from television into cinema, matured into a respected leader in the media industry, and, more recently, re-sinicized as a 'Greater Chinese star'.

Lau released his first album in 1985, but his Cantopop success only came in 1990 with the triple platinum album *Would It Be Possible* and the TVB (Jade) Solid Gold Award for Most Popular Male Singer. Andy Lau had many hits in the early 1990s and became known as one of the Four Heavenly Kings of Cantopop, a title first appearing in 1991. Lau claimed, 'I'm probably the most successful example of an actor-turned-singer' (HKIFF 2005, p.47). His most prolific period as a pop singer was in the 1990s and early 2000s. From 1985–2012, Andy Lau released 123 records in total, including singles, EPs and compilations, and at least half of these were in Mandarin or contained a mixture of Mandarin and Cantonese songs.[12] Lau's first Mandarin album was released in 1989, while his Cantonese-only records became increasingly rare, the last being in 2009, a shift that reflected the refocusing of the star's target market to Mainland China.

Many of Lau's hits were the theme songs of films he starred in, such as *A Moment of Romance 3* (Johnnie To, 1996) and *Shanghai Grand* (Tsui Hark, 1996). Like his contemporaries, the popular multimedia stars of the 1980s and 1990s, Lau was also engaged in super-concerting, including the 1993 series of 20 shows at the Hong Kong Coliseum. Lau never left his music work behind, although his popularity as a singer has subsided since the late 1990s. Despite this, his 2004 Vision Tour, a series of 15 concerts, was a typically high-budget spectacle with eight different set changes, acrobats, tap dancers, waltzes and Chinese lion dances. In a cross-media reference, he even appeared on stage in the bodysuit that he wore for the film *Running on Karma*. Four series of the Wonderful World Tour took place, mostly in China, from 2007–9, a total of 47 concerts (Figure 4.1). Lau then completed The Unforgettable Tour in Hong Kong in 2010 (20 shows) and China in 2011 (11 concerts).

The 2005 HKIFF included a retrospective on Lau, entitled *Andy Lau: Actor in Focus,* another indication of the recognition of his success as a star. A panel discussion on 3 April, made up of three local critics, focused on how Lau can be considered an exemplar of a Hong Kong style of acting that derives from television training. Athena Tsui pointed out that Andy Lau emerged during the 1980s and early 1990s when Hong Kong cinema was focused on mainstream and popular entertainment, mainly producing genre films which were reliant on stars. The Hong Kong film industry's commercial nature meant that actors were restricted by the types of films made and the short duration of production. Lau was initially limited by both his age and the kind of popular films being produced at the time, and therefore his career can be mapped onto the changing entertainment world in Hong Kong since the early 1980s. Lau's career trajectory was typical of many of the 1980s generation of actors, with its initial association with an idol image and background in television performance training. Like those in each generation of young stars, Lau too was criticized as an inexperienced performer with good looks but no acting skills. The more recent acknowledgement of Lau's acting skills indicates a re-evaluation of the television-influenced acting style in Hong Kong, constituting a changing discourse of performance as a result of the recognition of the specific characteristics of the media industries.

Figure 4.1 Andy Lau in concert (December 2008), with dancers and 'period' costumes. © CC-Ashley Lim.

Andy Lau showed an awareness of the popular discourse about him. He attributed the period in his career when he made many commercial films, particularly in the action genre, to the restrictions of the industry, which was also an acknowledge-ment that acting skills were not of prime importance in some productions:

> [When] I left TV for film, comedy and action genres occupied the whole film industry. Very few films were about solemn and thoughtful topics. So I changed my plan and began to improve my skills for action films . . . so people forgot that Andy Lau could act . . . At the time, people knew very little about Andy Lau's acting skills. They all thought I was a James Dean. In fact, I watched a lot of Marlon Brando films. He was a first-generation method actor. I imitated him almost completely.
>
> (cited in HKIFF 2005, pp.42–3)

In addition to the critics' use of Andy Lau as a tool to re-evaluate acting in Hong Kong, the star himself also asserted his adoption of Method acting in order to counteract early criticisms of his acting ability. He commented, 'I did a lot of research for every role, even if it was just a small role' (HKIFF 2005, p.41), indicating his work ethic.

Lau gained acting awards for his work in the films of Johnnie To, and his trust and respect for the director and producer were clear. To in turn claimed,

> I think his transformation came about during *Running Out of Time* . . . Since then, he has used the 'Andy Lau' way of acting less and less. He puts more weight on the character, whereas in the past he was always Andy Lau all the time.
>
> (cited in HKIFF 2005, p.46)

Johnnie To expressed the view that the pop idol Andy Lau had a specific image that overshadowed his onscreen characters. It was while working for To that the star twice donned bodysuits (in *Love On A Diet* and *Running On Karma*) that obscured his 'handsome' physique. Instead of relying on facial expression typical of television acting, Lau developed his performance skills through an increased emphasis on body transformation in *Running Out of Time,* occasionally cross-dressing in the part of a dying thief. Lau won Best Actor at the Hong Kong Film Awards for these reasons, another manifestation of the re-evaluation and accept-ance of the star as a performer by other professionals and critics. Lau's later image moved away from the depiction of working-class anti-heroes that had dominated his television and early film careers. In the *Infernal Affairs* trilogy (2002–3), he played a grown-up, tortured man who aspires to the middle-class lifestyle of a high-ranking policeman while harbouring dark personal secrets as a gangster mole in the police. Much of the story examines the protagonist's psychological torment, especially in the third instalment in which Lau's role becomes central. *A Simple Life* depicts the relationship between Roger (played by Lau), a middle-aged film producer, and Tao Jie ('Sister Peach'), a domestic servant who has worked for the family all her adult life. The star's understated performance won him his third Best Actor award at the Hong Kong Film Awards.

Lau's advertising contracts in recent years have reflected this change of image as well as the rising importance of star-fronted advertising campaigns. His campaign for LG mobile phones included a 'special edition' featuring the star's own calligraphy engraved on the back of the handset;[13] an advertisement stated that the first purchasers of the model would receive his latest Mandarin album, *Miracle World,* and a poster. The later cross-marketing of Lau, with an eye on the mainland and international markets, relied on his newfound image of middle-aged, charitable and hardworking respectability. For example, the poster for his Wonderful World Tour in 2007 shows the star in a dark suit, his airbrushed, youthful face (Lau was 46) half obscured and the lighting accentuating his angular features. His finger-to-lips gesture denotes mystery and puts a diamond ring by MaBelle Leo, the main sponsor of the concerts, in the centre. In a 2006 advertisement for Suntory Whisky, the star is shown imagining an alternative career as a suited, bespectacled engineer.[14] After successfully leading a team project, the protagonist celebrates with colleagues by drinking the whisky, proclaiming *fengfu rensheng, rensheng fengfu* ('enrich your life and you will live life to the full'). Some of Lau's other commercials in the 2000s were for Nescafe, *Daodi* green tea, Adidas trainers, and Baleno, a Hong Kong-based fashion chain. Increasingly, these campaigns were for mainland as well as Hong Kong markets, with the whisky and diamond ring ads targeting the aspirational middle-class male consumer.

In 2005, Lau became the ambassador in Southeast Asia for Swiss watch maker Cyma, chosen for his 'well-proven versatility'.[15] The watch maker's choice of the younger, mainland actor Liu Ye (b.1978) to replace Lau as their new ambassador in 2011 was taken 'to further raise the brand's profile in mainland China'.[16] Lau's commercial work in the Mainland was typical of Hong Kong stars since the early 2000s, as the Chinese advertisers often paid more than companies based in Hong Kong, resulting in more and more stars' northbound advertising assignments. It has also become an increasingly competitive market because of the rise of home-grown mainland and other Asian popular stars who appeal to Chinese consumers, as shown by CYMA's replacement of Lau by a younger mainland actor.

Andy Lau, like many of his contemporaries, has been part of the re-sinicization of Hong Kong's media industry since the late 1990s. As a result, his career has combined elements that speak to both local and Greater Chinese audiences, creating a tension that has become more apparent throughout the early 2000s. In 1995, Lau used an old song, *Last Night on the Star Ferry,* to rekindle a sense of belonging to the city through the pathos of the Star Ferry ride, a much-loved and traditional local means of transport between Kowloon and Hong Kong Island:[17]

Last night on the ferry

I faced the north wind . . .

In memory of you

I don the armour

And the spirit of a warrior

To start afresh

Today I laugh easily in a drunken haze

Early morn

Begin the sobering day

Erni suggests that following the massacre in Tiananmen Square in 1989, 'Cantopop went from being passionately in search of identity in the moment of crisis to being disillusioned and disinterested under the realization of political helplessness' (2007, p.98). With *Last Night on the Star Ferry,* Andy Lau showed how 'political feelings [were] repackageable in opportunistic ways' (p.98). Conversely, in 1997 on the eve of the handover, he re-released a song entitled *Chinese* that contained 'new and old patriotic feelings' (p.98), signalling a shift towards the Greater Chinese market. The chorus is as follows (note 33):

There is no you or I

We step forward

Let the world know that we are Chinese

This was the beginning of the repeated employment of Lau's newfound status and respectability in post-handover official, quasi-national articulations, celebrating abstract patriotic feelings towards an imaginary 'China'. Sabrina Yu notes that in the post-socialist period, 'patriotism' has become

> a basic criterion [that] Chinese actors have to meet if they want to establish their stardom in the PRC . . . For Hong Kong and Taiwan stars, it is even more important to package themselves as patriotic stars in order to consolidate their star status and expand their fan base in the mainland.
>
> (2012b, pp.234–5)

Lau and the other three Heavenly Kings recorded the theme song for the tenth anniversary of the establishment of the Hong Kong SAR and sang alongside Jackie Chan, the other 'model' Hong Kong star, during the 2008 Summer Olympics closing ceremony. Lau's song *Everyone is No. 1* was also adopted as the theme song for the Paralympics. In the music video, Lau plays a postman who has lost his lower leg in a car accident, a situation that does not stop him from continuing to work, training as an athlete or encouraging others to do the same.[18] All these assignments confirmed his status in the entertainment world in Hong Kong and increasingly in Mainland China. In a 2011 *Forbes China* list of the most powerful celebrities in the Mainland, Andy Lau was in second place (behind Jay Chou), his popularity recently enhanced by an extensive concert tour of China (Flannery 2012).

Andy Lau's career as a television-turned-pop and -film star and its evaluation by other media professionals illustrates the changing discourse of performance in Hong Kong. While acknowledging the nature of commercial cinema in Hong Kong, he insisted that he was a Method actor who worked hard on every role. His image changed from that of a young idol to a representative of the Hong Kong dream, a facet duly employed to promote a range of consumer products. In the 1990s, in anticipation of the handover, Andy Lau released numerous records in Mandarin, and his filmography gradually came to consist of high-profile China-Hong Kong co-productions and mainland blockbusters as he attempted to re-sinicize his career while accommodating his local supporters. Of his own career, the star states, 'I want to have a form that fits the time, so I just keep on changing and that makes people feel I'm a hardworking guy trying to do my best' (cited in Gough 2004). Despite his recent efforts to establish himself and succeed as a patriotic Chinese star, his public persona remains deeply rooted in the received Hong Kong ethic, just like the disabled athlete he played in the video for the Beijing Paralympics who never gave up. Andy Lau's comment, 'I work hard. Hong Kong spirit? Every era must have its own representative models' (cited in Yu 2004, p.78), sums up my argument that the discourse of performance in Hong Kong is uniquely connected to the history of the media industry, in which multimedia stars like Lau were expected to acquire skills over time while their hard work could be articulated to the social mobility ideal. Andy Lau, a star who established a multi-faceted career during the 1980s, was able to gradually move into a leadership position in the media industries in Hong Kong. He asserted his role as a model for the entertainment world and even as a representative of a Hong Kong spirit built on the foundation of a strong work ethic, a most pertinent aspect of multimedia stardom.

Concluding remarks

A unique tradition in the practices and discourse of performance in Hong Kong involves the narrow scope in commercial cinema for performances requiring time-consuming preparation by the actors. Many popular commercial genres allow little space for the sort of performance that might lend itself to Method acting, the Western standard. Most actors are trained informally, and many, especially those from the previous generation, started in television drama and presenting. In the early 2000s, cultural critics began to suggest a distinctive Hong Kong style of acting that emphasizes facial expression as a result of television performance training, the existence or significance of such a style having been previously ignored. Some filmmakers accept that the quality of multimedia stars' onscreen performance cannot be assumed. Another facet of the distinctiveness of multimedia stardom in Hong Kong is that pop singers perform and interpret pre-existing songs, often composed and written for them specifically, but they are not expected to be individual creative talents.

There is evidence that the notion of performance skills in Hong Kong is associated with traditional opera rather than with modern theatre, although neither is a mass cultural pursuit. The influence of Chinese opera was two-fold: respect for the multiple skills evident in the stars' stage performance and their ability to cross media. Life experience and hard work were also perceived as vital for the acquisition of performance skills by those who worked in the entertainment industry during the 1980s and 1990s. This discourse of an imagined collective Hong Kong ethos built on skills and diligence continues despite the changing nature of labour, as many multimedia stars are increasingly engaged in immaterial production. Therefore, the discourse on stardom in Hong Kong continues to assume artistry among the previous generation of stars, while young stars' success may be seen as accidental, purely a matter of luck and good looks, but without evidence of hard work and real skills. The career of Andy Lau, a television-turned-film and -pop star, is exemplary because he started from the 1980s as a young, handsome singer-actor criticized for his lack of skills. The change in his image from young anti-hero to middle-aged, respectable leader is reflected particularly in recent advertising campaigns, and his films, music, and commercials have been increasingly oriented towards the mainland market, with Lau depicted as a patriot in a re-sinicizing trend replicated in many Hong Kong stars' careers.

Cultural production and consumption in Hong Kong since the early 2000s has moved towards immaterial goods such as the creation of image, a change that has heightened anxiety in a society built on the myth of the mobility ideal. Andy Lau emphasized his performance skills and hard work and put himself forward as a representative of the authentic, collective Hong Kong spirit. The specific discourse of performance in Hong Kong makes reference to ideas about work and success, therefore providing evidence of stardom as a symbolic form that must be understood through the prescribed role of the individual in that specific society and culture. The comments of industry professionals and stars about performance in response to the changing nature of multimedia stardom represent an articulatory practice that allows them to rethink their own identity. This rethinking is also an assertion of a collective Hong Kong identity found in the star-related discourse manifested in a city under continuous flux.

5 Identity

In this chapter I argue that the discourse of a collective Hong Kong identity can be explained through cultural and social specificities revealed through an examination of the phenomenon of multimedia stardom. Identity, often assumed to be fixed, coherent and stable, becomes an issue when it is in crisis and certainty is challenged (Mercer 1990). This is highly relevant in the case of Hong Kong, as the city experienced political, economic and social uncertainties beginning in the early 1980s, when the issue of the handover to China was first raised. The 1997 handover, the focus of much existing research from the last three decades, should not be viewed as a watershed but rather as a significant date in the history of the continuous transformation of Hong Kong culture. In this chapter I examine how multimedia stardom has been discursively articulated to an imagined Hong Kong identity in order to create a sense of fixity and certainty in times of crisis. I incorporate analysis of the longstanding cultural discourse in support of collectivity and explain why the search for a unified identity continues to be an urgent issue in the post-handover city.

Self, identities and Hong Kong

My discussion of identity in Hong Kong is a response to existing writing that is dominated by debates about whether people in Hong Kong accept or resist a quasi-national identity resulting from the city's changing relationship with China. The complexity of the notion of Hong Kong identity is marked by historical, economic, political, social and cultural differences: subjectivities in the city during the 1980s and up to 1997 were constructed in the process of negotiating the mutations and permutations of colonialism, nationalism, and capitalism (Abbas 1996). The lack of attention towards the conceptualization of Hong Kong identity 'in the recesses of social and cultural life' may be understood as part of the 'disappearance' (Abbas 1996, p.7) of culture, resulting from a misrecognition rather than an absence of culture. The imminence of its disappearance engendered an intense and unprecedented interest in Hong Kong culture (Abbas 1996). In this analysis I advance the discussion of this pre-handover search for an identity to the continuation of the urgent need to assert collectivity in post-1997 Hong Kong.

Many existing debates regarding the media and identity in Hong Kong are positioned in relation to China and the handover. Eric Ma (1995), for instance, examines the contrasts between television drama serials, asserting that those in the 1970s helped to form and maintain indigenous cultural identity, while the 1990s serials reflected the residents' handover-related identity confusion. The audiences' concern was sometimes shared by media professionals; Peter Chan, the director of *Comrades, Almost a Love Story* (1996), states that he 'realized that the story [in the film] is also a reflection on the lives of Hong Kong natives of my generation, people like me who are trying to cope with a deadline called 1997' (cited in Lo 2001, pp.272–3).[1] However, another filmmaker, Gordon Chan, suggests that films could not represent the complex feelings of audiences with different psychological profiles in anticipation of the handover (cited in HKIFF 2000). As audiences are complex and their identities are contingent, cultural analysts need to recognize that media contents are not direct reflections of elusive feelings about geopolitical contexts; any discussion of the relationship between the media and identity must also take into account the conditions under which media products are produced and received.

My debate focuses on a particular media practice, stardom, as a subject in the cultural analysis of identity. Since the personal lives of media stars are widely reported and scrutinized, so the debates about the roles stars play in contemporary society lend themselves to a wider discourse about private individuals who are seen in public. Existing discussion of stardom often starts from the premise that stars are related to a particular ideology in which human individuality is based on a unique essence (Dyer 1986). Paradoxically, stars exemplify the contingent nature of individual identities in contemporary society because their 'selves' are represented in public are in constant flux, endlessly produced and remade in representation. Individual identities therefore can be conceived as *positionalities* in the contingent permutations of society (Laclau 1990, pp.89–92, original emphasis). Stars are people who are frequently in the public eye and whose 'authentic' selves are performed in public. Their representations change all the time, whether as onscreen characters or figures in entertainment news and advertising. The result of these contradictory demands is that 'persona is elastic rather than plastic, closer to a procedure for surviving, a heuristic of the self, than an essence' (King 2003, p.60). Stars thereby demonstrate the struggle for individuality within and against the relational or contextual ideas of the self. Celebrity as a status illustrates the social rules and knowledge that regulate the relationship between being an individual and being part of a wider collective identity (Marshall 1997). Stars in Hong Kong, a secular, colonial and post-colonial, advanced capitalist city, are best at reflecting social meanings at the intersections between the individual and the collective.

Existing studies of stardom are also based mostly on American culture, where the 'self seems to be characterized by individualism', while 'the traditional Chinese self, on the other hand, appears to be relatively more orientated towards the significant others' (Chu 1985, pp.257–8). The notion of the relational self, which is central in traditional Chinese culture, has been written about widely, particularly in relation to how it would be expected to contribute to a strong collective view of society (Blowers 1991; Leung 1996; Sun 1989; Tam 1995; Tu 1985). Human beings exist somewhere between individual, social and cultural orientations; therefore 'the interpersonal concept *jen* is more useful as a basis for understanding human behaviour with reference to social and cultural stability and change than the individualistic concept of personality' (Hsu 1985, p.33).[2] The unique social and cultural development of Hong Kong as a British colony offers an explanation of how self-reliance emerged as an important personal ethic; as Benjamin Leung writes, 'materialism and a pragmatic orientation prevailed over Confucian ethics in the evolution of Hong Kong culture' (1996, p.51). The issue is not simply about the determination of the exclusive existence of traditional Chinese ethics or Western individualism in Hong Kong, but about how and to what extent social and cultural changes might have influenced the discourse of the self.

Identity in modern society has become increasingly complex and is marked by cultural, national, personal and social differences, and it is often constructed in relation to conceptions of 'otherness'. Furthermore, individuals exist not at the extremes of binary conceptions but rather between the extremes and within the consternation of simultaneous overlapping systems of difference. Kathryn Woodward suggests that two different processes are necessary for the marking and maintaining of identities. Social differentiation is how differences are 'lived out' in social relations, while 'symbolic marking is how we make sense of social relations and practices; for example, regarding who is excluded and who is included' (1997, p.12). Stars in Hong Kong should be studied with reference to the existing analytical frameworks of social science because, by virtue of their public presence, they are treated as model individuals who embody the different social roles available while also being symbolically assigned a collective identity. The search for an essential identity in Hong Kong that obscured differences among social groups was affected by the city's social and cultural development long before the issue of the handover, especially as the result of a post-war, government-endorsed cultural discourse, discussed in Chapter 1, which perpetuated a grand narrative of Hong Kong as a capitalist success. Hong Kong Chinese were supposed to work hard due to the perceived possibility for social mobility, and they exerted themselves to fulfil the 'rags-to-riches' Hong Kong dream. This discourse of a collective ethos explained Hong Kong's economic progress and erased social and cultural differences as well as the increasing class divisions resulting from economic stratification. In the following discussion I examine how stardom in Hong Kong became a symbolic marker of a collective identity that masked such social divisions.

In post-war Hong Kong, diverse cultural forms including Mandarin, Hokkien entertainment, *huangmei diao* and Cantonese opera catered for different social groups, particularly the new migrants.[3] Cantonese media produced in Hong Kong, including television, cinema and music, dominated from the 1970s onwards in a process of indigenization. These media assumed a unified Hong Kong identity and catered for a mass audience, a generation born and raised in the city and who had become increasingly affluent consumers. Despite the socially destabilizing effects of the approaching handover, the indigenous entertainment industry did not wane until the mid-1990s because the prosperity enjoyed by the children of post-war mainland refugees sustained the demand for popular culture. These contexts were instrumental in the development of stardom-related practices and discourse. For my argument, I conceptualize stardom as a discursive construct, a symbolic marker of essential identity, and a key element in the continual search for collectivity in post-handover Hong Kong society.

Generational identities and stars

The anonymous publisher of the book *Great Idol,* written by local critic Tao Jie (2004), states that to understand Hong Kong there is no need to read its history; one need only examine the entertainment news because the whole of the city is like the entertainment business. If the government wanted to run a campaign of civic education, a concert would be organized using stars and capitalizing on their role as model individuals. Commentators like this publisher suggest that stars have a powerful influence in galvanizing communal support in Hong Kong. After the tsunami that hit Indonesia in late 2004 and killed thousands, people in the Asian region were quick to offer help. Many stars in Hong Kong immediately donated cash and participated in fundraising activities. More than 100 celebrities took part in a 7-hour Crossing Borders Fundraising Show at the Hong Kong Stadium on 7 January 2005 to raise money for disaster victims and to promote the message, 'Caring for the Earth'. The show was broadcast by major television channels and radio stations. A 100-strong group of singers recorded the song *Love (Sihai Yixin)* – a Chinese cover of the Band Aid song, *We Are the World* – with alternate Cantonese and Mandarin lines. Even the CEO at the time, Tung Chee-hwa, attended the show and sang alongside the singers. The concert took place shortly after Tung's chief of staff resigned, and the appearance was seen to be part of his 'efforts to get closer to the people' and restore confidence in his office (Leung & Cheung 2005, p.A2). The staging of large-scale fundraising concerts is typical of the responses from stars in Hong Kong in times of crisis that were, as indicated in this example, officially endorsed by the government. As part of a cultural discourse, stars help to bridge the individual and the two meanings of *ren,* the collective and civic. The goal of the government's cultural discourse, a project since the end of the Second World War, is to engender a shared ethos through civic education, and well-known individuals such as stars have been increasingly co-opted as spokespersons.

Chow Yun-fat is an exemplar of the group of 1970s indigenous Hong Kong stars who were expected to act as model citizens.[4] Writing in 1987, before Chow's career became international, Sek Kei states:

> The strongest attraction about Chow is that he belongs totally to Hong Kong. He is a star but he has at the same time a down-to-earth quality that enables the audience to identify with him. Few other stars have this rapport with the audience. This closeness we feel about him comes in part from his television

career and in part from his total accessibility. We know about his history – he was brought up on Lamma Island and is very much a native of Hong Kong. He started from the lowest rung [on] the ladder (TVB actors training class) and as he worked his way up step by step, we were there to witness the process.

(HKIFF 2000, p.108)

Lamma is one of the offshore islands of Hong Kong. At the time of Chow's upbringing, it would have been inhabited mainly by members of a poor fishing community. Sek Kei's comment asserts that stars like Chow are symbolic of the progress narrative which seeks to explain the development of Hong Kong, but this narrative also obscures social and economic inequalities. Vivian Tam cites the producer of a 1998 Smartone Stormfighter commercial that featured Chow Yun-fat: 'The crises in the plot symbolize social problems Hong Kong has experienced in [the] late 90s, including the Asian economic crisis, the E. Coli and bird's flu crises, and the diminishing confidence of the Hong Kong people' (2002, p.77). The producer also states that Chow symbolized the 'Hong Kong spirit', which is about using the right tools and self-confidence to overcome problems. In popular commentaries, the rags-to-riches stories of stars like Chow Yun-fat have paralleled the rise of Hong Kong's economic power. The biographies of stars, a frequent subject of circulation by the media, have become part of the articulatory practices between stardom, local history, and a collective cultural and social identity.

After the death of James Wong (1941–2004), an article entitled 'Farewell to the Era of Popular Media' by a columnist in *The Hong Kong Economic News* proclaimed that the passing of several famous stars signalled the end of the most glorious period in Hong Kong entertainment media (Liang 2004). Little-known outside of the city, James Wong was principally a prolific Cantonese pop songwriter, though he was also a popular television and film personality. He penned some of the most memorable Cantonese pop songs from the 1970s and 1980s, with lyrics that referred to everyday life in Hong Kong, and Wong's death produced a sense of nostalgia for the popular culture of those decades. In his theme song for the popular 1970s RTHK series *Below the Lion Rock*, he wrote:[5]

People in the same boat in search of a common ideal

Without fear

. . .

Hand in hand, we smooth the rocky path

Let us strive hard

To write a glorious script of Hong Kong together

Wong's sentiment supports my argument that the search for a collective Hong Kong identity did not begin in the early 1980s but started as a colonial project endorsed by the post-war cultural discourse. His lyrics for numerous theme songs from 1970s popular television drama series highlighted and served to engender a particular world-view of Hong Kong that corroborated a unifying ethos of social and industrial progress. When he died, the media lamented the loss of a spiritual leader. This discourse of the passing of a collective identity continued with the media outpouring of grief after Roman Tam (1945–2002), the popular singer of *Below the Lion Rock,* died from cancer. Like Wong, Tam performed many theme songs for popular television drama series of the 1970s, and he was associated with these daily viewings during family dinners.

Stars as model individuals embody a range of roles; specifically they are successful and respected performers who are able to represent their community, especially in public charitable and civic duties. Why should discursive constructions about a particular generation of Hong Kong stars, especially those from the 1970s and 1980s, and the stars' ability to embody a communal or collective identity, be evoked since the handover? In the 1970s and 1980s the stars who were featured in the front rooms of numerous viewers before crossing media from television to film and pop held an unprecedented sense of familiarity for that generation of local audiences, and the indigenous media masked cultural and ethnic differences that had characterized the immigrants, refugees and Hong Kong natives before this time. During the 1990s and beyond, the mass media began to lose the popular appeal it had once enjoyed; the media landscape shifted into new fields, as shown by a re-emergence of the youth market and an increasing necessity to cater for external markets, especially the Mainland. Recognition that the media industry was in crisis and was over-reliant on the previous generation of stars was most prevalent among professionals who had seen the rise and fall of local popular culture, typified by my professional contact Cheung Tung-joe's comment, 'This is not an industry but a crisis. You can only find a market with mega-stars from the 1980s' (29 July 2005). Bey Logan also observed the continuous influence of the previous generation of stars, although he suggested a shift in their status to character actors:

> There are people from the ages of 16 to early 20s who actively worship younger idols. In the 1980s, you had these amazing actors like Chow Yun-fat and Maggie Cheung. Even if new idols can act and sing, can they sing as well as Jacky Cheung and Leslie Cheung? . . . All we have in the industry are character actors now. *Infernal Affairs 2* (Andrew Lau & Mak Siu-fai, 2003) was the return of the character actors, Anthony Wong, Francis Ng (b.1961), Eric Tsang and even Carina Lau, who's not an ingénue any more. They are all great character players.
>
> (6 January 2005)

These stars from the earlier generation assumed their subject position as representatives of the collective and essential within the discourse of identity, a position supported mainly by those who previously benefited most from the success of local media. In the face of post-handover difficulties, these professionals had to look back to a cultural 'golden age' in order to explain the current crisis. For a generation of commentators, a collective cultural identity was at stake in post-1997 Hong Kong because they perceived that the pre-handover mass society had disintegrated. The new discourse of identity therefore demarcated between 'we' and 'they', between the vanguards of a Hong Kong way of life and the twin challenges of young consumers and the mainland market.

In 2005, *Ming Pao,* a longstanding quality newspaper, featured a debate about the state of culture in Hong Kong by criticizing the post-1990s generation. Bono (Lee), a local writer, commented on the lack of successors to the generation of cultural critics that included himself and his peers: 'People between 25 and 30 were polluted by these fast food style magazines, so no other cultural magazines could attract "these first generation fast food consumers". Young people are not interested in culture' (cited in Zheng 2005). The last generation of 'Hong Kong people', according to Bono, were those raised under the colonial educational system, and he predicted that the cherished 'Hong Kong spirit [would] disappear long before 2046' (Zheng 2005).[6] He linked this disappearance to the handover of Hong Kong and to the fact that Mainland China was also changing rapidly and emerging as a regional and global political and cultural power. Nonetheless, another culture, favoured by what Bono called 'a generation of fast food consumers', clearly existed in post-handover Hong Kong. The cultural commentators who criticized the young for their desertion of a Hong Kong spirit were to some extent side-lined by the new waves of emerging youth culture. The disappearance of the pre-1997 collective identity, discursively constructed since the end of the Second World War, was most acutely felt by this middle generation after the handover. The hostility toward the young, individualistic 'other' is summed up as follows by the journalist Liang Lijuan:

> In this individualistic time, fewer and fewer cultural products attract common interest. It is harder and harder to build collective and shared memory. Mass media no longer attract a popular response especially among young people influenced by individualism who have no idea about the Hong Kong miracle, Hong Kong spirit. They have no interest in the traditional mass media.
>
> (2004)

Liang and other local writers discussed a shared, essential identity and collective memory that seemed to belong only to the middle generation, those who were most economically and culturally active during the transition period, and not to the 'individualistic' younger people. Traditional media decreased in importance around the time of and after the handover, but they were partly replaced by different media products and a new generation of stars who appealed to the young people in Hong Kong. The middle generation felt that the new stars lacked influence and that the shifting focus of media interest was a sign of the death of the Hong Kong identity. This generation therefore negotiated the differences in social relations and the symbolic marking between self and other through the stars.

The construction of the self and other in Hong Kong identity has often appeared ambiguous as the city has increasingly had to face the rising cultural power of one of its most important others, Mainland China. Hong Kong's relationship with China has seen successive changes and ruptures, such as those resulting from the

Cultural Revolution. In the 1970s, Hong Kong media, casting new Chinese immigrants as the other, often portrayed them as unsophisticated 'country bumpkins'
(Lilley 1993; Ma 1995). China's status as the other took on a more subtle form
during the 1990s, with the country's rising political, economic and cultural power
and the Hong Kong media's process of re-sinicization into the Greater Chinese
mediasphere. Popular songs in Hong Kong often demonstrate the ambiguities of
identity as they make reference to the quasi-national, while they also depoliticize
through their focus on everyday life. John Erni contends that although questions of cultural identity and social collectivity are rarely addressed in Cantopop
directly, it 'has ironically enabled a series of cultural surfaces upon which Hong
Kong's uniquely contradictory historical experience finds its own expression'
(2007, p.99). This appears contradictory, since representations of the 'everyday'
in Cantopop, seen in the songs of artistes including Sam Hui, Roman Tam and
James Wong, were a form of symbolic marking that suggested a powerful construction of cultural identity and social collectivity.[7]

Faced with the prospect of the 1997 handover and the subsequent reality of
integration into the Chinese state, it was natural for media professionals to consider what this change might mean for their identity. The director Fruit Chan is
best known for his independent productions such as the film *Made in Hong Kong*
(1997), which directly comments on the experiences of a group of young people
in Hong Kong around the time of the handover. He followed this with two more
films that centred on different experiences of 1997. *The Longest Summer* (1998)
deals with a group of Hong Kong soldiers who served in the British army and
were made redundant at the time of the handover, while *Little Cheung* (1999)
is a story about two children, one from Hong Kong, the other a mainland illegal
migrant. Chan started working in the film industry in Hong Kong in the 1980s,
directing two films during that decade. *Made in Hong Kong* was the first film for
which he achieved wide recognition. In his conversation with me, Chan was interested in the notion of the Hong Kong ideology and spirit, a theme that appeared
to dominate the aforementioned independent productions, with the three titles
becoming known collectively as the Handover Trilogy. Chan associated the loss
of a distinctive Hong Kong ideology with the city's new status as part of China:

> If Hong Kong does not have a local spirit (*jingshen*), then the whole society
> will change. Now our identity is confused. After the handover, we don't have
> a say. The society's economy, politics, even culture are slowly . . . becoming
> less distinctive, without a local ideology (*yishi*). Gradually, we're becoming
> just part of China, a province . . . When we make a film now, the first ques-
> tion is, 'Can you go to China to recoup the money?' If you try to cater for
> the Chinese market, you need to put Chinese elements in the script and use
> mainland actors for no good reason. So, this will weaken the local culture
>
> (24 August 2005)

To explain the media industry's decline, Chan considered not only economic
factors but also the demise of a distinctive essential Hong Kong identity since

the handover. In Fruit Chan's comment, Hong Kong ideology or spirit appears to be central in the creation of a distinctive society, and the inevitable rise in co-productions with Mainland China therefore confirmed what he saw as the weakening of the 'local characteristics'. His colleague Jimmy Choi, on the other hand, questioned the basis of a distinctive cultural identity:

> Hong Kong is part of China now but we haven't left the [colonial] burden behind. Shanghai, Shenzhen and Beijing are all parts of China. But they can make films with distinctive characteristics. The handover has affected us because we're willing to let it affect us.
>
> (24 August 2005)

Choi questioned the existence of a distinctive Hong Kong identity, although this was something the colonial government had promoted in order to support its developmental modernity project. China's rising political, economic and cultural power became the other in post-handover Hong Kong, and it is with this that the post-colonial Hong Kong self has had to reconcile.

One celebrity whose career appropriately demonstrates this confused identity is the influential Jackie Chan, the martial arts star who had a lengthy career in Hong Kong starting in the 1970s and who made several successful Hollywood films beginning in the 1990s. His post-handover career took on new dimensions that included a decrease in film output, increasing sinicization and a developing notoriety in Hong Kong. Chan's pre-2000s position in the public domain is summed up here:

> In Hong Kong Chan endows university scholarships and contributes to many other philanthropic causes, is regularly photographed posing with government officials at various ceremonial functions, has substantial business and real estate investments in the territory, and is handsomely paid to appear in local and regional advertisements for consumer goods. His winning grin is featured in television spots produced by the Hong Kong Tourist Association.
>
> (Fore 2001, pp.118–9)

Stars' social backgrounds are often articulated in media commentaries to particular generational experiences. Chan is described as 'a product – though not necessarily a very typical one – of Hong Kong's turbulent post-1949 era' (Fore 2001, p.127). His family background is well known; his parents, who were too poor to bring him up, placed him in a Peking Opera school for ten years. It was this opera training that enabled him to move into stunt work and martial arts film-making. While this description suggests Chan is an exemplar of the post-war Hong Kong generation, his recent attempts to become a 'Greater Chinese star' have challenged the established notion of a local, collective Hong Kong ethos.

In addition to Chan's star status in Hong Kong, he is also a global brand. Before his blockbuster successes in Hollywood, including *Rumble in the Bronx* (Stanley Tong, 1995), *Rush Hour* (Brett Ratner, 1998), *Shanghai Noon* (Tom Dey, 2000) and

Rush Hour 2 (Brett Ratner, 2001), he had made several failed attempts (for instance, *Cannonball Run II,* Hal Needham, 1984) to conquer Hollywood. In Hollywood, Chan teamed up with black sidekicks and partners in order to capture an African American market that had been historically interested in the 'chopsocky' films (1970s kung fu movies from Hong Kong following the craze for Bruce Lee as a global martial arts star) and the subsequent martial arts and action genres from Hong Kong. Steve Fore (1997, p.247) comments that the 'Chineseness' of Chan's persona in East Asia, where he was already a major star, was closely aligned with the cultural heritage and life experiences of the average moviegoer in the Asian region. Globally, however, Chan's persona was culturally deodorized, to use a phrase proffered by Iwabuchi Koichi (2002); even though he beats his mainly Western opponents, Chan's characters are harmless. In *Rumble in the Bronx,* the protagonist tells the gang of American thugs after defeating them, 'I hope that the next time we meet we can sit down and have tea together', diffusing racial tension with comic relief (Shu 2003). On other occasions, his Hollywood roles were no more than sidekicks to his white and African American co-stars, as in *Around the World in Eighty Days* (Frank Coraci, 2004). After becoming a transnational star, the ageing actor's output in Hollywood slowed down, but he utilized his global appeal in branding the cartoon series *Jackie Chan Adventures* for Kids WB (Warner Brothers) and Cartoon Network, as well as spin-off video games. He also voiced the character Monkey in *Kung Fu Panda* (Mark Osborne & John Stevenson, 2008), giving the film added credence as a martial arts animation and gaining the star an even wider young global audience.

Like many of his contemporaries, such as Chow Yun-fat, Chan re-immigrated in the early 2000s and began making Mandarin Chinese films, such as *The Myth* (Stanley Tong, 2005), and co-productions with mainland Chinese companies, including *The Forbidden Kingdom* (Rob Minkoff, 2008). Released in the year of the Beijing Olympics, the latter is an English-language film aimed at the global market, including Chinese territories. Chan was cast against the other Chinese heavyweight global star, Jet Li, and financiers included China Film Group and the successful private company, Huayi Brothers. Chan demonstrated his Chinese patriotism with a cameo role in *The Founding of a Republic* and by starring in the Sun Yat-sen biography, *1911* (Jackie Chan & Zhang Li, 2011); Sun is considered a national father by both the PRC and Taiwan. *CZ12* (2012), directed by and starring Chan, tells the story of a bounty hunter, JC (Chan's initials), trying to recover loot from British and French soldiers during the Second Opium War. After pressure from international activist groups to return a stolen dragon bronze to China, JC successfully recovers the relic in a dare-devil rescue mission. This veiled critique of colonialist expansion in nineteenth century China indicated Chan's efforts to become not only a local but a global and mainland Chinese hero. Even the mainly Hollywood production, *The Karate Kid* (Harald Zwart, 2010), was partially funded by China Film Group and could be mistaken for a long tourism promotion video, with locations including the Forbidden City and the Great Wall.

At times Chan has taken his status as the big brother of Hong Kong cinema and a patriotic Chinese star too far, developing a pro-China public persona reflected by his criticisms of the Taiwanese and Hong Kong governments. In 2004, the star publicly said that the Taiwanese presidential election was 'the biggest joke in the world', which angered not only the Taiwanese government and population but also residents in Hong Kong who were pro-democracy or otherwise valued the city's autonomy.[8] Chan also took an active part in the Beijing 2008 Olympic Games, one of the most visible soft-power triumphs of the PRC.[9] Chan reportedly dismissed pro-Tibet demonstrators against the torch relay as 'some naughty boys [who] just want to be on TV' (Wardrop 2008). He was the most prominent Hong Kong star to play a major role during the Olympics, including leading the theme song, *Beijing Welcomes You,* which was ubiquitous on Chinese and international media throughout the Games. The messages in the song and the promotional video combined traditional Chinese emblems such as the Great Wall with words like 'brand new', consistent with the overall campaign of branding the Beijing Olympics as an important event to welcome foreigners to a changed China and to show the world its important, 'real' cultural heritage (Latham 2009).

Chan's pro-China stance continued; in 2009, he spoke about Chinese people having too much freedom; 'I'm gradually beginning to feel that we Chinese need to be controlled', he said, this time annoying commentators from all three Chinas – Hong Kong, Taiwan and the PRC (Jacobs 2009). The Hong Kong Tourism Board received 164 complaints (Li 2013), and this was likely the reason why Chan has rarely been seen in the Board's campaigns in recent years. In December 2012, he once again came under criticism for stating that the Hong Kong administration should stipulate what people could protest about, directly challenging the freedom to protest that people in Hong Kong cherish. The recognition of his pro-China stance could be seen in his appointment to the political advisory body, the Chinese People's Political Consultative Conference (CPPCC) standing committee, in February 2013 (Cheung & Ng 2013).[10] Although the CPPCC did not have real political power, this was a symbolic moment in Chan's efforts to be a public figure in China. This development also occurred shortly after the release of *CZ12,* with its patriotic storyline, and the star's statement in an interview on Phoenix Television, a Hong Kong-based Mandarin cable channel, that the USA was the 'most corrupt' country (Bloomberg News 2013).

Although existing literature has focused on Hong Kong identity as part of the discussion of the handover in 1997, the cultural discourse of a collective ethos in support of a narrative of personal, societal and economic progress had been a colonial project since the post-war period (Grant 2001). Stars, as model individuals in their public support for collective and benevolent causes, had a role in cementing this ethos. The humble backgrounds of many of the earlier generations of stars were used as symbolic markers; their success was the result of diligence, and they embodied the 'Hong Kong spirit' associated with the mobility ideal. Subsequently, local critics claimed that the difference between their generation and the young, whose cultural pursuits appeared to be moving away from traditional media, signified the death of an essential Hong Kong identity. The sense of impending doom since the handover had more to do with the economic, social and cultural situation as reported by media professionals and cultural commentators than with changes in government. A crisis of confidence forged the discourse of an essential identity, manifested in the symbolic marking of 'we' and 'they', 'they' especially being the young who represented imagined differences and social divisions which the longstanding cultural discourse had tried hard to suppress. The rising economic and cultural power of China, Hong Kong's enduring other, brought new challenges. Jackie Chan, who had gained the status of a 'big brother' in Hong Kong in the 1980s and 1990s and succeeded in Hollywood (albeit under limited terms), became increasingly pro-China throughout the early 2000s. After re-immigrating to Hong Kong, Chan's popularity in his native city rapidly declined as he spoke out overtly against freedom of speech and the right to protest. Stars' efforts at re-sinicization, as in Chan's case, could therefore contradict their ability to represent the collective Hong Kong ideology. This chapter's case study, Anita Mui, who died in 2003 before the fervent re-sinicization of Hong Kong media, was constructed by media discourse as a worthy Hong Kong subject representing the imagined cultural golden age, further supporting my discussion of the discourse of identity.

Anita Mui: Image and the performer

Prior to the death of James Wong, there was already an extensive discourse in the early 2000s about the passing of the group of stars who emerged in the 1970s and 1980s, most prominently Leslie Cheung, who committed suicide in April 2003 (Figures 5.1 and 5.2), and Anita Mui, who died of cancer in December of the same year at the age of 40. In various newspaper articles, the deaths of Mui and Cheung were reported as the end of a chapter in the history of popular culture in Hong Kong. The writer Li Pik-wah (Lillian Lee) called Mui the 'Daughter of

Figure 5.1. A tribute to Leslie Cheung outside the Oriental Mandarin Hotel where he committed suicide, taken on 1 April 2011, marking the eighth anniversary of his death. © CC-Ding Yuin Shan.

Figure 5.2. A display of books and DVDs related to Leslie Cheung in a Beijing bookshop in 2013, marking the tenth anniversary of his death. © Leung Wing-Fai.

Hong Kong': '[She] went at 40. Even if we wait another ten, hundred years, there will not be another Anita Mui' (2004). The comment asserts the uniqueness of the star while suggesting that she embodied a Hong Kong identity as a daughter of the city. If Hong Kong is framed as the miraculous economic offspring of a marriage between Britain and China, then stars like Mui are symbolic representations of a particular generation, a chapter in the story of progress. The 'family' and 'growth' metaphors were extended to the assumption by the popular press of a mass audience, illustrated by this comment in *Sing Tao:* 'The death within a year of two entertainers who have accompanied the growing up of people in Hong Kong, Anita Mui and Leslie Cheung, touched many people' (Staff Reporters 2004, p.B7). The close relationship between the careers of the two stars and the 'growing up of people in Hong Kong' was assumed; they were then discursively articulated to a specific period in recent history at the perceived height of the importance of the post-war generation. After Mui's death, a member of the Legislative Council immediately suggested that the government should build a Museum of the Entertainment World in order to record the glorious history of the media industry.[11] Both Anita Mui and Leslie Cheung were held up as symbolic markers of Hong Kong worthy of the creation of an officially endorsed memorial at a time when there was widespread dissatisfaction about Hong Kong's economic performance and the government's political competence. This dissatisfaction was also partly a response to difficulties arising from the SARS epidemic, resulting in a mass public demonstration on 1 July 2003 that had a scale of popular support rarely seen since the riots of the 1950s and 1960s. The articulation of popular stars to a collective identity was a timely throwback to the discourse of progress and self-reliance that so successfully constructed the stereotypical Hong Kong *ren*.

Mui, who entered the entertainment industry by winning a song contest staged by TVB in 1982, remained primarily a singer, but she gradually built up a reputation as an actress and appeared in over 40 films. She cultivated her own support band made up of young male pop idols, whose budding singing careers she was supposed to have helped establish. These male idols, who were called her 'disciples' (*tudi*), appeared repeatedly in the tribute programmes after her death and were central figures at her funeral. They referred to Mui as *Mui Jie* or *Jie Jie* (older sister Mui or older sister). Leslie Cheung, on the other hand, was *ge ge* (older brother), a continuation of the family metaphor.

In the many media tributes to Mui in the days after her death, her success was attributed to her extraordinary performance skills and work ethic, indicating that she embodied the essential elements of a Hong Kong identity. This Hong Kong daughter was therefore a particularly powerful symbolic marker, an exemplar of the stars from the previous generation who were associated with a time period when the city was perceived to be at its peak. Mui's success supported the myth of social mobility. Her biography, widely circulated in the media, included her training in Cantonese opera at her single mother's opera school after her father died when she was still an infant. She also became a child performer in a theme park, an experience that supported the subsequent discourse about her performance skills and long commitment to the stage.

Mui was called the 'Queen of Pop', a term suggesting her status as the matriarch of the media industry. Mui's personal relationships were reported in the media, but she never married, a fact she attributed to her not being pretty enough and too masculine for most men (from an interview in 1990, *Forever Remembrance: Anita Mui* 2004). In 1992 she 'retired' from live performance but 'returned' four years later.[12] She sold more than 10 million units from her discography of over 40 albums, played more than 300 concerts, and won over 30 music awards during her career. In 1991 she broke all Asian records by playing 28 consecutive nights at the Hong Kong Coliseum, the city's premier venue with 12,500 seats (Witzleben 1999). In late 2003, despite undergoing chemotherapy for her illness, the tireless Mui planned to appear in a series of sold-out concerts in November, signed an advertising contract with a beauty salon and started the shooting of the film *House of Flying Daggers*. She was unable to fulfil the contract or finish the filming. The ten concerts in November 2003 were reduced to three.

Her public image changed frequently throughout her career; in the 1980s Anita Mui promoted the image of a 'bad girl' after a hit song of the same title, a cover version of *Strut* by Sheena Easton with a disco dance beat. *Bad Girl* was branded 'spiritual pollution' by Chinese officials because its lyrics depict sexual desire, but Mui still performed it during a series of 35 concerts on the Mainland in 1995, indicative of her image as a strong rebellious woman who was not afraid to challenge authority (Fung & Curtin 2002).[13] This anti-Chinese authority move would not have been wise were Mui still alive today, with the importance of the mainland market to most Hong Kong pop stars. She was known for her 'hundred changes',[14] a reference to the extraordinary number of costume changes during her concerts, and for being Hong Kong's Madonna because of her multiple star images. William So Wing-hong (b.1967), one of her 'disciples', commented, 'Before Mui, no one talked about image in the pop industry . . . she started it' (*Forever Remembrance: Anita Mui* 2004); therefore, like later multimedia idols, Mui's career was characterized by ever-changing images. Yet the star's reliance on image-making as a transparent practice was not considered in the media discourse as a simulacrum. Instead, in the many televised tributes to her during the days after her death (*Forever Remembrance: Anita Mui* 2004; *Anita Mui and Friends* 2003; *In Memory of Anita Mui* 2004), the common themes were her extraordinary performance skills and descriptions of her as 'a natural performer', being 'married to the stage', and 'a true professional', asserted mainly by her colleagues and disciples. Her comments on her own illness in late 2003 perpetuated the idea of her being a natural-born performer: 'I will fight this battle. I am a professional performer. Every time you see me, I will be in high spirits' (*Anita Mui and Friends* 2003). During her final series of concerts in November 2003, one of the many costumes was a wedding dress that famously denoted that Mui was still 'married to the stage' despite her terminal illness. Even though Mui's career was about image-making, her success was asserted to be the result of her extraordinary performance skills and work ethic, and she was therefore considered an embodiment of the essential Hong Kong identity.

Mui's multimedia performance skills were seen in her acting career in roles that demonstrated a diverse repertoire. In *Rouge* (Stanley Kwan, 1988), she played a 1930s courtesan returning to contemporary Hong Kong as a female ghost, a role that won her the Best Actress Award at the Hong Kong Film Awards and the Taiwan Golden Horse Awards. Later films saw her play more mature characters, such as the unhappy wives in *Midnight Fly* (Jacob Cheung, 2001) and *July Rhapsody* (Ann Hui, 2001). Because of the limited presence of an art cinema or other non-mainstream media practices in Hong Kong, Mui, like other film actors, worked mostly in commercial cinema. Despite gaining awards for roles in films like *Rouge,* her film stardom was based on largely stereotypical parts, including many comic characters, within entertainment genre films. In her later films, Mui's Queen of Pop persona was directly employed, as with the enigmatic singer she played in *Who's the Woman, Who's the Man?* (Peter Chan, 1996). The self-referential nature of the narrative is reflected by the character's name, Fong Yim Mui, the reversal of her Chinese name, Mui Yim Fong.

In contrast with other younger idols whose images were considered simulacra, Mui was discursively constructed as someone who deserved her rags-to-riches success. All the participants, including many work colleagues, disciples and friends, in the aforementioned televised tributes after Mui's death were keen to claim privileged personal knowledge that showed that she deserved their respect.

Aside from the diligence and professionalism associated with Mui as a successful singer-actress, her humble upbringing was an element of the discourse of her multimedia stardom that further defined Mui as a representative star with a unique, specifically local background rooted in post-war Hong Kong. John Sham (b.1952), an actor-producer in Hong Kong, explained why Mui's upbringing contributed to perceptions of her as an authentic performer: 'It is her background. She could see the suffering' (*Forever Remembrance: Anita Mui* 2004). The notion that suffering leads to good performance might seem intriguing if not for my previous discussion of the importance of life experience and arduous training as elements of stardom in Hong Kong.

The authenticity of her performances came from her suffering and childhood hardship, as with many of the older generation of stars; there is a perception that the pre-1997 generation, including Anita Mui and Chow Yun-fat, would not be such great stars without their poverty-stricken upbringings. In the 1970s and 1980s, young people who wanted a career alternative to further education could enter song contests or the acting classes run by the local television stations and then strive to become successful performers. Tao Jie even calls Chow Yun-fat the 'last real man on the Hong Kong screen', claiming that the public estates and apartment blocks of subsequent decades were no longer environments that created 'men with substance' (2004, pp.143–5). The 1970s and 1980s stars are therefore particularly potent metaphors for Hong Kong's collective identity as an island that grew from fishing villages to an urban metropolis through commercial success, while many young stars of the early 2000s, coming from more comfortable, middle-class backgrounds, are not regarded as desperate for success.[15]

Anita Mui is a prominent example of a star from the previous generation who has been discursively constructed to be a representative of that age; her death signified the passing of an era and her performance skills are held up and admired. Mui's disadvantaged background resonates with the post-war social history of the city and adds to the concept that good performance has to be achieved through diligence and professionalism. In these discussions, Anita Mui is presented as the true authentic star who embodied an essential local identity of a cultural golden age. This successful Hong Kong daughter was a particularly powerful symbol of social mobility, and she was qualitatively different from the younger, more affluent generation. The fact that many of the younger stars have come from the newly emerged middle class is seen as an indication that they are not desperate for success, unlike the more authentic Hong Kong stars who grew up in post-war hardship and emerged in the 1970s and 1980s. The discourse surrounding the stars is a continuation of the cultural discourse that began in the late 1940s, resurrected at a time of economic, political and social crisis in the early 2000s. The notion of identity in modern society has become increasingly complex, often underpinned by relations to others marked by difference; therefore the assertion of a communal notion of identity associated with a generation of stars and articulated to pre-handover Hong Kong demonstrates a long-term project seeking the meaning of the authentic self.

Nostalgia for the subject in Hong Kong

Intense discussion regarding the demise of Hong Kong culture in the 2000s was often sparked by the death of stars who had emerged when local mass media was at its height. Anita Mui was seen as representative of Hong Kong's 'collective spiritual capital', as were a group of similarly revered stars including Danny Chan (1958–93), Roman Tam, Wong Ka-kui and Leslie Cheung (Tao Jie 2004, pp.21–3).[16] Though the Museum of the Entertainment World was never built, a stamp set honouring these five stars was issued by the Hong Kong Post Office in November 2005, signalling their importance in the recent history of the city.

The idea of an authentic identity associated with pre-1997 Hong Kong demonstrates a will to assert a dominant world-view and a continuous cultural history. The discourse on the previous generation of multimedia stars was connected to a past imagined as more unified and collective. Nostalgia is a yearning for an origin, sometimes one that is imagined: 'Nostalgia is most commonly understood as the sentiment of homesickness, which may extend into a tendency to reminisce about old times or to romanticize what happened in the irretrievable past' (Chow 1999, p.33). Nostalgia, seen in many media forms, was part of the construction of a continuous narrative of progress. Eric Ma's (2001) study of a television commercial for the Hong Kong and Shanghai Bank in 1995 is a case in point. The commercial featured the story of a fisherman and his family in nostalgic black and white:

> Although the history of Hong Kong represented in the TV commercial is highly selective, the text is produced and consumed with a strong commitment to modernist ideas of progress and factual historicity. On a microlevel, these nostalgic practices of textual production and consumption are also regulated by the strong social desire for continuity at a time of extraordinary change.
>
> (Ma 2001, p.132)

By locating the story alongside major events in modern Hong Kong history and showing how the poor family survived, the commercial historicized the development of the city from a collection of poor fishing villages to a cosmopolitan metropolis. The protagonist's declaration, 'Don't depend on the sky, depend on yourself', was another example of the propagation of the myth of the Hong Kong dream and the 'macro-history' of miraculous growth that paradoxically leaves out the uneven development and exploitation of many social groups, including the original farming and fishing communities. Similarly, nostalgia for the past success of local popular media featured strongly in the discourse surrounding stardom in post-handover Hong Kong. Chan Pak-sun, the editor of *City Entertainment,* exemplified this nostalgia:

> In the 1960s and 1970s, the sense of distance between stars and audiences was wide. The stars were a class above and you could only see them on screen. It was very difficult to see stars in real life unless you went to really classy

places like the Peninsula Hotel. Now stars are everywhere on the streets, so I don't think they are real [stars].

(11 April 2005)

'Stars are not how they used to be' is a well-rehearsed sentiment. Chan perpetuated the idea that the earlier generations of stars were models of a consumer culture, living a lifestyle that could be aspired to by all and yet was beyond the reach of ordinary audiences. Chan's comments have to be understood in the context of his personal history as the founder of the city's (then) only film magazine and its editor for nearly three decades. In the interview he discussed how the decline of local cinema had deeply affected the survival of the magazine. The closing of the magazine in 2007 after 28 years symbolized the crisis of identity experienced in post-colonial Hong Kong for Chan, and explained his sense of nostalgia. For Chan's generation, coming of age and wielding cultural power in the 1980s and 1990s caused them to believe that an essential identity, often in an abstract form, stemmed from that era, as 'to grapple with the real, present-day political and other reasons [is] why essentialist identities continue to be invoked and are often deeply felt' (Calhoun 1994, p.14). My discussion therefore focuses on the world-view of a particular generation of media professionals and commentators that should be seen as a micro-narrative about a collective Hong Kong identity.

The middle generation's nostalgia as a yearning for an essential identity was associated with an earlier period in Hong Kong's history because 'being true to one's self, possessing depth of character, and searching for one's identity all become old-fashioned phrases; they are nicely suited to earlier times but no longer profitable' (Gergen 2000, p.208). People in Hong Kong from a vague past before the handover were assumed to be more like self-determined, unified subjects; they did not passively accept media products dominated by the young, who were qualitatively different and inferior to their predecessors. It is this nostalgia for the subject with an essential identity that unites the generation who experienced the changes in Hong Kong since the 1970s.

Concluding remarks

The media in the early 2000s saw the death of aura twice, firstly through the literal death of stars as an embodiment of Hong Kong identity and secondly through the death of a glorious era of pre-1997 local culture. This assertion of a unified identity articulated to a generation of stars has to be understood with reference to the practices and discourse of multimedia stardom that are specific to the cultural and social contexts of Hong Kong.

The middle generation in Hong Kong are sceptical about contemporary stardom, while no doubt is expressed about the professional performer status of stars from a previous generation in inter-media commentaries or by cultural critics who shared the experience of a unique time in the city's recent history, namely the transition period (the early 1980s to 1997) and the handover of Hong Kong. Entertainers like Anita Mui are markers of an authentic self as the archetypical

Hong Kong *ren* because they embody both meanings of the Chinese word: the individual, and the communal and benevolent self. The humble backgrounds of many of the earlier generations of stars explain why they are symbolic markers; their success was the result of diligence, and they embody the 'Hong Kong spirit' associated with the mobility ideal. The fact that many of the newer stars have come from the newly emerged middle class is an indication that they are not desperate for success like the more authentic Hong Kong stars who grew up in post-war hardship and emerged in the 1970s and 1980s.

Stars are symbolic in the marking of differences that distinguish between a constructed identity and imagined others. In the 1970s and 1980s, the stars who featured in the front rooms of numerous viewers before crossing media from television to film and pop music had an unprecedented sense of familiarity for that generation of local audiences, as indigenous media masked the cultural and ethnic differences that characterized the immigrants, refugees and Hong Kong natives before this time. Since the 1990s the mass media has lost the popular appeal it once enjoyed. The media landscape has moved into new fields, including video games, karaoke, the Internet and mobile technology, signalling the emergence of social groups such as the young and an increasing necessity to cater for external markets, especially Mainland China. Local critics claim that the difference between their generation and the young, whose cultural pursuits appear to have moved away from traditional media, signifies the death of an essential Hong Kong identity. The sense of impending doom in the early 2000s had less to do with changes in government than with perceptions of the economic, social and cultural situation by media professionals and cultural commentators. Additionally, the crisis in confidence forged the discourse of an essential identity, manifesting in the symbolic marking of a 'we' and 'they' and responding to the imagining of social differences and divisions that the government-endorsed cultural discourse had tried hard to suppress. As stars have left Hong Kong to pursue careers elsewhere, first in Hollywood and more recently via re-immigration to work on mainland Chinese productions, the strong connection between local stars and a collective identity has been challenged. In the case of Jackie Chan, his campaign to succeed in the PRC has drawn negative reactions from audiences in other countries and cultural critics in his native city, especially when he began to comment on political freedom and autonomy in a mediasphere that had been hitherto largely apolitical.

The disruption of the cultural, social, and political lives of those who experienced the transition period and post-handover Hong Kong explains the prominence of a discourse of an imagined identity suggesting collectivity. The discourse of stardom in Hong Kong attempts to recuperate the aura of the earlier era against the 'phoney spell' of the personality (Benjamin 1936, p.231) circulated in the mediasphere. Respected stars are able to galvanize communal effort through civic education without politicizing social and cultural issues, asserting qualities such as work and diligence as part of a unified, collective Hong Kong identity. This essential identity is assigned to the previous generation of stars as representatives of the recent history of Hong Kong, especially those who experienced post-war hardship, while widely-seen young stars are felt to lack the diligence, professionalism and drive to succeed through personal effort. The discourse of stardom therefore perpetuates the myth of the Hong Kong dream of social mobility based on work ethic. While existing writing on Hong Kong identity focuses on the effects of the handover, this search for a unified society has been a long-term modernity project since the Second World War, when a cultural discourse, endorsed by official policies, engendered an apolitical, hard-working Hong Kong *ren*.

Since the idea of the individual as an essential self may be under attack in contemporary society (Laclau & Mouffe 1985; Laclau 1990), nostalgia for the true subject is central to the discourse of stardom in Hong Kong, in that the relational character of social identities must be limited by their inclusion in an essential and coherent view of the object-world. The discourse about media stars, therefore, is also a debate about an object-world that should have a shared internal essence resembling an identity. 'Individuals incorporate [symbolic forms] into their own understanding of themselves and others. They use them as a vehicle for reflection and self-reflection, as a basis for thinking about themselves, about others and about the world to which they belong' (Thompson 1995, p.42). In order to explain the changing fortunes of the media industry, continuity with the past is discursively constructed by those who see themselves as vanguards of a distinctive Hong Kong identity. Associated with this vague past is a fixed, essential Hong Kong identity, to which the authentic stars from the 1980s and 1990s are articulated as symbolic markers. This nostalgia for the subject manifested itself at a time when Hong Kong seemed most vulnerable economically, socially and politically. Paradoxically, this assertion of a communal identity highlights the proliferation of cultural and social differences since the 1990s. Ien Ang argues:

> Any identity of a 'culture', a 'society', and any other social entity ('nation', 'ethnicity', 'gender', 'audience', 'the people', and so on) is merely the conjunctural articulation of constantly changing positionalities, a precarious positivity formed out of a temporary fixation of meaning within the capitalist world-system.
>
> (1996, p.176)

The 1980s generation of multimedia stars in Hong Kong, despite their divided public selves, held the individual and the collective together in the early 2000s, articulating a fixed and seemingly one-dimensional cultural identity. The notion of identity in Hong Kong as constructed through stardom is part of an ongoing cultural discourse that refuses to recognize the cultural, social, personal, national, ethnic, political and economic differences which all contribute to the shaping of identity. The longstanding cultural discourse of a unified ethos constructed Hong Kong before 1997 as 'one of the few places in the modern world that fostered a strong local culture without a nationalistic discourse' (Ma 2001, p.154). The strong tradition of stardom in Hong Kong and its widespread influence in Asia and beyond has allowed stars to become depoliticized and apolitical, 'quasi-national' symbols for an imagined community (Anderson 1983). In response to the re-emergence of social and cultural differences since the mid-1990s, the discourse of stardom has become central in a philosophical debate about a return to the Hong Kong subject, with respected stars viewed as exemplary individuals and embodiments of an essential identity. This Hong Kong identity perpetuates the myth of social mobility and influences the discourse on how individuals should behave in a late capitalist society.

Conclusions
Stardom in and beyond Hong Kong

In this book I argue that the practices and discourse of multimedia stardom in Hong Kong are unique. Stardom is influenced by and is a major component of the popular culture and social landscapes of the city. In particular, my analysis moves away from a textual approach to individual stars to an embrace of the cultural and sociological significance of stardom, that is, the conditions that gave rise to these famous individuals in their specific culture and society. Through this study I demonstrate the importance of multimedia stardom as part of the 'cultural Chinese' mediasphere in both historical and contemporary contexts. In addition, I elaborate the distinction between multimedia stardom and celebrity, and assert that the former in Hong Kong has been central in the production and consumption of many aspects of popular culture. Multimedia stardom is distinguishable from celebrity in that it is a concept related to a range of cultural productions, while celebrity relates to fame and the quality of being well-known, even though stars by nature are notable individuals. The concept of multimedia stardom highlights the contradictions and similarities between stardom and celebrity, namely the rise of new media and new forms of image-making, the expectation of stars' performance-as-work by 'invested audiences' (Marshall 2006, p.316), and stars' ability to reflect a collective identity while commenting on how individuals should behave in public.

Hong Kong at the beginning of the 1980s witnessed the rising anticipation of the handover in 1997, which continued to affect the social, political and personal lives of the residents throughout the transition period, particularly in their search for a distinctive identity. The search for collectivity during the transition period sought to maintain the cultural discourse endorsed by the post-war government that had attempted to construct a unified society in response to political and social divisions. The emergence in the 1970s of commercially successful and prolific indigenous cultural productions in cinema, pop music and terrestrial television was due to the coming of age of a generation who were born and bred in the city and formed a mass market for media products. The indigenization of popular culture in the 1970s was reflected in the media, especially television, film and pop music, which became the cultural forms that Abbas suggests were about 'the cultural self-invention of the Hong Kong subject in . . . a space of disappearance' (1996, p.1).

A central feature of the historical development of the popular media in Hong Kong is stars' permeation of various popular cultural forms. Hong Kong stars have always traversed different media, with a multifarious and often simultaneous existence in the entertainment press, advertising, Cantonese opera films, the martial arts genre, musicals and as recording artists. From the 1970s onwards, the emergence and maintenance of stars in Hong Kong were closely related to the popularity of television, cinema and pop music. The interlocking relationship between these media in the 1970s and 1980s capitalized on the mass audiences' familiarity with television, making this medium a main source of multimedia stardom. As stars moved between media, this familiarity was fluidly employed in the building of their popularity. The mass market for these media and for multimedia stars during the 1980s and early 1990s explains the continued reverence for this previous generation of stars. Although stars from the 1980s and early 1990s were still able to capture the attention of adult audiences at the beginning of the millennium, new cultural and leisure activities and a group of multimedia idols aimed at the youth market began to crowd the Hong Kong entertainment world. The difficulties facing the traditionally successful media since the mid-1990s were tied to changes in leisure and the reorganization of the everyday lives of people in the city, from which emerged a more diverse range of media productions, a fragmented marketplace and an urgent need to cater for other markets, especially the Mainland.

Increasing tension between Mainland China and Hong Kong after 1997, despite closer economic, social and cultural ties, came from the latest wave of immigrants – the 'other' – and potential threats to the continuation of the local way of life. There has been a close and unique relationship between stardom in China and Hong Kong from both historical and contemporary perspectives. Since the handover in 1997, the media industries in Hong Kong and China have become increasingly integrated, and this book pays particular attention to how stars from the former colony have adapted to the wider Chinese market, such as by participating in Asian film and television co-productions that involved the Mainland. Hong Kong stars' participation in the 2008 Beijing Olympics, a major triumph for China's international soft-power strategy, epitomizes the re-sinicization of these famous individuals. To become Greater Chinese patriotic celebrities, many of the multimedia Hong Kong stars have had to de-emphasize what contributes to their popularity in the local market. Jackie Chan's outspoken pro-China stance contradicts the 'big brother' status he earned in Hong Kong during the 1980s and 1990s. In Chan's case, his campaign to succeed in the PRC has drawn negative reactions from audiences and cultural critics in his native city and in other Chinese diasporic communities, especially when he commented on political freedom and autonomy in a Hong Kong mediasphere that had been largely apolitical.

The central themes of image, performance and identity addressed in this book enable a discussion of multimedia stardom under the influence of these specific historical junctures. As the traditional media has declined, the previous generation of stars has lost many of the work opportunities they had in the 1980s, and their commercial survival has become more reliant on appearances in the printed press and advertising that continue to rely on the stars' cross-media existence. The criticism that younger idols lack substance often focuses on their commodification as simulacra without real qualities. The Edison Chen scandal demonstrated how new means of telecommunications have changed how entertainment news is produced and consumed. My professional contacts have responded to the perceived lack of depth of manufactured stars through the practice of clawback, whereby an attempt is made to regain credibility through reasserting the importance of skills and of stars as representations of collective values.

I assert that there has been a unique tradition in the practices of performance in Hong Kong and that the surrounding discourse is part of a collective strategy of clawback. Most actors have been trained informally, especially through on-the-job training in television, and cultural critics have suggested a distinctive Hong Kong style of acting emphasizing televisual aesthetics, seen especially through a reliance on facial expressions. Pop singers perform and interpret pre-existing songs but are not expected to display individual creative talent, another distinctive facet of Hong Kong stardom. Reverence for multimedia stars who can perform numerous spectacular concerts and are also known to be able actors is evidence that the notion of performance skills in Hong Kong is associated with traditional Chinese opera and its multiple required skills. Many stars from the 1970s and 1980s generation have been able to endure and earn recognition for their skills after years of working in the media industry, as life experience and hard work are also perceived as vital for the acquisition of performance skills within the specific discourse connected to Chinese theatrical arts. The fact that cultural production and consumption in Hong Kong in the early 2000s had moved towards immaterial goods such as the creation of image has conjured up anxiety in a society built on the social mobility myth. Therefore, the discourse on stardom in Hong Kong continues to assume the possession of artistic skills among the previous generation of stars.

Another concept central to this discussion is that of identity as a collective notion, a feature that distinguishes stardom in Hong Kong from Western conceptualizations of celebrity, which place primary social meaning on the ability to express individualism. Identity is a concept that allows a set of problems to emerge (Hall 1996), thus enabling me to demonstrate how stars and their presence across media create a set of questions related to the changing constitution and recognition of cultural subjects. Stars are symbolic markers adopted as unofficial symbols of the city and individual representatives of a Hong Kong identity that resonates with notions of collective effort and the social mobility ideal associated with a longstanding modernity project. With Hong Kong under economic and social pressures and media practices moving into new fields of operation, the post-1990s generation of young stars and their fans are seen to be indicative of the fragmentation of the mass society, as they fail to exemplify the rags to riches Hong Kong dream. At the same time, the Hong Kong media industry has had to increasingly rely on collaborations with Mainland China as the latter's cultural, economic and political power has grown. As the cultural and social landscapes have continued to evolve since the mid-1990s, evident in the changing practices of multimedia stardom, an imagined collective identity articulated to the previous generation of stars is the result of nostalgia for the golden age of pre-handover Hong Kong and its mass society. In the discourse of Hong Kong identity, stardom remains a symbolic marker through which social and cultural differences are temporarily fixed for a return of the essential subject and to foster a coherent world-view that differentiates the self and the other. Multimedia stardom in Hong Kong is a specific set of practices, the development of which is embedded in unique social and cultural contexts: multimedia stardom in the city is a form of image-making associated with a distinctive discourse of performance and a symbolic marker in the discursive construction of a collective identity.

While this book has focused on multimedia stardom in the domestic market and its changing relationship with Mainland China, stars from the city have also been part of international popular culture, and their works are widely circulated among and consumed by the Chinese diaspora. However, multimedia stars from Hong Kong are often caught between international and local-regional contexts in a paradoxical way. Non-Chinese audiences know very little of these stars' work outside of film; Cantonese and Mandarin pop is virtually unknown to most Western listeners; the stars' appearance on television is usually of interest only to Chinese-speaking communities; and they rarely appear in entertainment magazines or commercials outside of Asia. Nonetheless, a cursory consideration of the few significant Hong Kong stars in the international mediasphere reveals the uniqueness of the stardom emerging from the city while communicating something about an imaginary Cultural China. Lo Kwai-cheung characterizes Chineseness in Hollywood cinema as 'an empty concept without a specific ethnic object', and in Hong Kong film as 'an ethnic object without a proper concept of Chinese national identity' (2005, p.136). This serves as a starting point for considering the role Hong Kong stars play in global popular culture, as they act as symbolic markers of Chineseness and represent the discourses on ethnic and national identities to diverse producers and consumers across different times and markets.

Bruce Lee, arguably the most famous Hong Kong actor, achieved transnational stardom long before the temporal focus of this book. Lee was born in San Francisco in 1940, but his parents were from Hong Kong and Lee returned there while still a child. His father was a Cantonese opera star, and Lee became a child actor in several local films before moving back to the USA at the age of 18, where he attended college and began his martial arts career. He acted in film and television, his most famous role being that of Kato in *The Green Hornet* television series (1966–7), but the lack of opportunities in the US prompted him to return to Hong Kong.[1] The five kung fu films he made in Hong Kong between 1971 and 1973 and his premature death brought him worldwide fame. The amount of academic and popular literature on the stardom of Lee demonstrates his legacy and importance, and more recent debates have focused on the proliferation of Bruce Lee-inspired 'clones' (Bruceploitation, to use Brian Hu's [2008] neologism) and the posthumous documentaries that keep on appearing. The stardom of Bruce Lee demonstrates precisely Lo Kwai-cheung's above-cited argument; the abstract nationalism in his most popular films, a reaction against racism (Teo 1997, p.113), allowed him to break out of the ethnic ghettoization of Asian actors in Hollywood and carve out a brand of Chineseness that could be appropriated by different audiences at different times. Hu's (2008) article on Bruceploitation, for instance, discusses how this brand of Chineseness has been hijacked by Asian Americans to interrogate Asian-ness.

Lee, despite being the most famous Hong Kong star, did not initially escape the Hollywood practice of conflating Asian-ness, in which East Asian actors were employed as arbitrary others, with little recognition of the subtle differences between ethnic and national identities. This conflation continues today even with prominent Asian actors in Hollywood, as shown by the discussions of the American careers of Chow Yun-fat (Chapter 2) and Jackie Chan (Chapter 5) in this book. The Beijing-born Jet Li has been correctly identified as the first post-Mao superstar (Farquhar 2010), but most of his film career was developed in Hong Kong and then transnationally in Hollywood. Li's career, from national *wushu* champion to international star, via Hong Kong, demonstrates the important long-term connection between media in Mainland China and Hong Kong. Li's career trajectory was rather different from those of the Hong Kong stars of the 1980s. The young Jet Li assumed the role of a national treasure and soft-power export when, as China's *wushu* champion, he performed martial arts for national and international political leaders (Farquhar 2010). Initially known for his authentic martial arts skills, the film that solidified Li's fame was the early China-Hong Kong co-production *Shaolin Temple* (Chang Hsin-yen, 1982), the first martial arts film made since the ban by the Republicans in 1931.

It is important to note that many Hong Kong stars were known in Hollywood only for film acting and participated in a relatively small number of genres, especially action and martial arts.[2] Shu Yuan states, 'Action as performance and performance as action have indeed become the language of Kung Fu cinema' (2003, p.54).[3] The adaptation of their star image to cater for the American market was clear. When Jackie Chan first tried to conquer Hollywood, with films such as *The Big Brawl* (Robert Clouse, 1980) and the *Cannonball Run* films (1981, 1984), American producers regarded him as nothing but a standard kung fu star and created films that were popular neither in the USA nor Asia. Chan did not try the American market again until the mid-1990s, with *Rumble in the Bronx*. Although Shu (2003) suggests that kung fu films changed the Hollywood market, it can also be argued that the stardom of Jackie Chan and the success of other Hong Kong actors in the American film industry has always been the result of negotiation. Chan's roles in Hollywood movies are de-sexualized, and his American sidekicks provide both comic relief (for example, Owen Wilson) and a hook for specific target audience groups (for instance, Chris Tucker for the African American market). In other words, no matter how big a star Chan was in Asia, he could not be relied upon to be the sole lead in American films.

The re-migration into the Asian film industries during the early 2000s of stars such as Chow Yun-fat and Jackie Chan exemplifies a new breed of transnational star able to appear in both Hollywood productions and Chinese-language films. The re-migration of these stars has also helped them reconnect to their multimedia stardom that originated from Hong Kong. Chinese-language films have typically offered a more varied and diverse range of roles. Chow worked with the director Ann Hui in *The Story of Woo Viet* and *Love in a Fallen City* in the 1980s. In 2006, the two were reunited in a tragic-comedy, *The Postmodern Life of My Aunt* (Figure 6.1), the kind of dramatic role that is not usually available to Hong Kong stars beyond Chinese-language cinema.

Notwithstanding the success of these global stars, other Hong Kong stars have succeeded only in Chinese-speaking territories. Miriam Yeung, the case study in Chapter 3, has acted mainly in comedies and is not as transnational as the stars mentioned above. It can therefore be argued that some film genres are more locally specific, and the case of Yeung also suggests that the stardom of actresses from Hong Kong is less translatable to non-Chinese audiences than that of male stars. This is partly due to the fact that, other than films, few star-products, such as television, pop music, commercials and entertainment news, are exported beyond Chinese and Asian communities. Maggie Cheung, however, is an exception in many ways. Although she came from a background in beauty contests and acted in many formulaic popular films in the 1980s, she later began to be associated with New Wave directors and art cinema, such as Ann Hui's *Song of the Exile* (1990), Wong Kar-wai's *Days of Being Wild* and Stanley Kwan's *Actress,* the latter winning her the Best Actress Award at the Berlin Film Festival. These and other collaborations with Wong Kar-wai, including *In the Mood for Love* (2000),

Figure 6.1 Chow Yun-fat as an ageing dandy in the tragi-comic film *The Postmodern Life of My Aunt* (Ann Hui, 2006). Reproduced with kind permission from Qinxinran.

solidified Cheung's international stardom. Although the actress also began to appear in transnational productions in the mid-1990s, including *Irma Vep* (Olivier Assayas, 1996) (see An 2000; Hudson 2006), *Chinese Box* (Wayne Wang, 1997), *Augustin, King of Kung-Fu* (Anne Fontaine, 1999) and *Clean* (Olivier Assayas, 2004), her destination was not mainstream Hollywood but independent and French (co-)productions, to the extent that a *New York Times* critic asked, 'Why isn't Maggie Cheung a Hollywood star?' (Dominus 2004). Felicia Chan (2014) considers how Cheung's roles in her two film collaborations with Assayas, who was her husband from 1998 to 2001, relate to her star image and to constructions of Chineseness. My assertion of Cheung's uniqueness among Hong Kong stars is illustrated by *Clean,* in which Cheung plays the cosmopolitan, cross-border, rock-star widow Emily Wang. While Chan questions whether Maggie Cheung was 'playing herself' in the role of Emily Wang, as the star and Assayas asserted, the role won her the Best Actress Award at the Cannes Film Festival; she was the first Asian actress to do so. Cheung's transnational multi-lingualism enabled her to become internationally recognized, in contrast to most of her female con-temporaries. Furthermore, with the exception of *Hero,* Cheung made less of an effort than her fellow Hong Kong stars to appear in mainland Chinese productions. Cheung's international stardom demonstrates more about the relationships between European art and independent cinema and Hollywood than about Hong Kong stars as symbolic markers of ethnic and national identities. Though she has made few films since *Clean,* Cheung can be considered a Hong Kong star who has carved out a unique brand of transnational stardom through her international career.

Since the 1950s and 1960s, the cosmopolitan life of Hong Kong has been reflected by its cinema and embodied by its famous stars (Desser 2014). The stars also represent the paradoxes; citizens feel a sense of loyalty to the city but they also have a sense of the world (Appiah 2006). The Hong Kong Tourism Board continues to emphasize the cosmopolitanism and cultural fusion of the city by branding it 'Asia's World City'. This makes Hong Kong stars eminently suitable to be cast in the transnational film productions that are part of Hollywood's recent bid to capture the domestic Asian American market, audiences in the Asia Pacific, and even the global film market. However, such a role could lead to stars being seen as interlopers, as with Jackie Chan, who was embraced as a representative of Hong Kong until his strategy of re-sinicization, described in Chapter 5, alienated the public of his native city.

Throughout this book I assert the importance of multimedia stardom within the popular culture and social landscapes in Hong Kong, as well as the increasing popularity of Hong Kong stars in China and internationally. The book is the result of ten years of empirical research into the media in Hong Kong, during which time I gained privileged access to 33 media practitioners, stars, critics and other key contacts. My interviews gave them a voice not often heard in existing writing on the media in Hong Kong. I have also relied on extensive historical materials, often in under-researched areas such as the discourse of performance and the enduring influence of Cantonese opera, to build on already existing knowledge about the entertainment industry. The robust primary and secondary datasets from a wide range of sources demonstrate the depth and scope of the research that led to this book. Empirical research into media producers, performers and cultural critics has not been the mainstay of methods in the disciplines of media, especially film studies, to which star studies are closely aligned. This book represents the first substantive research focusing on stardom as a symbolic form in understanding the notion of Hong Kong identity. No previous book-length publication exists in English concerning stardom in Hong Kong, and comparatively little has been written about post-1997 Hong Kong media, in contrast to the level of interest in the British colony before the handover. More than an analysis of films as a direct allegory of Hong Kong's relationship to the question of handover, this monograph examines the city's cultural forms and social contexts with a wide scope in terms of both the spectrum of media practices included and temporal span.

The research contained in this monograph contributes to existing knowledge within star, film, media, and regional studies. In particular, star studies tend to be dominated by Hollywood examples and focus on examining image and film texts without reference to their production and consumption, and few studies explore the multimedia nature of contemporary stardom. In contrast I present historically and culturally specific research about Hong Kong and argue that multimedia stardom is central to a whole spectrum of contemporary cultural practices that must be analysed through an exploration of the contexts from which they emerge. As multimedia stardom has been a longstanding and central, albeit changing, media practice in Hong Kong, I focus in this book on this unique feature and argue for its cultural and social significance when explored within the discussions of image, performance, and identity.

I argue that the characteristics of multimedia stardom illustrate that the centrality of film in star studies is often over-emphasized in existing writing, and I point out the need to re-evaluate the relationships between a spectrum of media and stardom. The multimedia nature of stardom has only been recently recognized in Euro-American star studies, and it is sometimes subsumed under the concept of celebrity. In this book I shed light on how elements within the discipline of star studies are appropriate for the analysis of multimedia stardom, but I challenge the existing demarcation between the understanding of film stars only within film at the expense of an understanding of their participation in other media, which will be a useful contribution to star studies.

My research has shown how multimedia stardom in Hong Kong is an important aspect of the changing nature of media stars worldwide. I distinguish the concept of multimedia stardom from celebrity by asserting its closer proximity to a range of cultural productions and their consumption, rather than focusing on fame, an abstract condition of being well-known. This is a useful distinction to interrogate the contemporary production and consumption of popular culture in which stardom plays a central role. I also contend that multimedia stardom is a concept that raises questions about the roles of the individual in society, especially given the persistent discourses on authenticity and work. Stars in Hong Kong are best at reflecting social meanings at the intersection between individualism and the collective, indicative of modern and contemporary stars' status in secular, advanced and late capitalist societies. I conclude by examining how stars from Hong Kong, who have long been transnational and internationally known, possess an ability to illustrate changing notions of ethnic identities in diverse markets. I argue that because of China's rising economic, cultural and political power since 1978 and its Open Door Policy, re-sinicization has made multimedia stardom in Hong Kong firmly part of the mediasphere of Mainland China and, therefore, an important facet of its expanding global soft power.

Appendix 1

List of interviewees and public events cited in the book

Interviewees (in alphabetical order) and interview dates:

Chan, Fruit 陳果 (director and producer) and Jimmy Choi 蔡甘銓 (independent filmmaker and programmer of independent films at the Hong Kong Arts Centre, HKIFF and the Hong Kong Independent Short Film and Video Awards). 24 August 2005.

Chan, Pak-sun 陳柏生, founder and editor of *City Entertainment* magazine since the 1970s. 11 April 2005.

Chan, Rowena, Media Relations Manager at Gold Label Entertainment, the company that managed Miriam Yeung. 23 August 2005.

Chang, Sylvia 張艾嘉, filmmaker. 7 July 2005.

Cheng, Bede 鄭子宏 was the Programme Assistant (Film Programme) at the HKFA and, later, a Programme Manager at the HKIFF. 3 January 2005.

Cheung Tung-joe 張同祖, a producer/director/actor since the 1970s and the Vice Chairman (2005–8) and Special Executive Member (2008–present) of the Federation of Hong Kong Filmmakers. 29 July 2005.

Choi, Jimmy – See Fruit Chan

Chua, Robert 蔡和平. Chua is one of the most experienced television producers in Hong Kong. He helped launch TVB in 1967 and created the live show *Enjoy Yourself Tonight* and the annual Miss Hong Kong Pageant, both of which provided opportunities for the first generation of Cantonese television stars. He later started his own production house making television programmes and commercials. A full biography is contained on Chua's official website. Available: http://www. robertchua.com (accessed 27 October 2013). 17 June 2009.

Jiang, David 蔣維國, then Dean of Performance Arts, Academy for Performing Arts, Hong Kong. 21 February 2005.

Lam, Edward 林奕華, theatre director, writer and screenwriter. 3 August 2005.

Lam Suet 林雪, actor. Interview as part of the press meetings at Far East Film Festival, Udine, Italy. 26 April 2008.

Lam Tze-chung 林子聰, actor, writer and director. Interview as part of the press meetings at Far East Film Festival, Udine, Italy. 25 April 2006.

Lau Ching-wan 劉青雲, actor. Interview as part of the press meetings at Far East Film Festival, Udine, Italy. 26 April 2008.

Lau, Jeff 劉鎮偉. Lau has been a producer and director in Hong Kong since 1980. He directed and produced (and occasionally acted in) many comedies and was also a long-term collaborator with director Wong Kar-wai. 5 August 2005.

Lee Sinje 李心潔, actress. 6 June 2005.

Logan, Bey, British director and producer who moved to Hong Kong in the early 1990s. Logan described how he arrived in Hong Kong just as the film industry was at the beginning of the current decline and how his English background helped to facilitate international co-productions. 6 January 2005.

NR, an assistant director who has worked in film and advertising since the early 1990s. 4 August 2005.

Sze Man-hung 史文鴻, a writer and critic who taught at the University of Science and Technology, Hong Kong. 4 March 2005.

Wai Ka-fai 韋家輝, director, writer and producer. Personal interview as part of Far East Film Festival press meetings in Udine, Italy. 24 April 2006.

Wu, Flora 胡穎怡. Wu was a gossip columnist for the *South China Morning Post*. She invited me to shadow her at the opening of *Eros* (Wong Kar-wai, M. Antonioni & S. Soderbergh, 2005) in the Central District on the evening of 13 May 2005.

Public events:

29 January 2005 – Seminar 香港演藝—從舞台到銀幕 (*Performance Arts in Hong Kong: From Stage to Silver Screen*) with Cheung Tat-ming 張達明 (actor, playwright and director) and To Kwok-wai 杜國威 (screenwriter and playwright).

6 February 2005 – 文化沙龍 (Cultural Salon) with members of the Hong Kong Film Critics Society.

3 April 2005 – Seminar 劉德華的星味與演技 (*Andy Lau: Actor and Star*) with Bryan Chang 張偉雄, Athena Tsui 馮若芷 and Thomas Shin 登徒 (critics).

Appendix 2

List of terms, proper names and titles

Chinese terms:

A Can	阿燦
Baibian Mui Yim Fong	百變梅艷芳
Cao gen	草根
Dan	旦(see also *Huadan*)
Daodi Green Tea	道地綠茶
Fei	妃
Fengfu rensheng, rensheng fengfu	豐富人生, 人生豐富
Ge ge	哥哥
Genü	歌女
Geshou	歌手
Gēxīng	歌星
Gèxìng	個性
Gouzaidui	狗仔隊
Hakka	客家人
Hanyu pinyin	漢語拼音
Hokkien	福建話
Huadan	花旦(see also *dan*)
Huangmei diao	黃梅調
Huayi Brothers	華儀兄弟
Jiannan	賤男
Jiejie	姐姐

Jincao yanyuan	甘草演員
Jingshen	精神
Lantau Island	大嶼山
Mongkok	旺角
Mou lei tou	無厘頭
Mui jie	梅姐
Ouxiang	偶像
Pak-dong	拍檔
Punti	本地
Ren	人 or 仁
Renyan kewei	人言可畏
Sha dajie	傻大姐
Sha Tin	沙田
Shek Kip Mei	石硤尾
Sheng	生
Sheng, se, yi	聲色藝
Shidaiqu	時代曲
Tanka	蛋家／蛋民
Tiananmen	天安門
Tian ci	填詞
Tianya	天涯社區
Tudi	徒弟
Tuen Mun	屯門
Wong Fei-hung (Huang Feihong)	黃飛鴻
Wushu	武術
Wuxia	武俠
Xingxiang	形像
Xinshan ze daochu tiantang	心善則到處天堂
Yam-Pak	任白
Yishi	意識
Yiyuan	藝員

Yunü	玉女
Zhongguofeng	中國風

Translations of English terms:

Academy for Performing Arts (APA)	香港演藝學院
Asia Television (ATV)	亞洲電線
Basic Law	基本法
Beijing Film Academy	北京電影學院
Capital Artists	華星唱片
Cathay Studio/MP & GI	國泰
China Film Group	中國电影集團公司
China Television (CTV)	中國電視
Chinese People's Political Consultative Conference (CPPCC)	中國人民政治協商會議
Cinepoly Records	新藝寶
Closer Economic Partnership Agreement (CEPA)	更緊密經貿關係
Commercial Television (CTV)	佳藝電視
Cultural Revolution	文化大革命
Diocesan Girls' School	拔萃女書院
Emperor Entertainment Group (EEG)	英皇娛樂集團
Federation of Hong Kong Filmmakers	香港電影工作者總會
Festival Walk	又一城
Focus Group (formerly Teamwork)	映藝
Four Heavenly Kings	四大天王
Gold Label	金牌（大風）娛樂
Golden Harvest	嘉禾
Hong Kong Audit Bureau of Circulations	香港出版銷數公證會
Hong Kong Autonomy Movement	香港自治運動
Hong Kong Coliseum	香港體育館
Hong Kong Film Awards (HKFA)	香港電影金像獎
Hong Kong Film Critics Society	香港影評人協會

Hong Kong Heritage Museum	香港文化博物館
Hong Kong International Film Festival (HKIFF)	香港國際電影節
Hong Kong Journalists Association	香港記者協會
Hong Kong, Kowloon and New Territories Motion Picture Industry Association	香港影業協會
Hong Kong Special Administrative Region (SAR)	香港特區
Hong Kong Stadium	香港大球場
Individual Visit Scheme (IVS)	個人游
International Federation of the Phonographic Industry (IFPI)	國際唱片業協會（香港會）
IFPI Hong Kong Digital Music Award	香港數碼音樂大獎
IFPI Hong Kong Top Sales Music Awards	香港唱片銷量大獎
Jade Solid Gold (see *Television programme and series titles*)	
KMT or Kuomintang or Guomindang	國民黨
Lamma Island	南丫島
May Fourth Movement	五四運動
Media Asia	寰亞綜藝集團
Mingxing Film Company	明星影片公司
Museum of the Hong Kong Entertainment World	演藝博物館
New Light Theatre	新光戲院
New Talent Singing Awards	新秀歌唱大賽
New Woman Incident	新女性事件
Next Media	壹蘋果
Opium War	鴉片戰爭
Phoenix Television	鳳凰衛星電視
Radio Television Hong Kong (RTHK)	香港電台
RTHK Ten Gold Song Awards Presentation	十大中文金曲獎
Rediffusion (RTV)	麗的呼聲
Shaw Brothers	邵氏片場
Star Ferry	渡海小輪
Suntory (Whisky)	三得利

Teamwork Motion Pictures (see also Focus Group)	天幕製作
Television Broadcasts/TVB (Jade)	無線電視 （翡翠台）
Treaty of Nanking	南京條約
West Kowloon Cultural District	西九龍文娛藝術區

Names of performers and bands:

Ai Xia	艾霞
Bai Guang	白光
Chan, Bobo	陳文媛
Chan, Danny	陳百強
Chan, Eason	陳奕信
Chan, Jackie	成龍
Chan, Kelly	陳慧琳
Chan Po-chu, Connie	陳寶珠
Chang, Grace (see Ge Lan)	
Chang, Sylvia	張艾嘉
Chen, Edison	陳冠希
Chen Hou, Peter	陳厚
Cheng, Sammi	鄭秀文
Cheung, Cecilia	張柏芝
Cheung, Jacky	張學友
Cheung, Leslie	張國榮
Cheung, Maggie	張曼玉
Cheung Tat-ming	張達明
Choi, Charlene	蔡卓妍
Chou, Jay	周杰倫
Chow, Niki	周麗洪
Chow, Stephen	周星馳
Chow, Vivian	周慧敏
Chow Yun-fat	周潤發

Chu Kong	朱江
Chung, Gillian	鍾欣桐
Deng Lijun (see Teresa Teng)	
Fu Sheng	傅聲
Ge Lan (Grace Chang)	葛蘭
Ho, Denise	何韻詩
Ho, Josie	何超儀
Hu Die	蝴蝶
Hui, Alfred	許廷鏗
Hui, Michael	許冠文
Hui, Ricky	許冠英
Hui, Sam	許冠傑
Hung, Sammo	洪金寶
Ku, Leo	古巨基
Kwan Tak-hing	關德興
Kwok, Aaron	郭富城
Lai, Leon	黎明
Lam, George	林子祥
Lam, Sandy	林憶蓮
Lam Suet	林雪
Lau, Andy	劉德華
Lau, Carina	劉嘉玲
Lau Ching-wan	劉青雲
Lee, Bruce	李小龍
Lee, Danny	李修賢
Lee, Deborah	狄波拉
Lee, Hacken	李克勤
Lee Sinje, Angelica	李心潔
Leong, Isabella	梁洛施
Leung Chiu-wai, Tony	梁朝偉
Leung Kar-fai, Tony	梁家輝

Li, Jet	李連杰
Li Lihua	李麗華
Li Lili	黎麗麗
Lin Ching-hsia, Brigitte	林青霞
Lin Dai	林黛
Liu, Gordon	劉家良
Liu, Rene	劉若英
Liu Ye	劉燁
Lo Lieh	羅烈
Lotus, The	蓮花樂團
Lung Kim-sheng	龍劍笙
Lung Kong (Patrick Lung Kong)	龍剛
Mok, Karen	莫文蔚
Morris, Karen (see Karen Mok)	
Mui, Anita	梅艷芳
Mui Shet-sze	梅雪詩
Ng, Francis	吳鎮宇
Ng, May	吳碗芳
Ngan, Rachel	顏穎思
Pak Suet-sin	白雪仙
Reis, Michelle	李嘉欣
Ruan Lingyu	阮玲玉
Sham, John	岑健勳
Siao Fong-fong, Josephine	蕭芳芳
Sit, Fiona	薛凱琪
So Wing-hong, William	蘇永康
Tam, Alan	譚詠麟
Tam, Roman	羅文
Tang Zhi-kei (G.E.M.)	鄧紫棋
Teng, Teresa (Deng Lijun)	鄧麗君
Ti Lung	狄龍

Tsang, Eric	曾志偉
Tsang Kong	曾江
Tse, Nicholas	謝霆蜂
Tse Yin	謝賢
Tseng, Jenny	甄妮
Tsui, Paula	徐小鳳
Wang Hanlun	王漢倫
Wang, Lisa	汪明荃
Wang Yu	王羽
Wong, Anthony	黃秋生
Wong, Faye (Shirley Wong)	王菲 (王靖雯)
Wong, Ivana	王菀之
Wong Ka-kui (of Beyond)	黃家駒
Wu, Daniel	吳彥祖
Wynners, The	溫拿樂團
Yam Kim-fai	任劍輝
Yam, Simon	任達華
Yeh, Sally	葉倩文
Yeung, Miriam	楊千嬅
Yip, Veronica	葉玉卿
Yuen, Anita	袁詠儀
Yung, Joey	容祖兒
Zhang Yang	張揚
Zhou Xuan	周璇

Other names:

Cai Chusheng	蔡楚生
Chan, Benny	陳木勝
Chan, Fruit	陳果
Chan, Gordon	陳嘉上
Chan, Peter	陳可辛

Chang, Bryan	張偉雄
Chang Hsin-yen	張鑫炎
Chen Kaige	陳凱歌
Cheung, Alfred	張堅庭
Cheung, Jacob	張之亮
Chin Chi-ming	錢志明
Chiu, Samson	趙良駿
Chong, John	莊澄
Chor Yuen	楚原
Chu Pui-hing	朱培慶
Deng Xiaoping	鄧小平
Feng Xiaogang	馮小剛
Han Sanping	韓三平
Ho, Stanley	何鴻燊
Hu Mei	胡玫
Huang Jianxin	黃建新
Hui, Ann	許鞍華
Ip Kam-hung, Riley	葉錦鴻
Ip Wai-shun, Wilson	葉偉信
Jiang Wen	姜文
Kam Kwok-leong	甘國亮
Keeto (Lam)	記陶
Kong Qingdong	孔慶東
Kwan, Stanley	關錦鵬
Lai, Jimmy	黎智英
Lam, Peter	林健岳
Lam Tze-chung	林子聰
Lau, Andrew	劉偉強
Law Wing-cheong	羅永昌
Lee, Ang	李安
Lee, Bono	李照興

Leong Po-chih	梁普智
Leung Chun-ying	梁振英
Leung, Longmen	梁樂民
Li Cheuk-to	李焯桃
Li Ka-shing	李家誠
Li Minwei	黎民偉
Li Pik-wah (Lillian Lee)	李碧華
Li, Richard	李澤楷
Lo, Lowell	盧冠廷
Lu Xun	魯迅
Luk, Sunny	陸劍青
Ma Wai-ho, Joe	馬偉豪
Mak Kai-gwong	麥啟光
Mak Siu-fai	麥兆輝
Pang Ho-cheung	彭浩翔
Sek Kei	石棋
Sham, John	岑建勳
Shaw, Run Run	邵逸夫
Shi Nansun	施南生
Sun Yat-sen	孫中山
Tang, Susan	唐書琛
To, Johnnie	杜棋鋒
Tong Hok-tak, Daffy	唐鶴德
Tong, Stanley	唐季禮
Tsang, Donald	曾蔭權
Tsui, Athena	馮若芷
Tsui Hark	徐克
Tsung, Woody	叢運滋
Tung Chee-hwa	董健華
Wai Ka-fai	韋家輝
Wang Tianlin	王天林

Wong, James	黃霑
Wong Jing	王晶
Wong Kar-wai	王家衛
Woo, John	吳宇森
Yee Tung-sing, Derek	爾東陞
Yi Wen (Evan Yang)	易文
Yuen Kin-to, Toe	袁健滔
Yuen Sai-sang, James	袁世生
Zhang Che	張徹
Zhang Li	張黎
Zhang Shichuan	張石川
Zhang Yimou	張藝謀

Song and album titles:

Bad Girl	壞女孩
Beijing Welcomes You	北京歡迎你
Below the Lion Rock (theme song)	獅子山下
Chinese	中國人
Dream Person	夢中人
Drunken Life	淺醉一生
Half a Pound, Eight Taels	半金八兩
I Love Cha Cha	我愛恰恰
Last Night on the Star Ferry	昨夜的渡輪上
Lies	謊言
Long Qing Shi Yi Ban Shi Ji	龍情詩意半世紀
Love/We Are the World	四海一心
Miracle World	一隻牛的異想世界
Please Myself	討好自己
Woman Who Easily Gets Hurt, The	容易受傷的女人
Would It Be Possible	可不可以

Magazine and newspaper titles:

Apple Daily	蘋果日報
City Entertainment	電影雙周刊
Cantonese Opera Monthly	粵劇曲藝月刊
Eastweek	東周刊
Headline Daily	頭條日報
Headline Finance	頭條財經
Hong Kong Daily News (*Sun Pao*)	新報
Hong Kong Economic News	信報財經新聞
International Screen	國際電影
Metro	都市日報
Ming Pao	明報
Ming Pao Weekly	明報周刊
New Monday	新Monday
Next	壹周刊
Oriental Daily	東方日報
Oriental Sunday	東方新地
People's Daily	人民日報
Sharp Daily	爽報
Sing Pao	成報
Sing Tao (Daily)	星島日報
Sing Tao Weekly	星島周刊
South China Morning Post (SCMP)	南華早報
Southern Screen	南國電影
(Hong Kong) Standard	英文虎報
Sudden Weekly	突然一周
Weekend Weekly	新假期

Television programme and series titles:

Anita Mui and Friends	真心相聚梅艷芳
Below the Lion Rock (series)	獅子山下

Boy from Vietnam, The	來客
Duke of Mount Deer, The	鹿鼎記
Emissary, The	花艇小英雄
Enjoy Yourself Tonight (EYT)	歡樂今宵
Forever Remembrance: Anita Mui	永遠紀念梅艷芳
Hong Kong Hong Kong	香港香港
Hotel	狂潮
Hui Brothers Show	雙星報喜
In Memory of Anita Mui	回憶梅艷芳
Inbound Troubles	老表你好嘢！
Jade Solid Gold	勁歌金曲
Legend of the Condors	射雕英雄傳
Miss Hong Kong Pageant	香港小姐競選
See You on the Other Side	江湖再見

Theatre performances:

A Sentimental Story	劍雪浮生

Feature film titles:

1911	辛亥革命
Actress	阮玲玉
All About Love	得閒炒飯
Better Tomorrow, A	英雄本色
Better Tomorrow, A, 2	英雄本色 2
Better Tomorrow, A, 3: Love and Death in Saigon	英雄本色 3
Blind Detective	盲探
Boat People	投奔怒海
Chinese Zodiac (CZ12)	十二生肖
Chungking Express	重慶森林
Cold War	寒戰
Comrades, Almost a Love Story	甜蜜蜜

Confucius	孔子
Crouching Tiger, Hidden Dragon	臥虎藏龍
Curse of the Golden Flower	滿城盡帶黃金甲
CZ12	十二生肖
Days of Being Wild	阿飛正傳
Detective Dee and the Mystery of the Phantom Flame	狄仁傑之通天帝國
Drink Drank Drunk	千杯不醉
Dummy Mommy, Without a Baby	玉女添丁
Dumplings	餃子
Dry Wood, Fierce Fire	乾柴烈火
Farewell My Concubine	霸王別姬
Feel 100% 2	百分百感覺 II
Forbidden Kingdom, The	功夫之王
Founding of a Party, The	建黨偉業
Founding of a Republic, The	建國大業
Fulltime Killer	全職殺手
Golden Chicken 2	金雞 2
Group, The	全職大盜
Happy Together	春光乍洩
Her Fatal Ways	表姊，你好嘢！
Hero	英雄
Homecoming	似水流年
Hooked on You	每當變幻時
House of Flying Daggers	十面埋伏
House of 72 Tenants, The	七十二家房客
In the Mood for Love	花樣年華
Infernal Affairs	無間道
Initial D	頭文字D
July Rhapsody	男人四十
Jumping Ash	跳灰

Killer, The	諜血雙雄
Kung Fu Hustle	功夫
Let the Bullets Fly	讓子彈飛
Life Without Principle	奪命金
Little Cheung	細路祥
Long Arm of the Law	省港旗兵
Longest Summer, The	去年煙花特別多
Lost in Time	忘不了
Love in a Fallen City	傾城之戀
Love in a Puff	志明與春嬌
Love in the Buff	春嬌與志明
Love on a Diet	瘦身男女
Love Undercover	新紮師妹
Love Undercover 2: Love Mission	新紮師妹 II
Made in Hong Kong	香港製造
Mambo Girl	曼波女郎
McDull: Prince de la Bun	麥兜菠蘿油王子
Midnight Fly	慌心假期
Moment of Romance	天若有情
Moment of Romance 3	天若有情 III：烽火佳人
Myth, The	神話
Needing You	孤男寡女
New Woman	新女性
Orphan Saves His Grandfather, The	孤兒救祖記
Police Story	警察故事
Postmodern Life of My Aunt, The	姨媽的後現代生活
Private Eyes, The	半斤八兩
Rouge	胭脂扣
Rumble Ages	烈火青春
Rumble in the Bronx	紅番區
Running on Karma	大隻佬

Running Out of Time	暗戰
Shanghai Grand	新上海灘
Shaolin Soccer	少林足球
Shaolin Temple	少林寺
Simple Life, A	桃姐
Song of the Exile	客途秋恨
Spooky Bunch, The	撞到正
Story of Woo Viet, The	胡越的故事
Summer Snow	女人四十
Teddy Girls	飛女正傳
True Mob Story, A	龍在江湖
Warlords, The	投名狀
Who's the Woman, Who's the Man?	金枝玉葉 2
Wild Wild Rose, The	野玫瑰之戀
World Without Thieves, A	天下無賊
Yesterday Once More	龍鳳鬥
Zhuangzi Tests His Wife	莊子試妻

Notes

Introduction

1 Chen's statement on 21 February 2008. Online. Available: http://news.sina.com.hk/cgi-bin/nw/show.cgi/32/1/1/645837/1.html (accessed 23 February 2008).

2 For a collection of essays on class and social stratification, see Lau Siu-kai et al. (1994) and, especially, Benjamin Leung's (1994) chapter on the study of class and class formation in Hong Kong.

3 1997 was the year when the lease of the colony, or more specifically the New Territories, would expire.

4 The transition period comprises the years 1984–97.

5 See Fung (2001), Leung (2000), Lo (1999, pp.67–8) and Ma (1995).

6 The notion of 'the subject', defined later in this chapter, will be discussed in Chapter 5; for the time being, the term is considered to be broadly synonymous with identity.

7 Discourse, according to Michel Foucault, means 'a group of statements which provide a language for talking about—a way of representing the knowledge about—a particular topic at a particular historical moment . . . Discourse is about the production of knowledge through language' (Hall 1992, p.291).

8 See for instance Leung (2000), Lo (2001) and Yau (2001).

9 Allegory is 'a form of narrative or a visual image whose literal or obvious meaning masks one or more other meanings, often with a didactic purpose' (Macey 2000, p.8). For instance, the success of the *A Better Tomorrow* series (John Woo 1986, 1987 and Tsui Hark, 1989) is attributed to anxiety over the then-upcoming 1997 handover. The title of the series is often used as an illustration of its relevance to Hong Kong's future (Williams 1995; Williams 1997), although the Chinese title translates simply as 'The Essence of Heroes'.

10 This is despite the fact that consciousness of 1997 did not solidify until after Margaret Thatcher's visit to Beijing in 1982, and the director herself denied that the films were political (Ho 1999).

11 These include Richard Dyer's (1979) seminal work, *Stars;* fan studies such as that by Jackie Stacey (1994); and updated volumes, including those by Martin Barker and Thomas Austin (2003) and McDonald's chapter in the second edition of *Stars* (McDonald 1998). A collection of articles, *Stardom: Industry of Desire,* edited by Christine Gledhill (1997), includes seminal studies by Dyer (1991) and Thomas Harris (1991). Paul McDonald (2000) also examines the history of the star system in Hollywood. Other collections of case studies include the edited volume by Andy Willis (2004). Ginette Vincendeau's work extends film star studies to European actors and their transatlantic

fame in the American film industry (Phillips & Vincendeau 2006; Vincendeau 2000). The most recent survey of the development of star studies is by Martin Shingler (2012).

12 My analysis employs the definition of transnationality as 'the cultural and economic flows of globalisation, the erosion of the nation state, a "borderless world", de-territorialisation, debates about whether we live in a "global village" or are witness to ever more sophisticated forms of "global pillage"' (Hunt & Leung 2008, p.3).

13 Turner's article, published in the inaugural issue of the journal *Celebrity Studies,* represents the emergence of the subject as a distinct academic field, following seminal publications such as those by Jessica Evans and David Hesmondhalgh (2005) and Chris Rojek (2001).

14 The mediasphere, cultural production in the visual and textual fields characterized by endless expansion (Debray 1991), can be understood to include film, television, and new and social media.

15 See Appendix 1 for a list of the interviewees included in the book.

1 Transformations in Hong Kong society and popular culture

1 See Jan Morris (1988) and Jack Potter (1969) on the culture and society of rural communities in the New Territories (many of whom were non-Cantonese ethnic groups).

2 Data are available: http://hkupop.hku.hk/english/popexpress/trust/conhkfuture/poll/datatables.html (accessed 4 June 2013).

3 Details available: http://www.tid.gov.hk/english/cepa/cepa_overview.html (accessed 4 June 2013).

4 Interview with Helen Mak (Senior Director of Retail Services, Colliers International Asia). Online. Available: http://www.youtube.com/watch?v=4_SzDMa_GUE (accessed 31 May 2013).

5 See for instance the report by *SCMP.* Online. Available: http://www.scmp.com/topics/individual-visit-scheme (accessed 31 May 2013).

6 Video available: http://badcanto.wordpress.com/2012/01/20/mainland-scholar-many-hongkonger-are-dogs/ (accessed 1 June 2013).

7 See the Hong Kong Journalists Association's 2013 annual report, which expressed a fear of threats to freedom of expression. Online. Available: http://www.hkja.org.hk/site/Host/hkja/UserFiles/file/annualreport/e_annual_report_2013.pdf (accessed 3 November 2013).

8 See report available: http://chinadigitaltimes.net/2012/02/running-dogs-and-locusts/ (accessed 10 August 2014).

9 Motion Pictures and General Industries, renamed Cathay in 1965.

10 *Huangmei diao* were folk songs adapted from those sung by tea-picking women in the Anhui Province of China.

11 The Hui brothers, Michael (b.1942), Ricky (b.1946) and Sam (b.1948), emerged from a comedy sketch show on TVB.

12 It was owned by Run Run Shaw.

13 The show was briefly resurrected in 2007, showing highlights from the original series, to mark the 40th anniversary.

14 This translates to approximately US$ 6.47 million at the November 1995 exchange rate.

15 A TVB series called *Inbound Troubles* broadcast in 2013 represents the tensions between mainlanders and Hong Kong citizens, including the aforementioned baby

milk formula shortage. The drama depicts the lives of two cousins, one from the Mainland, one a Hong Kong native; the Chinese title, *Laobiao, nihao ye!* (literally 'Old cousin, you are great!'), makes reference to *Her Fatal Ways. Inbound Troubles* was seen as realistic and was one of the highest-rated series of the year in Hong Kong (Mullany 2013), but Chinese censors deleted scenes which disparaged mainlanders when the show was aired there.

16 Data from Hong Kong Trade Development Council. Online. Available: http://hong-kong-economy-research.hktdc.com/business-news/article/Hong-Kong-Industry-Profiles/Film-Entertainment-Industry-in-Hong-Kong/hkip/en/1/1X000000/1X0018PN.htm (accessed 14 May 2013).

17 The survey interviewed 1,013 people about the film and music industries and stars.

18 See Cahiers du Cinema (2006); Chu (2003); *City Entertainment* (1990).

19 There is also another famous actor in Hong Kong named Tony Leung Kar-fai. In this study, Tony Leung refers to Leung Chiu-wai unless otherwise stated.

20 Available: http://www.robertchua.com/robertchua.com/PROFESSIONAL/recentpress/20071113_MediaC21.html (accessed 2 June 2009). His view on competition as the cause of decline seems to contradict that of the above-cited Shi Nansun, though both agreed on the poor quality of local television.

21 Data from China Internet Watch. Online. Available: http://www.chinainternetwatch.com/1337/charts-internet-usage-hk-v-s-sea/#more-1337 (accessed 7 June 2013).

22 Note that not all films produced in China were released in the cinemas. Film exhibition in China should take into account theatrical releases, DVDs and piracy in combination, which makes quantifying production difficult. Greater China refers to China, Hong Kong, Taiwan, and the Chinese diaspora, notwithstanding the longstanding debates around the use of the term (Harding 1993).

23 There has been a similar trend in the Taiwanese film industry in which many high-budget commercial films rely on cross-strait co-financing and feature stars from China, Hong Kong and Taiwan. Several successful Taiwanese directors have migrated to China to develop their careers (Cremin 2013).

24 *Next,* 2 May 2002. p.38. In Chinese.

2 Multimedia stardom in Hong Kong

1 See Richard deCordova (1991) for a discussion of the origin of stardom in Hollywood and the role of the studios; see also Chapters 2 and 3 in McDonald (2000).

2 Ruan Lingyu's suicide note contained the sentences, '我何罪可畏？不過是人言可畏罷了！' ('What punishment did I have to fear … but gossip is still a frightening thing') (Elley 1997, p.143).

3 This brief discussion of Ge Lan should be supplemented by the detailed study of the star's career by David Desser (2014).

4 See Gary Needham (2008) for a detailed discussion of the link between modernity and Cathay musicals.

5 *International Screen* was produced by Cathay, *Southern Screen* by Shaw.

6 Siao was a teenage idol who grew into a respected actress and filmmaker, infrequently working in films since the 1970s. For instance she co-directed *Jumping Ash* (with Leong Po-chih, 1976), which is seen as a precursor to the Hong Kong New Wave Cinema that emerged at the end of the 1970s, and she acted in Ann Hui's *The Spooky Bunch* (1980) and *Summer Snow* (1995).

7 Chan's recent comeback career, including stage plays and concerts, continued to exploit her girlish image even though both she and her fans were now of advancing years.

8 Tse Yin was married to Deborah Lee, an actress; they are the parents of the actor and singer Nicholas Tse (b.1980), who was married to another singer-actress, Cecilia Cheung, one of the 'victims' of Edison Chen's Internet photographs scandal. The couple divorced in 2011. These details demonstrate the close-knit nature of the entertainment industry in Hong Kong.

9 Background details of the female stars of varying popularity were taken from a selection of infotainment magazines. They were not all 'top-billing' stars at the time but were selected to represent a range.

10 In Hollywood, 'for many film performers, a great deal of their working time involves the unwaged labour of "studying acting, seeking agents, going to casting interviews . . . keeping the body in shape, socialising with other actors, and making [influential] contacts"' (Anne Peters & Muriel Cantor, cited in McDonald 1998, p.196, original omission and parenthesis). In Hong Kong the emergence of artiste management companies is a comparatively recent phenomenon, with many being part of multimedia corporations (see Chapter 3).

11 Comedy became the top genre in television after the coming of terrestrial channels in Hong Kong (Cheuk 1999).

12 The other popular group in Hong Kong during this time was The Wynners; members included Alan Tam (b.1950), who later became a successful Cantopop singer. The Wynners was a deliberate misspelling just like The Beatles.

13 This was the translation of the film's Chinese title *Banjin Baliang*. The film also starred the Hui brothers.

14 Male-to-female cross-dressing part in Chinese opera; *huadan* can be shortened to *dan*.

15 Eastweek, 24 April 2004, pp.50–4. In Chinese.

16 Yip was famous for acting in Category III movies, a category reserved for audiences over 18 years of age. 'Veronica Yip [has] come up through the ranks of Category III films to mainstream respectability' (Teo 1997, p.244).

17 Available: http://www.echinacities.com/news/The-Elite-Payroll-How-Much-Chinas-Wealthiest-Actors-Get-Paid (accessed 25 August 2014).

18 It was Kwok's dancing ability that first got him noticed, and later he was known as 'Hong Kong's Michael Jackson' for his extraordinary onstage dance routines.

19 Details from IFPI. Online. Available: http://www.ifpihk.org (accessed 10 July 2009).

20 The Chinese title of the song is *Qianzui Yisheng* ('Drunken Life'), with music by Lowell Lo and words by Susan Tang and James Wong. The translation comes from the subtitles of the Cantonese version of the song from a recording of the broadcast on Channel 4 (UK) on 14 April 2003 (they likely came from new subtitles submitted to the British Board of Film Classification in 2002 by the UK distributor Medusa), with a minor change from 'just enough for tomorrow' to 'enough for the future'.

21 In the subtitles, he is called Jeff. This was probably due to the fact that Woo was inspired by *Le Samouraï* (Jean-Pierre Melville, 1967) in making *The Killer*. In Melville's film, Alain Delon plays the protagonist, named Jef Costello. The Chinese title, *Diexue shuangxiong*, literally translates as 'Bloodshed, twin heroes'.

22 See Chapter 1 Table 1.2. The details of the albums were taken from a fan website. Available: http://www.alan-tam.com (accessed 30 June 2009).

23 See Chapter 1 Table 1.2.

24 *Next*, 2 May 2002, p.8. In Chinese.

25 It had to be abandoned due to a technical fault, so the 2013 contest was the first to allow viewers to vote at the final.

26 *Ming Pao*, 9 February 2005, p.C5. In Chinese. The Chinese New Year releases occupy one of the most important periods in the film calendar in Hong Kong, and films released at this time traditionally include major stars in order to maximize box office returns.

27 Telephone interviews were conducted with 1,026 people.

28 The poll took place from 29 April to 22 May 2005 on the Internet, as well as at the UA chain of cinemas and selected malls in Hong Kong.

29 Local films garnered only 22 per cent of the Hong Kong market in 2012 (Law 2012).

30 For the purposes of this discussion, Jay Chou is excluded since he originated from Taiwan; he began his pop career in Taiwan in 2000.

31 The album does not have a Chinese title.

32 The reason for the change is suggested by Anthony Fung and Michael Curtin (2002), although their interpretation of *fei* as 'queen' is not strictly correct.

33 *Faye's Story*, 1997. Online. Available: http://wongfei.tumblr.com/post/1202947591/realistically-we-who-work-in-the-entertainment (accessed 20 September 2013).

34 She later married, had a child with one of the musicians, and divorced. This personal history further confirmed her independent and uncompromising image, although her family commitments were also cited by women in Hong Kong as reasons for their identification with Wong and in discussions of gender roles (Fung & Curtin 2002).

35 Wong has been in 'semi-retirement' since 2005, though she completed comeback concert tours in 2010–2.

36 Next, 23 January 2003, p.52. In Chinese.

37 Chow subsequently released a record in 2011 and starred in the film *All About Love* (Ann Hui, 2010).

38 Beyond was a pop group in Hong Kong that formed in 1983. Their lead singer, Wong Ka-kui (1962–93), died after falling from a broken stage in Japan. In 2013, a major concert featuring Faye Wong and Andy Lau was staged on the twentieth anniversary of his death.

39 See Steve Fore (1997) for a discussion of Jackie Chan's transnational career and the tension created in trying to use his star persona to cater for global and local audiences.

40 See Chapter 1 and Teo (1997).

41 Her Japanese name in *kanji* ('Chinese characters') is 鈴木杏.

3 Image

1 Persona is 'the aspect of someone's character that is presented to or perceived by others' or 'a role or character adopted by an author or an actor', and its origin is from Latin, meaning mask. *Oxford English Dictionary*. Online. Available: http://www.oxforddictionaries.com/definition/english/persona?q=persona (accessed 4 January 2013).

2 Hong Kong Audit Bureau of Circulations. Available: http://www.hkabc.com.hk/en/index.htm (accessed 1 July 2013).

3 Hong Kong Audit Bureau of Circulations. Available: http://www.hkabc.com.hk/en/index.htm (accessed 1 July 2013).

4 Hong Kong Audit Bureau of Circulations. Available: http://www.hkabc.com.hk/en/index.htm (accessed 1 July 2013).

5 See the group's website. Available: http://www.emperorgroup.com/ct/ourbusinesses.php?id=4 (accessed 11 July 2013).

6 Details from *Next*, 14 March 2002, pp.42–4. In Chinese.

7 Data available: http://www.jaynestars.com/news/hong-kong-film-stars-and-tvbs-artist-appearance-fees-exposed/ (accessed 17 July 2013).

8 Leong married Richard Li (son of one of the richest businessmen in Hong Kong, Li Ka-shing) in 2008 when she was 20. The couple, who had three sons, divorced in 2011.

9 *Eastweek,* 24 April 2004, p.5. In Chinese.

10 The term refers to a group of paparazzi who follow the stars.

11 The united front might be a result of the fact that Lee was managed by Chang's company, having been discovered by Chang in a competition. She was initially a pop singer in Taiwan before focusing on film acting in Hong Kong.

12 'Films were often built around star images. Stories might be written expressly to feature a given star, or books might be bought for production with a star in mind' (Dyer 1979, p.62).

13 *Monday,* 22 April 2005, cover and pp.57–60. In Chinese. The album and magazine do not have Chinese titles.

14 Product placement can be defined as the 'placement of a brand or a firm in a movie or in a television program by different means and for promotional purposes' (d'Astous & Séguin 1999, p.896).

15 OL is a term from popular usage in Japan referring to young unmarried women who work in offices in relatively junior positions.

16 *Next,* 2 May 2002, p.186. In Chinese.

17 *Next,* 18 July 2002, p.70. In Chinese.

18 'Grassroots' (*cao gen*) is a term often used in Hong Kong to refer to those belonging to the lower social class; more generally it means 'being ordinary'.

4 Performance

1 'Above the line' is a film financing term that refers to investment needed mainly in pre-production and paid out to creative talents (producers, directors, writers and actors). 'Below the line' refers to other departments such as art, costumes, camera and set design.

2 See Chapter 3 for a discussion of the term idol.

3 The seminar took place on 3 April 2005 as part of the Hong Kong International Film Festival.

4 During the Cultural Salon with the Hong Kong Film Critics Society on 6 February 2005.

5 During a seminar on 29 January 2005.

6 Yam Kim-fai and Pak Suet-sin were the most notable opera film actresses.

7 Cantopop stars were renowned for concerts staged in large stadiums. See Chapter 2.

8 Mui will be the case study in the next chapter.

9 In *The Theory of the Leisure Class* (1899), Thorstein Veblen discusses the notion of conspicuous consumption as the way that the wealthy display the fact that they are wealthy.

10 I (Leung 2008a) argue elsewhere that through the director Johnnie To, many actors who came mainly from the television series of the 1980s were able to reinvent their acting careers. Andy Lau has been one of To's regular lead actors.

11 See also Leung (2009) for an exploration of the actor's position in the post-1997 Hong Kong film industry.

12 Details from Andy Lau's official fan club site. Available: www.awc618.com (accessed 1 July 2013).

13 It reads *xinshan ze daochu tiantang,* meaning 'those with kind hearts will go to heaven'. Available: http://www.intomobile.com/2007/08/08/lg-shine-x-andy-lau-special-edition-phone/ (posted on 8 August 2007, accessed 25 August 2014).

14 Suntory is a brand of Japanese whisky (the company's website is available: http://www.suntory.com.tw).

15 *Today* (Singapore), 5 December 2005. Available: http://newspapers.nl.sg/Digitised/Article/today20050905-2.2.71.5.2.aspx (accessed 5 July 2013).

16 Available: http://www.cyma.ch/ambassadors/liuye (accessed 5 July 2013).

17 Author's partial translation.

18 Available: http://www.youtube.com/watch?v=k7R6Pkx_4kU (accessed 10 November 2013).

5 Identity

1 The film is about a ten-year romance between two mainlanders who first meet in Hong Kong in 1986, and it ends with the death of the Taiwanese singer Teresa Teng (Deng Lijun) in 1995. As a singer who was popular first in Taiwan and Hong Kong in the 1970s and then on the Mainland in the 1980s, Teng was an example of a floating signifier of pan-Chinese culture.

2 The writer uses the Wade-Giles system of romanization. *Jen* is *ren* in *hanyu pinyin*. The possible translations of *ren* are (1) human being, man, person, people; (2) personality, character; (3) everybody, each, all; (4) benevolence, kind-heartedness, humanity (from *A Chinese-English Dictionary,* 1978, published by Beijing College of Foreign Languages Department of English). Taken together, these definitions explain Hsu's comment that individuals are understood in relation to their societal and communal roles.

3 For a discussion of Hokkien media, see Taylor (2008).

4 See Chapter 2 for a discussion of Chow's career from local Hong Kong star to Hollywood (mainly) action man to an actor of Greater Chinese cinema.

5 Author's partial translation.

6 The Chinese government promised that there would be no change to Hong Kong's way of life for 50 years after the handover; hence the date 2046, which was also used as the title of a Wong Kar-wai film (2004).

7 See also Chapter 4 on Andy Lau's rendition of *Last Night on the Star Ferry* and *Chinese.*

8 The Hong Kong Autonomy Movement began around 2011 (see Sung 2012).

9 See the seminal work on soft power by Joseph Nye (2004).

10 Actress Lisa Wang was also a member, and Stephen Chow was a delegate to the Guangdong chapter of the CPPCC.

11 At the time of writing, no such museum had been built, though a major Bruce Lee exhibition opened in Hong Kong in July 2013 at the Heritage Museum, leading to a newspaper report's title, 'A Major Bruce Lee Exhibition at Last Honors the Memory of a Native Son' (Cheng 2013).

12 Media speculation at the time attributed her retirement to plans to marry, as well as to death threats from the Triads. (For a summary of Mui's career, see the obituary in *The Guardian* [Anon 2004]; for a brief discussion of the connection between organized criminal gangs and the film industry in Hong Kong, and the threats to Mui in 1992, see http://www.bbc.co.uk/worldservice/specials/163_wag_globalcrime/page4.shtml [accessed 25 August 2014].)

13 Mui was also deemed rebellious within the confines of a Hong Kong entertainment industry that was in fact rather conservative. Erni (2007) describes how strong sexual content in songs would be immediately banned by RTHK.
14 *Baibian* Mui Yim Fong. See my discussion of her spectacular stage set during a concert tour in the previous chapter.
15 Examples include the aforementioned Eason Chan; Josie Ho (b.1974), the daughter of Stanley Ho who owns the Lisboa Casino in Macao; Karen Mok (Karen Morris, b.1970), who is a graduate from the prestigious Diocesan Girls' School in Hong Kong and University College London (with a degree in Italian Literature); and Fiona Sit (b.1981), who studied Creative Media at City University Hong Kong.
16 Chan died after falling into a coma following a suicide attempt and became another pop legend in Hong Kong, a predecessor to Anita Mui and Leslie Cheung. In the same year, Wong Ka-kui of the band Beyond was killed in an onstage accident while touring Japan, as described in the notes to Chapter 2.

Conclusions: Stardom in and beyond Hong Kong

1 David Carradine famously played Kwai Chang Caine, a mixed-race Shaolin monk, in the 1970s television drama *Kung Fu,* a role that Bruce Lee was denied.
2 Some stars from Hong Kong appeared in American drama series, but only Sammo Hung had a sustained lead role in the CBS series *Martial Law* (1998–2000).
3 There was little interest beyond Chinese audiences in Jackie Chan as anything other than an action star, even though he had long toured to Chinese diasporic communities with his stage show, 'JC and friends'.

Bibliography

Abbas, A., 1996. *Hong Kong: Culture and the Politics of Disappearance*, Minneapolis: University of Minnesota Press.

Abbas, A., 1997. Hong Kong: Other Histories, Other Politics. *Public Culture*, 9, pp.293–313.

Abbas, A., 2001. (H)edge City: A Response to 'Becoming (Postcolonial) Hong Kong'. *Cultural Studies*, 15(3/4), pp.621–6.

Adut, A., 2009. *On Scandal: Moral Disturbances in Society, Politics, and Art*, Cambridge: Cambridge University Press.

Ahonen, L., 2007. In the Spotlight and Underground – Constructing (Anti)Stardom in Popular Music. In K. Kallioniemi, K. Kärki, J. Mäkelä, & H. Salmi, eds. *History of Stardom Reconsidered*. Turku: International Institute for Popular Culture. Available: http://iipc.utu.fi/reconsidered/.

Alberoni, F., 2007. The Powerless 'Elite': Theory and Sociological Research on the Phenomenon of the Stars. In S. Redmond & S. Holmes, eds. *Stardom and Celebrity: A Reader*. Los Angeles & London: SAGE, pp.65–77.

Althusser, L., 1971. *Lenin and Philosophy and Other Essays*, London: New Left Books.

An, G., 2000. Pan-Asian Screen Women and Film Identities: The Vampiric in Olivier Assayas' *Irma Vep*. *Sites: The Journal of Twentieth-Century Contemporary French Studies*, 4(2), pp.399–416.

Anderson, B., 1983. *Imagined Communities: Reflections on the Origins and Spread of Nationalism*, London: Verso.

Ang, I., 1996. *Living Room Wars: Rethinking Media Audiences for a Postmodern World*, London: Routledge.

Anita Mui and Friends, 2003, television broadcast, TVB (Europe).

Anon, 2004. Obituary: Anita Mui. *The Guardian*, 20 January, p.25.

Appiah, K.A., 2006. *Cosmopolitanism: Ethics in a World of Strangers*, New York: W.W. Norton & Co.

Asia Sentinel, 2011. Free Newspaper War to Escalate in Hong Kong. *Jakarta Globe*. Available: http://www.thejakartaglobe.com/archive/free-newspaper-war-to-escalate-in-hong-kong/ (accessed 15 July 2013).

Auslander, P., 1999 *Liveness: Performance in a Mediatized Culture*, London & New York: Routledge.

Barbieri, M., 2004. Perseverance Pays Off: Chinese Cinema in the Year of the Goat. In Far East Film, ed. *Far East Film 6 Festival Catalogue*. Udine: CEC, pp.24–7.

Barker, M. & Thomas, A., eds. 2003. *Contemporary Hollywood Stardom,* London: Arnold.

Basic Law of the Hong Kong Special Administrative Region of the People's Republic of China 1990. Beijing: National People's Congress.

Baudrillard, J., 1981. Simulacra and Simulation. In M. Poster, ed. *Jean Baudrillard: Selected Writing*. Cambridge: Polity, pp.166–84.

Benjamin, W., 1936. The Work of Art in the Age of Mechanical Reproduction. In H. Arendt, ed. *Illuminations*. London: Fontana, pp.217–52.

Bergfelder, T., 2004. Negotiating Exoticism: Hollywood, Film Europe and the Cultural Reception of Anna May Wong. In L. Fischer & M. Landy, eds. *Stars: The Film Reader*. London & New York: Routledge, pp.59–76.

Birch, A., 1991. *The Colony That Never Was*, Hong Kong: Twin Age Ltd.

Bloomberg News, 2013. Jackie Chan Becomes China CPPCC Committee Member, Phoenix Says. *Bloomberg News,* 31 January. Available: http://www.bloomberg.com/news/2013-01-31/jackie-chan-becomes-china-cppcc-committee-member-phoenix-says.html (accessed 30 June 2013).

Blowers, G.H., 1991. Assessing the Impact of Western Psychology in Hong Kong. *International Journal of Psychology*, 26(2), pp.254–68.

Boorstin, D.J., 1961. *The Image: A Guide to Pseudo-Events in America,* 1992 ed., New York: Vintage Books.

Bordwell, D., 2000. *Planet Hong Kong: Popular Cinema and the Art of Entertainment*, Cambridge, MA: Harvard University Press.

Brace, T., 1991. Popular Music in Contemporary Beijing: Modernism and Cultural Identity. *Asian Music*, XXII(2), pp.43–66.

Brackett, D., 2000. *Interpreting Popular Music*, Berkeley: University of California Press.

Brett Erens, P., 2000. Crossing Borders: Time, Memory, and the Construction of Identity in *Song of the Exile. Cinema Journal*, 39(4), pp.43–59.

Burgess, R., 1984. *In the Field: An Introduction to Field Research*, London & New York: Routledge.

Butler, J., 1993. *Bodies that Matter: On the Discursive Limits of 'Sex'*, New York & London: Routledge.

Cahiers du Cinema, 2006. *Atlas 2006,* Paris: Cahiers du Cinema.

Calhoun, C., 1994. *Social Theory and the Politics of Identity*, Oxford: Blackwell.

Cameron, N., 1991. *An Illustrated History of Hong Kong*, Hong Kong: Oxford University Press.

CFO Innovation Asia Staff, 2012. Hong Kong's Ad Spend Continues Growth, But Rate of Increase Slows Down. *CFO Innovation Asia,* 25 April. Available: http://www.cfoinnovation.com/content/hong-kongs-ad-spend-continues-growth-rate-increase-slows-down (accessed 3 July 2013).

Chan, A.H., 2000. Middle-Class Formation and Consumption in Hong Kong. In B.H. Chua, ed. *Consumption in Asia: Lifestyles and Identities*. London & New York: Routledge, pp.98–134.

Chan, F., 2014. Maggie Cheung, 'une Chinoise': Acting and Agency in the Realm of Transnational Stardom. In W.F. Leung & A. Willis, eds. *East Asian Film Stars*. Basingstoke, Hampshire: Palgrave Macmillan, pp. 83–95.

Chan, J.M. & Lee, C.C., 1991. *Mass Media and Political Transition: The Hong Kong Press in China's Orbit*, New York: Guilford.

Chan, K., 2012. Hong Kong Asserts Identity to Beijing's Dismay. *The Guardian,* 10 February. Available: http://www.guardian.co.uk/world/feedarticle/10086593 (accessed 4 September 2013).

Chang, M.G., 1999. The Good, the Bad, and the Beautiful: Movie Actresses and Public Discourse in Shanghai, 1920s–1930s. In Y. Zhang, ed. *Cinema and Urban Culture in Shanghai, 1922–1943*. Stanford: Stanford University Press, pp.128–59.

Chen, T.P. & Yung, C., 2012. Hong Kong Taps Beijing Ally. *The Wall Street Journal,* 25 March. Available: http://online.wsj.com/articles/SB1000142405270230463640457730 2602761238734 (accessed 4 November 2014).

Cheng, J., 2013. In Hong Kong, a Major Bruce Lee Exhibition at Last Honors the Memory of a Native Son. *Time Magazine,* 26 July. Available: http://world.time.com/2013/07/26/ in-hong-kong-a-major-bruce-lee-exhibition-at-last-honors-the-memory-of-a-native-son/ (accessed 4 December 2013).

Cheuk, P., 1999. Television in the 90s: Its State of Being. In HKIFF香港國際電影節, ed. *Hong Kong New Wave – Twenty Years After.* 香港電影新浪潮. Hong Kong: Provisional Urban Council of Hong Kong, pp.28–31.

Cheung, E.M.K., 2001. The Hi/stories of Hong Kong. *Cultural Studies,* 15(3/4), pp.564–90.

Cheung, G. & Ng, K., 2013. Jackie Chan Appointed to Beijing's Top Advisory Body. *South China Morning Post,* 1 February. Available: http://www.scmp.com/news/hong-kong/article/1140490/jackie-chan-appointed-beijings-top-advisory-body?page=all (accessed 26 October 2013).

Chiang, Y.M., n.d. *Taiwan and Hong Kong's Film Industries in the Context of Globalization.* Available: http://homepage.newschool.edu/~chakravs/YMCessay.html (accessed 5 May 2008).

Chow, R., 1998. Between Colonizers: Hong Kong's Postcolonial Self-Writing in the 1990s. In R. Chow, ed. *Ethics After Idealism: Theory, Culture, Ethnicity, Reading.* Bloomington: University of Indiana Press, pp.149–67.

Chow, R., 1999. Nostalgia of the New Wave: Structure in Wong Kar-wai's *Happy Together. Camera Obscura,* 14(42), pp.30–49.

Chow, V., 2005a. Fadeout on the Set as Filmmakers Play Safe. *South China Morning Post,* 10 January, p.C1.

Chow, V., 2005b. Stars Getting a Bit Long in the Tooth. *South China Morning Post,* 21 January, p.C1.

Chow, V., 2005c. Star Shortage Forces Director to Look Elsewhere. *South China Morning Post,* 8 July, p.C3.

Chow, Y.F. & de Kloet, J., 2011. Blowing in the China Wind: Engagements with Chineseness in Hong Kong Zhongguofeng Music Videos. *Visual Anthropology,* 24, pp.59–76.

Chu, D., 2000. Evergreen Li Lihua. In HKFA 香港電影資料館, ed. *Monographs of Hong Kong Film Veterans 1: Hong Kong Here I Come.* 香港電影人口述歷史叢書：南來香港. Hong Kong: HKFA, pp.163–80.

Chu, G.C., 1985. The Changing Concept of Self in Contemporary China. In A. Marsella, G. Devos, & F.L.K. Hsu, eds. *Culture and Self: Asian and Western Perspectives.* New York & London: Tavistock, pp.252–77.

Chu, Y., 2003. *Hong Kong Cinema: Coloniser, Motherland and Self,* London & New York: Routledge Curzon.

Chua, B.H., ed. 2000. *Consumption in Asia: Lifestyles and Identities,* London & New York: Routledge.

Chua, S.K., 1998. *Song of the Exile:* The Politics of 'Home'. *Jump Cut,* (42), pp.90–3.

Chun, A., 1996. Discourses of Identity in the Changing Spaces of Public Culture in Taiwan, Hong Kong and Singapore. *Theory, Culture & Society,* 13(1), pp.51–75

*City Entertainment*電影雙周刊, 1990. 香港電影製作一覽表. A List of Hong Kong Film Productions. 電影雙周刊 *City Entertainment,* (25 January), pp.56–7.

*City Entertainment*電影雙周刊, 2002a. 香港電影 下半年復甦無望？Is there no Hope of a Hong Kong Cinema Revival in the Next Six Months? 電影雙周刊 *City Entertainment,* (15–28 August, 609), pp.18–22.

City Entertainment 電影雙周刊, 2002b. 無間道 梁朝偉. *Infernal Affairs* Tony Leung. 電影雙周刊 *City Entertainment*, (21 November–4 December, 616), pp.38–41.

City Entertainment 電影雙周刊, 2004. 梁朝偉 縱橫影圈經驗談. Interview of Tony Leung about His Experience in the Film Industry. 電影雙周刊 *City Entertainment*, (10–23 March, 676), pp.32–3.

Corliss, R., 2001. Cantopop: Cantopop Kingdom. *Time Magazine,* 15 September. Available: http://www.time.com/time/magazine/article/0,9171,1000778,00.html (accessed 4 August 2013).

Cremin, S., 2013. Looking North and South: Taiwan Cinema in 2012. *Far East Film Festival 15.* Available: http://www.fareastfilm.com/EasyNe2/LYT.aspx?IDLYT=7803 &CODE=FEFJ&ST=SQL&SQL=ID_Documento=4082 (accessed 3 June 2013).

Curtin, M., 2007. *Playing to the World's Biggest Audience: The Globalization of Chinese Film and TV,* Berkeley: University of California Press.

d'Astous, A. & Séguin, N., 1999. Consumer Reactions to Product Placement Strategies in Television Sponsorship. *European Journal of Marketing*, 33(9/19), pp.896–910.

Debray, R., 1991. *Cours de Médiologie Générale*, Paris: Éditions Gallimard.

DeCordova, R., 1991. The Emergence of the Star System in America. In C. Gledhill, ed. *Stardom: Industry of Desire.* London: Routledge, pp.17–29.

Desser, D., 2014. Grace Chang: Dreaming Hong Kong. In W.F. Leung & A. Willis, eds. *East Asian Film Stars.* Basingstoke, Hampshire: Palgrave Macmillan.

Dominus, S., 2004. Why Isn't Maggie Cheung a Hollywood Star? *New York Times,* 14 November, pp.110–5.

Dyer, R., 1979. *Stars,* 1998 ed., London: British Film Institute.

Dyer, R., 1986. *Heavenly Bodies: Film Stars and Society*, London: MacMillan.

Dyer, R., 1991. A Star is Born and the Construction of Authenticity. In C. Gledhill, ed. *Stardom: Industry of Desire.* London: Routledge, pp.132–40.

Eastweek Entertainment Editorial, 2009. 玉照女星: 生活大追逐Nude Photograph Female Stars: Life After the Scandal. *Eastweek,* 7 March, pp.48–9.

Elley, D., 1997. Peach Blossom Dreams: Silent Chinese Cinema Remembered. *Griffithiana*, 60/61, pp.127–79.

Ellis, J., 1997. From Visible Fictions: Stars as a Cinematic Phenomenon. In L. Braudy & M. Cohen, eds. *Film Theory and Criticism: Introductory Readings.* New York & Oxford: Oxford University Press, pp.539–46.

Erni, J.N., 2007. Gender and Everyday Evasions: Moving with Cantopop. *Inter-Asia Cultural Studies*, 8(1), pp.86–106.

Evans, J. & Hesmondhalgh, D., 2005. *Understanding Media: Inside Celebrity*, Maidenhead: Open University Press.

Farquhar, M., 2010. Jet Li: 'Wushu Master' in Sport and Film. In E. Jeffreys & L. Edwards, eds. *Celebrity in China.* Hong Kong: Hong Kong University Press, pp.103–24.

Farquhar, M. & Zhang, Y., 2008. Introduction: Chinese Stars. *Journal of Chinese Cinemas*, 2(2), pp.85–9.

Farquhar, M. & Zhang, Y., eds. 2010. *Chinese Film Stars*, London & New York: Routledge.

Fiske, J., 1987. *Television Culture*, London & New York: Routledge.

Fiske, J. & Hartley, J., 1978. *Reading Television*, London: Methuen.

Flannery, R., 2012. Taiwan Singer Jay Chou Tops the 2012 Forbes China Celebrity List. *Forbes,* 21 May. Available: http://www.forbes.com/sites/russellflannery/2012/ 05/21/taiwan-singer-jay-chou-tops-the-2012-forbes-china-celebrity-list/ (accessed 10 July 2013).

Fore, S., 1997. Jackie Chan and the Cultural Dynamics of Global Entertainment. In S.H.P. Lu, ed. *Transnational Chinese Cinemas: Identity, Nationhood, Gender.* Honolulu: University of Hawaii Press, pp.239–62.

Fore, S., 2001. Life Imitates Entertainment: Home and Dislocation in the Films of Jackie Chan. In E.C.M. Yau, ed. *At Full Speed: Hong Kong Cinema in a Borderless World.* London & Minneapolis: University of Minnesota Press, pp.115–41.

Forever Remembrance: Anita Mui, 2004, television broadcast, TVB (Europe). January.

Foucault, M., 1980. *Power/Knowledge: Selected Interviews and Other Writings, 1972–1977.* C. Gordon, ed., New York: Pantheon Books.

Foucault, M., 1983. The Subject and Power. In H. Dreyfus & P. Rabinow, eds. *Michel Foucault: Beyond Structuralism and Hermeneutics.* Brighton: Harvester, pp.208–23.

Foucault, M., 1987. *The Use of Pleasure,* Harmondsworth: Penguin.

Fu, P., 2000. Going Global: A Cultural History of the Shaw Brothers Studio, 1960–1970. In HKIFF 香港國際電影節, ed. *Border Crossings in Hong Kong Cinema.* 跨界的香港電影. Hong Kong: HKIFF, pp.43–51.

Fung, A., 2001. What Makes the Local? A Brief Consideration of the Rejuvenation of Hong Kong Identity. *Cultural Studies,* 15(3/4), pp.591–601.

Fung, A. & Curtin, M., 2002. The Anomalies of Being Faye (Wong). *International Journal of Cultural Studies,* 5(3), pp.263–90.

Geertz, C., 1973. *The Interpretation of Cultures,* London: Harper Collins/Fontana.

Geraghty, C., 2000. Re-Examining Stardom: Questions of Texts, Bodies and Performance. In C. Gledhill & L. Williams, eds. *Reinventing Film Studies.* London: Arnold, pp.183–201.

Gergen, K., 2000. The Self in the Age of Information. *The Washington Quarterly,* 23(1), pp.201–14.

Gledhill, C., ed. 1991. *Stardom: Industry of Desire.* London: Routledge.

Gledhill, C., 1997. Genre and Gender: The Case of Soap Opera. In S. Hall, ed. *Representation: Cultural Representations and Signifying Practices.* Milton Keynes: The Open University in association with SAGE, pp.337–86.

Gold, T.B., 1993. Go with Your Feelings: Hong Kong and Taiwan Popular Culture in Greater China. *The China Quarterly,* 136, pp.907–25.

Gough, N., 2004. The Rule of Lau. *Time Magazine,* 12 April. Available: http://www.time.com/time/magazine/article/0,9171,610098,00.html (accessed 6 June 2013).

Grant, J., 2001. Cultural Formation in Postwar Hong Kong. In P. Lee, ed. *Hong Kong Reintegrating with China: Political, Cultural and Social Dimensions.* Hong Kong: Hong Kong University Press.

Grossberg, L., 1993. The Media Economy of Rock Culture: Cinema, Postmodernity and Authenticity. In S. Frith, A. Goodwin, & L. Grossberg, eds. *Sound and Vision: The Music Video Reader.* London & New York: Routledge.

Ha, L., 1998. Advertising in Hong Kong under Political Transition: A Longitudinal Analysis. *The Web Journal of Mass Communication Research,* 1(3). Available: http://www.scripps.ohiou.edu/wjmcr/vol01/1-3a.HTM (accessed 17 July 2008).

Hall, S., 1992. The West and the Rest. In S. Hall & B. Gieben, eds. *Formations of Modernity.* Cambridge: Polity Press, pp.275–332.

Hall, S., 1996. Who Needs Identity? In P. Du Gay, J. Evans, & P. Redman, eds. *Identity: A Reader.* London & Thousand Oaks: SAGE, pp.15–30.

Harding, H., 1993. The Concept of 'Greater China': Themes, Variations and Reservations. *The China Quarterly,* 136, pp.660–86.

Harris, K., 1997. The New Woman Incident: Cinema, Scandal, and Spectacle in 1935 Shanghai. In S.H.P. Lu, ed. *Transnational Chinese Cinemas: Identity, Nationhood, Gender*. Honolulu: University of Hawaii Press, pp.277–302.

Harris, T., 1991. The Building of Popular Images. In C. Gledhill, ed. *Stardom: Industry of Desire*. London: Routledge, pp.40–4.

Ho, E., 1999. Women on the Edges of Hong Kong Modernity: The Films of Ann Hui. In M.M.H. Yang, ed. *Spaces of Their Own: Women's Public Sphere in Transnational China*. Minneapolis: University of Minnesota Press, pp.162–87.

Ho, W.C., 2003. Between Globalisation and Localisation: A Study of Hong Kong Popular Music. *Popular Music*, 22(2), pp.143–57.

Hong Kong Film Archive 香港電影資料館, 2003. *Shaws Galaxy of Stars*. 邵氏星河圖. Hong Kong: HKFA.

Hong Kong International Film Festival 香港國際電影節, 1999. *Hong Kong New Wave – Twenty Years After*. 香港電影新浪潮. Hong Kong: HKIFF.

Hong Kong International Film Festival 香港國際電影節, 2000. *Hong Kong Cinema 79–89* 香港電影七九~八九. Hong Kong: HKIFF.

Hong Kong International Film Festival 香港國際電影節, 2005. *Andy Lau: Actor in Focus*. 焦點演員：劉德華. Hong Kong: HKIFF.

Hong Kong Trade Development Council, 2013. *Economic and Trade Information on Hong Kong*. Available: http://hong-kong-economy-research.hktdc.com/business-news/article/Market-Environment/Economic-and-Trade-Information-on-Hong-Kong/etihk/en/1/1X000000/1X09OVUL.htm (accessed 10 October 2013).

Hsu, F.L.K., 1985. The Self in Cross-Cultural Perspective. In A. Marsella, G. Devos, & F.L.K. Hsu, eds. *Culture and Self: Asian and Western Perspectives*. New York & London: Tavistock, pp.24–55.

Hu, B., 2006. The KTV Aesthetic: Popular Music Culture and Contemporary Hong Kong Cinema. *Screen*, 47(4), pp.407–25.

Hu, B., 2008. 'Bruce Lee' after Bruce Lee: A Life in Conjectures. *Journal of Chinese Cinemas*, 2(2), pp.123–35.

Hudson, D., 2006. Just Play Yourself, 'Maggie Cheung': *Irma Vep,* Rethinking Transnational Stardom and Unthinking National Cinemas. *Screen*, 47(2), pp.213–32.

Hunt, L., 2003. *Kung Fu Cult Masters: From Bruce Lee to Crouching Tiger*, London: Wallflower Press.

Hunt, L. & Leung, W.F., 2008. *East Asian Cinemas: Exploring Transnational Connections on Film*, London & New York: I.B.Tauris.

Hwang, A., 1998. The Irresistible: Hong Kong Movie *Once Upon A Time in China* Series: An Extensive Interview with Director/Producer Tsui Hark. *Asian Cinema*, 10(1), pp.10–23.

In Memory of Anita Mui, 2004, television broadcast, TVB (Europe). January.

Italian Trade Commission, 2011. *Overview of China Film Market*, Shanghai: Italian Trade Commission.

Iwabuchi, K., 2002. *Recentering Globalization: Popular Culture and Japanese Transnationalism*, Durham, NC & London: Duke University Press

Jacobs, A., 2009. Jackie Chan Strikes a Chinese Nerve. *The New York Times,* 24 April. Available: http://www.nytimes.com/2009/04/24/world/asia/24jackie.html (accessed 12 August 2013).

Jarvie, I.C., 1969. A Postscript on Riots and the Future of Hong Kong. In I.C. Jarvie & J. Agassi, eds. *Hong Kong: A Society in Transition*. London: Routledge & Kegan Paul, pp.361–9.

Jarvie, I.C. & Agassi, J., eds. 1969. *Hong Kong: A Society in Transition,* London: Routledge & Kegan Paul.

Jeffreys, E. & Edwards, L., eds. 2010. *Celebrity in China,* Hong Kong: Hong Kong University Press.

King, B., 2003. Embodying an Elastic Self: The Parametrics of Contemporary Stardom. In M. Barker & A. Thomas, eds. *Contemporary Hollywood Stardom.* Oxford: Oxford University Press, pp.45–61.

Kozo, 2001. *Fulltime Killer. Love HK Film.com.* Available: http://www.lovehkfilm.com/reviews/fulltime_killer.htm (accessed 13 July 2013).

Laclau, E., 1990. *New Reflections on the Revolution of Our Time*, London: Verso.

Laclau, E. & Mouffe, C., 1985. *Hegemony & Socialist Strategy: Towards a Radical Democratic Politics*, London & New York: Verso.

Lam, A., 2005. TVB a 'Turn-Off for Middle-Class and Young'. *South China Morning Post,* 11 March.

Lam, E. 林奕華, 2005. 等待香港：娛樂篇. *Waiting for Hong Kong: Entertainment*, Hong Kong: Oxford University Press.

Latham, K., 2000. Consuming Fantasies: Mediated Stardom in Hong Kong Cantonese Opera and Cinema. *Modern China*, 26(3), pp.309–47.

Latham, K., 2009. Media, the Olympics and the Search for the 'Real China'. *The China Quarterly*, 197, pp.1–24.

Lau, J.K.W., 1998. Besides Fists and Blood: Hong Kong Comedy and its Master of the Eighties. *Cinema Journal*, 37(2), pp.18–34.

Lau, S.K. & Kuan, H.C., 1988. *The Ethos of the Hong Kong Chinese,* Hong Kong: The Chinese University Press.

Lau, S.K., Lee, M.K., Wan, P.S., & Wong, S.L., 1994. *Inequalities and Development: Social Stratification in Chinese Societies*, Hong Kong: The Chinese University Press.

Law, R., 2004. Mixed Blessings: Hong Kong Box Office in 2003. In Far East Film, ed. *Far East Film 6 Festival Catalogue.* Udine: CEC, p.13.

Law, R., 2012. Keeping the Faith: Hong Kong in 2012. *Far East Film Festival 15*. Available: http://www.fareastfilm.com/EasyNe2/LYT.aspx?Code=FEFJ&IDLYT=7803&ST=SQL&SQL=ID_Documento=4067 (accessed 15 July 2013).

Lee, C.C., 1998. Press Self-Censorship and Political Transition in Hong Kong. *Harvard International Journal of Press/Politics*, 3(2), pp.55–73.

Lee, C.C., ed. 2000. *Power, Money, and Media: Communication Patterns and Bureaucratic Control in Cultural China,* Illinois: Northwestern University Press.

Lee, L.O.F., 1994. Two Films from Hong Kong: Parody and Allegory. In N. Browne et al., eds. *New Chinese Cinemas: Forms, Identities, Politics*. Cambridge: Cambridge University Press, pp.202–15.

Lee, P.S.N. 李少南, ed. 2003. 香港傳謀新世記. *New Perspectives on Hong Kong Media,* Hong Kong: The Chinese University Press.

Lee, T.D. & Huang, Y., 2002. We are Chinese: Music and Identity in Cultural China. In S H Donald, M. Keane, & Y. Hong, eds. *Media in China: Consumption, Content and Crisis*. Surrey: Curzon, pp.105–15.

Leung, A. & Cheung, G., 2005. Tung Shows It's Business as Usual after Exit of His Top Aide. *South China Morning Post*, 8 January, p.A2.

Leung, B.K.P., 1994. 'Class' and 'Class Formation' in Hong Kong Studies. In S. Lau et al., eds. *Inequalities and Development: Social Stratification in Chinese Societies*. Hong Kong: The Chinese University Press, pp.47–72.

Leung, B.K.P., 1996. *Perspectives on Hong Kong Society*, Hong Kong: Oxford University Press.

Leung, P., 2000. Urban Cinema and the Cultural Identity of Hong Kong. In P. Fu & D. Desser, eds. *The Cinema of Hong Kong: History, Arts, Identity*. London: Cambridge University Press, pp.227–51.

Leung, W.F., 2008a. Attori, Corpi, Costumi. Ovvero, Come Salvare il Cinema di Hong Kong e L'arte della Recitazione. Johnnie To and Body Suits: Saving Hong Kong Cinema and Performance. In M. di Giulio & F. Zanello, eds. *Non è Tempo di Eroi. Il Cinema di Johnnie To. No Time For Heroes: The Cinema of Johnnie To*. Piombino, Italy: Edizioni il Foglio, pp.132–40.

Leung, W.F., 2008b. *Infernal Affairs* and *Kung Fu Hustle*: Panacea, Placebo and Hong Kong Cinema. In L. Hunt & W.F. Leung, eds. *East Asian Cinemas: Exploring Transnational Connections on Film*. London & New York: I.B.Tauris, pp.71–87.

Leung, W.F., 2009. From Wah Dee to CEO: Andy Lau and Performing the Hong Kong Subject. *Film International*, 40(7), pp.19–28.

Leung, W.F., n.d. Local Hero Chow Yun Fat's Journey to Hollywood. *The Media Student's Book*. Available: http://www.mediastudentsbook.com/content/local-hero-chow-yun-fats-journey-hollywood (accessed 4 July 2013).

Li, C.T., 1994. The Return of the Father: Hong Kong New Wave and its Chinese Context in the 1980s. In N. Browne et al., eds. *New Chinese Cinemas: Forms, Identities, Politics*. Cambridge: Cambridge University Press, pp.160–79.

Li, P.W. 李碧華, 2004. 花開有時, 夢醒有時 A Time to Flower, A Time to Awake from a Dream. 壹周刊 *Next*, 15 January, pp.164–5.

Li, X. 李雪琪, 2002. 買一億保險 阿梅准坐不准企 $100,000,000 Insurance, Mui was Allowed to Sit, not Stand. *Next*, 4 April, pp.40–3.

Li, X., 2013. Netizens See Red over HK Actress' Weibo Posting. *The Straits Times,* 4 August. Available: http://www.straitstimes.com/the-big-story/asia-report/hong-kong/story/netizens-see-red-over-hk-actress-weibo-posting-20130804 (accessed 9 September 2013).

Liang, L. 梁麗娟, 2004. 告別大眾傳媒年代 Farewell to the Era of Popular Media. *Hong Kong Economic News,* 1 December.

Lii, D.T., 1998. A Colonized Empire: Reflections on the Expansion of Hong Kong Films in Asian Countries. In K.H. Chen, ed. *Trajectories: Inter-Asia Cultural Studies*. London & New York: Routledge, pp.122–41.

Lilley, R., 1993. Claiming Identity: Film and Television in Hong Kong. *History and Anthropology*, 6(2–3), pp.261–92.

Livingstone, S. & Markham, T., 2008. The Contribution of Media Consumption to Civic Participation. *British Journal of Sociology*, 59(2), pp.351–71.

Lo, K.C., 2001. Transnationalization of the Local in Hong Kong Cinema of the 1990s. In E.C.M. Yau, ed. *At Full Speed: Hong Kong Cinema in a Borderless World*. London & Minneapolis: University of Minnesota Press, pp.261–76.

Lo, K.C., 2005. *Chinese Face/Off: The Transnational Popular Culture of Hong Kong*, Urbana & Chicago: University of Illinois Press.

Lo, W.L., 1999. A Child without a Mother, An Adult without a Motherland: A Study of Ann Hui's Films. In IIКIГГ 香港國際電影節, ed. *Hong Kong New Wave – Twenty Years After*. 香港電影新浪潮. Hong Kong: Provisional Urban Council of Hong Kong, pp.65–71.

Lovell, A., 2003. I Went in Search of Deborah Kerr, Jodie Foster and Julianne Moore but got Waylaid . . . In M. Barker & A. Thomas, eds. *Contemporary Hollywood Stardom*. Oxford: Oxford University Press, pp.259–70.

Luo, L., 2011. Dispute over New Immigrants from the Mainland, Hong Kong is Unhappy? *Southern Weekly,* 18 May. Available: http://www.chinahush.com/2011/05/18/dispute-over-new-immigrants-from-the-mainland-hong-kong-is-unhappy/ (accessed 4 September 2013).

Ma, E.K.W., 1995. *Television Ideologies and Cultural Identities: The Case of Hong Kong Television.* PhD Thesis, Goldsmith College, University of London.

Ma, E.K.W., 1999. *Culture, Politics and Television in Hong Kong*, London: Routledge.

Ma, E.K.W., 2001. Re-Advertising Hong Kong: Nostalgia Industry and Popular History. *positions: asia critique*, 9(1), pp.131–59.

Macey, D., 2000. *The Penguin Dictionary of Critical Theory*, London: Penguin.

Marshall, D., 1997. *Celebrity and Power: Fame in Contemporary Culture*, Minneapolis: University of Minnesota Press.

Marshall, P.D., 2006. Intimately Intertwined in the Most Public Way: Celebrity and Journalism. In P.D. Marshall, ed. *The Celebrity Culture Reader*. London & New York: Routledge, pp.315–23.

Marshall, T.H., 1977. A Note on 'Status'. In P. Du Gay, J. Evans, & P. Redman, eds. *Identity: A Reader*. London & Thousand Oaks: SAGE, pp.304–10.

McDonald, P., 1998. Reconceptualising Stardom. In *Stars*. London: British Film Institute, pp.175–200.

McDonald, P., 2000. *The Star System: Hollywood's Production of Popular Identities*, London: Wallflower Press.

Mendik, X. & Mathijs, E., eds. 2007. *Cult Film Reader,* Maidenhead: Open University Press/McGraw-Hill.

Mercer, K., 1990. Welcome to the Jungle. In J. Rutherford, ed. *Identity: Community, Culture, Difference*. London: Lawrence & Wishart, pp.43–71.

Morris, J., 1988. *Hong Kong: Epilogue to an Empire*, London: Penguin.

Mullany, G., 2013. Hong Kong TV Drama Plays Out Uneasy Ties with China. *New York Times,* 11 February. Available: http://www.nytimes.com/2013/02/11/business/media/hong-kong-tv-drama-plays-out-uneasy-ties-with-china.html?_r=0 (accessed 15 February 2013).

Needham, G., 2008. Fashioning Social Change in the Hong Kong Musical 1957–1964. In L. Hunt & W.F. Leung, eds. *East Asian Cinemas: Exploring Transnational Connections on Film*. London & New York: I.B.Tauris, pp.41–56.

Nye Jr., J.S., 2004. *Soft Power: The Means to Success in World Politics*, New York: Public Affairs.

Pae, J.H., Samiee, S., & Tai, S., 2002. Global Advertising Strategy. *International Marketing Review*, 19(2), pp.176–89.

Phillips, A. & Vincendeau, G., eds. 2006. *Journeys of Desire: European Actors in Hollywood,* London: British Film Institute.

Potter, J., 1969. The Structure of Rural Chinese Society in New Territories. In I.C. Jarvie & J. Agassi, eds. *Hong Kong: A Society in Transition*. London: Routledge & Kegan Paul, pp.3–28.

Quan, K., 2004. Profile of Anna May Wong: Remembering the Silent Star. *Asia Pacific Arts*. Available. http://www1.international.ucla.edu/article.asp?parentid=6132 (accessed 26 August 2014).

Reynaud, B., 1993. Glamour and Suffering: Gong Li and the History of Chinese Stars. In P. Cook & P. Dodd, eds. *Woman and Film: A Sight and Sound Reader*. London: Scarlet Press, pp.21–9.

Rifkin, J., 1995. *The End of Work: The Decline of the Global Labor Force and the Dawn of the Post-Market Era*, New York: Putnam.

Robinson, L., 2006. Wong Kar-wai's Sensuous Histories. In K. Latham, S. Thompson, & J. Klein, eds. *Consuming China: Approaches to Cultural Change in Contemporary China*. London & New York: Routledge, pp.190–207.

Rodriguez, H., 1997. Hong Kong Popular Culture as an Interpretive Arena: The Huang Feihong Film Series. *Screen*, 38(1), pp.1–24.

Rojek, C., 2001. *Celebrity*, London: Reaktion.

Ruan, J. 阮記宏, 2003. 藝人與記者 破鏡難重圓. Artistes and Journalists: Broken Mirrors. In P.S.N. Lee李少南, ed. 香港傳謀新世記. *New Perspectives on Hong Kong Media*. Hong Kong: The Chinese University Press, pp.125–38.

Salaff, J. & Wong, S., 1994. Exiting Hong Kong: Social Class Experiences and the Adjustment to 1997. In S. Lau et al., eds. *Inequalities and Development: Social Stratification in Chinese Societies*. Hong Kong: The Chinese University Press, pp.205–49.

Schrøder, K.C. & Jensen, K.B., eds. 2002. *Handbook of Media and Communication Research,* London: Routledge.

Screen Daily Staff, 2011. China Box Office up 61% in 2010 for a New Record. *Screen Daily,* 5 January. Available: http://www.screendaily.com/china-box-office-up-61-in-2010-for-a-new-record/5021983.article (accessed 12 December 2012).

Screen Digest, 2003. *Global Cinema Exhibition Markets,* London: EMEA.

Sek Kei, 1988. The Social Psychology of Hong Kong Cinema. In HKIFF 香港國際電影節, ed. *Changes in Hong Kong Society Through Cinema.* 香港電影與社會變遷. Hong Kong: Urban Council of Hong Kong, pp.15–20.

Shingler, M., 2012. *Star Studies: A Critical Guide*, Basingstoke, Hampshire: Palgrave Macmillan.

Shu, Y., 2003. Reading the Kung Fu Film in an American Context: From Bruce Lee to Jackie Chan. *Journal of Popular Film and Television*, 31(2), pp.50–9.

Siu, H.F., 1996. Remade in Hong Kong: Weaving into the Chinese Cultural Tapestry. In T.T. Liu & D. Faure, eds. *Unity and Diversity: Local Cultures and Identities in China.* Hong Kong: Hong Kong University Press, pp.177–96.

So, C. 蘇鑰機, 2005. *Changing Hong Kong Media,* Hong Kong: School of Journalism and Communication, Chinese University of Hong Kong.

Stacey, J., 1994. *Star Gazing: Hollywood Cinema and Female Spectatorship*, London: Routledge.

Staff Reporters, 2004. 建巨星館留住光輝 Build a Museum to Preserve the Stars' Glory. *Sing Tao* 星島日報, 14 January, p.B7.

Stringer, J., 1997. 'Your tender smiles give me strength': Paradigms of Masculinity in John Woo's *A Better Tomorrow* and *The Killer. Screen*, 38(1), pp.24–41.

Stringer, J., 2003. Scrambling Hollywood: Asian Stars/Asian American Star Cultures. In T. Austin & M. Barker, eds. *Contemporary Hollywood Stardom*. London: Arnold, pp.229–42.

Sun, C., 2005. Chinese Opera in Need of Fresh Talent, Says Chan. *South China Morning Post*, 19 March, p.C6.

Sun, L., 1989. The Long March to Man. In G. Barmé & J. Minford, eds. *Seeds of Fire: Chinese Voices of Conscience*. New York: Noonday Press, pp.30–5.

Sung, V, 2012. Champions of HK Autonomy Should Embrace Full Colonial History. *South China Morning Post,* 1 November. Available: http://www.scmp.com/comment/insight-opinion/article/1074014/champions-hk-autonomy-should-embrace-full-colonial-history (accessed 3 November 2013).

Sze, M.H. 史文鴻, 世紀交接下香港電影的危機與轉機, n.d. Crises and Opportunities for Hong Kong Cinema at the End of the Millennium. Unpublished Paper.

Tam, K., 1995. Self-Identity and the Problematic of Chinese Modernity. *The Humanities Bulletin*, 4, pp.57–64.

Tam, V.W.W., 2002. *Domestication of the Cultural Icon Chow Yun Fat: From Subversion to Domination*. MPhil Thesis, Chinese University of Hong Kong.

Tao Jie, 陶傑, 2004. 大偶像 *Great Idol*, Hong Kong: CUP Publishing.

Taylor, J., 2008. From Transnationalism to Nativism? The Rise, Decline and Reinvention of a Regional Hokkien Entertainment Industry. *Inter-Asia Cultural Studies*, 9(1), pp.62–81.

Teo, S., 1997. *Hong Kong Cinema: The Extra Dimension*, London: British Film Institute.

Thompson, J.B., 1995. *The Media and Modernity: A Social Theory of the Media*, Cambridge: Polity Press.

Tsui, C., 2005. Chan the Man. *Sunday Morning Post*, 21 June, p.8.

Tu, W., 1985. Selfhood and Otherness in Confucian Thought. In A. Marsella, G. Devos, & F.L.K. Hsu, eds. *Culture and Self: Asian and Western Perspectives*. New York & London: Tavistock, pp.231–51.

Tu, W., 1991. Cultural China: The Periphery as Center. *Daedalus*, 120(2), pp.1–32.

Turner, G., 2010. Approaching Celebrity Studies. *Celebrity Studies*, 1(1), pp.11–20.

University of Hong Kong, 2005. *Hong Kong Entertainment Poll 2004*, Hong Kong: University of Hong Kong. Available: http://hkupop.hku.hk/english/cablecen04 (accessed 15 August 2005).

Veblen, T., 1899. *Theory of the Leisure Class,* 1970 ed., London: George Allen & Unwin.

Vincendeau, G., 2000. *Stars and Stardom in French Cinema*, London: Continuum.

Wang, Y., 2008. Anna May Wong: A Border-Crossing 'Minor' Star Mediating Performance. *Journal of Chinese Cinemas*, 2(2), pp.91–102.

Ward, B., 1979. Not Merely Players: Drama, Art and Ritual in Traditional China. *MAN*, 14(1), pp.18–39.

Wardrop, M., 2008. Beijing Olympics 2008: Jackie Chan Slams Protesters. *The Telegraph*, 3 August. Available: http://www.telegraph.co.uk/news/worldnews/asia/china/2240004/Beijing-Olympics-2008-Jackie-Chan-slams-protesters.html (accessed 25 June 2013).

Watts, J., 2008. China Riveted by Stolen Sex Photos of Hong Kong Stars. *The Guardian*, 13 February. Available: http://www.theguardian.com/world/2008/feb/13/china.news (accessed 3 July 2009).

Welsh, F., 1997. *A History of Hong Kong*, London: Harper Collins.

Williams, R., 1989. Culture is Ordinary. In *Resources of Hope: Culture, Democracy, Socialism*. London: Verso, pp.3–18.

Williams, R., 2002. Culture is Ordinary. In B. Highmore, ed. *The Everyday Life Reader*. London & New York: Routledge, pp.91–100.

Williams, T., 1995. To Live and Die in Hong Kong: The Crisis Cinema of John Woo. *cineAction*, 36, pp.42–52.

Williams, T., 1997. Space, Place, and Spectacle: The Crisis Cinema of John Woo. *Cinema Journal*, 36(2), pp.67–84.

Williams, T., 1998. *Song of the Exile:* Border-Crossing Melodrama. *Jump Cut*, (42), pp.94–100.

Willis, A., ed. 2004. *Film Stars: Hollywood and Beyond,* Manchester: Manchester University Press.

Wiseman, J.P., 1979. The Research Web. In J. Bynner & K. Stribley, eds. *Social Research: Principles and Procedures*. London: Longman, pp.113–36.

Witzleben, J.L., 1999. Cantopop and Mandopop in Pre-Postcolonial Hong Kong: Identity Negotiation in the Performances of Anita Mui Yim-Fong. *Popular Music*, 19(2), pp.241–58.

Wong, C.H.Y. & McDonogh, G., 2001a. Consuming Cinema: Reflections on Movies and Market-Places in Contemporary Hong Kong. In G. Mathews & T.L. Lui, eds. *Consuming Hong Kong*. Hong Kong: Hong Kong University Press, pp.81–116.

Wong, C.H.Y. & McDonogh, G., 2001b. The Mediated Metropolis: Anthropological Issues in Cities and Mass Communication. *American Anthropologist*, 103(1), pp.96–111.

Wong, D., 2005. Women's Reception of Mainstream Hong Kong Cinema. In L. Pang & D. Wong, eds. *Masculinities and Hong Kong Cinema*. Hong Kong: Hong Kong University Press, pp.239–60.

Wong, J.J., 2003. *The Rise and Decline of Cantopop: A Study of Hong Kong Popular Music (1949–1997)*. PhD Thesis, University of Hong Kong.

Woodward, K., 1997. *Identity and Difference*, Milton Keynes: Open University Press.

Xu, G.G., 2008. Remaking East Asia, Outsourcing Hollywood. In L. Hunt & W.F. Leung, eds. *East Asian Cinemas: Exploring Transnational Connections on Film*. London: I.B.Tauris, pp.191–202.

Yahuda, M., 1995. *Hong Kong: China's Challenge*, London: Routledge.

Yau, E., 1994. Border Crossing: Mainland China's Presence. In N. Browne et al., eds. *New Chinese Cinemas: Forms, Identities, Politics*. Cambridge: Cambridge University Press, pp.180–201.

Yau, K.F., 2001. Cinema 3: Towards a 'Minor Hong Kong Cinema'. *Cultural Studies*, 15(3/4), pp.463–543.

Youngs, T., 2003. Memories of Old Hong Kong: An Interview with Riley Ip. In Far East Film, ed. *Far East Film 5 Festival Catalogue*. Udine: CEC, pp. 20–23.

Yu, J. 余家強, 2004. 為人民服務 Service the People. *Next*, 15 July, pp.74–80.

Yu, M.W. 余慕雲, 1987. 香港戲劇電影發展史話 Hong Kong Opera Film Development History. In 香港國際電影節 HKIFF, ed. *Cantonese Opera Film Retrospective* 粵語戲曲片回顧. Hong Kong: The Urban Council of Hong Kong, pp.18–24.

Yu, S.Q., 2012a. *Jet Li: Chinese Masculinity and Transnational Film Stardom*, Edinburgh: Edinburgh University Press.

Yu, S.Q., 2012b. Vulnerable Chinese Stars: From *Xizi* to Film Worker. In Y. Zhang, ed. *A Companion to Chinese Cinema*. Chichester: Wiley, pp.218–38.

Zhang, J. 張鍵, 1998. 90年代港產片工業狀態一瞥. *A Brief Review of the State of the Hong Kong Film Industry in the 1990s*, Hong Kong: Hong Kong Society for the Concern of Hong Kong Film Industry.

Zhang, Y., 2004. *Chinese National Cinema*, London: Routledge.

Zheng, S. 鄭淑華, 2005. 帶菌者 李照興 The Carrier Bono. *Ming Pao,* 13 March.

Index

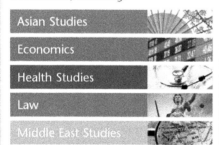
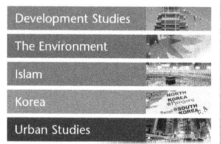

For Product Safety Concerns and Information please contact our EU
representative GPSR@taylorandfrancis.com
Taylor & Francis Verlag GmbH, Kaufingerstraße 24, 80331 München, Germany